READY OR NOT, HERE LIFE COMES

Mel Levine, M.D.

SIMON & SCHUSTER
NEW YORK   LONDON   TORONTO   SYDNEY

SIMON & SCHUSTER
Rockefeller Center
1230 Avenue of the Americas
New York, NY 10020

The names and certain characteristics of the individuals
in this book have been changed.

SIMON & SCHUSTER and colophon are registered trademarks
of Simon & Schuster, Inc.

Excerpt from "The Road Not Taken" from *The Poetry of Robert Frost,*
edited by Edward Connery Lathem. Copyright 1916, 1969 by
Henry Holt and Company, copyright 1944 by Robert Frost.
Reprinted by permission of Henry Holt and Company, LLC.

Designed by Karolina Harris

For information regarding special discounts for bulk purchases,
please contact Simon & Schuster Special Sales at
1-800-456-6798 or business@simonandschuster.com

Manufactured in the United States of America

10 9 8 7 6 5 4 3 2 1

Library of Congress Cataloging-in-Publication Data
Levine, Melvin D.
  Ready or not, here life comes / Mel Levine.
    p. cm.
  Includes bibliographical references and index.
  1. Young adults—Psychology. 2. Young adults—Vocational
guidance. 3. Young adults—Life skills guides. 4. Maturation
(Psychology) 5. Motivation (Psychology) I. Title.
HQ799.5.L56 2005
305.242—dc22   2004061602

ISBN 0-7432-6224-7

This book is dedicated to the memory of Justin Coleman—

from whose life there is much to be learned

CONTENTS

Part Two—WAYS TO GROW

6
DEFT NOVICES

7
INNER DIRECTION

8
INTERPRETATION

9
INSTRUMENTATION

10
INTERACTION

Part Three—MIND GROWERS

11
PARENTS

12
EDUCATORS

13
ADOLESCENTS

PREFACE

I doubt if any mother, father, or teacher ever actually posed the question to me, "What will he be like when he's in his twenties?" But I know they never stopped thinking about it and may have wondered and worried mostly in silence. As a pediatrician who for more than thirty years has treated children and adolescents struggling with their own brain wiring, I myself have come to realize that the core issue for any developing child is who he is turning into and, more specifically, what he will be like when he grows up.

I have accompanied countless kids on journeys through their school years. And I have been able to witness their varied outcomes. I have gotten to meet them and learn from them as they progressed toward and into young adult life. Now I find myself preoccupied with how and why different kids turn out so differently. I'm especially concerned with those who don't turn out so well, and I'd like to know what we could have done differently for them as children and adolescents.

In recent years I have been stunned by the plight of individuals—far too many—who seem unprepared for the crossover from education to work. There are convincing reasons to believe that a swirl of factors unique to our contemporary culture and embedded in our educational practices is harming children. In particular, these forces are stunting mental growth and leaving developing minds unready to launch themselves into productive and fulfilling adult lives.

I decided to write this book so that I could join others in exploring the various forms and manifestations of what I call work-life unreadiness. I also want to examine the lessons we have to learn from young adults who are currently buckling under anguish and confusion, young adults who lack a clear sense of identity or direction. I have relied substantially on my own clinical experiences and reading of the relevant research literature. In addition, my research assistant, Miles Harmon, and I compiled an interview format, and he then used this tool to study the earlier years, experiences, and challenges facing a group of individuals striving to define themselves during their twenties. Direct quotations from these interviews appear at each chapter heading.

Even though this book deals with an older age group, it is written very much from the perspective of a pediatrician. It is my hope that these collected insights can provide a stimulus for parents, educators, and policy makers to reconsider the manner in which we are educating and rearing children. Moreover, I would like caring readers to think about the ways in which we can counter the negative environmental/cultural influences, misguided educational priorities, and tragically misunderstood brain differences that may well be contributing to the growth of a young population unready to go to work. Life is coming at them. If we fail to apply updated strategies to help them get ready, they'll have to take what they can get in life. They will be forced to settle for less than they deserve!

Mel Levine
Sanctuary Farm
Rougemont, North Carolina
September 2004

ACKNOWLEDGMENTS

The support and advice of numerous individuals contributed richly to the creation of this book. Miles Harmon served as my research assistant. Miles, destined to be a great healer as a future physician, accomplished valuable bibliographic research and conducted highly informative interviews with his fellow startup adults.

I want to acknowledge the terrific help of my office staff, Pam McBane and Janet Furman. I also wish to express my appreciation to the many heroic patients I have seen over the years who have permitted me to step into and learn from the early pages of their biographies. This book has benefited immensely from the input of my editor at Simon & Schuster, Bob Bender, and his colleague Ruth Fecych, who have worked hard to teach me to say much more with many fewer words. I also want to thank my brilliant literary agent, Lane Zachary, who was instrumental in the birth and rearing of *Ready or Not, Here Life Comes*.

I am very grateful for the success of our extraordinary nonprofit institute All Kinds of Minds, whose board of trustees and staff have been invaluable allies in the effort to prevent the misinterpretation and mismanagement of kids with differences in learning (basically *all* kids). I am especially grateful to Mark Grayson, our CEO, and Mike Florio, our COO, as well as Mary Dean Barringer, the national director of Schools Attuned, and Paul Yellin, who heads our Student Success Programs. Charles Schwab, my cochairman of the board, and Bob Eubanks, board president, have been staunch facilitators of what we are trying to do, and their influence permeates the pages of this book as well as my career. This work has been greatly aided by Jeff Low, Tom Gray, and their talented staff within the information technology department of All Kinds of Minds and the Center for Development and Learning.

The University of North Carolina Medical School and the North Carolina legislature have consistently shown a commitment to individuals with differences in learning and have been highly supportive of our efforts. Governor Mike Easley, Senators Tony Rand and Marc Basnight, and Howard Lee, chairman of the North Carolina State School Board of Education, keep demonstrating that they are brilliant child advocates. Also, I have appreciated the encouragement and wisdom of Charles Moeser, chancellor of the University of North Carolina.

I extend special thanks and profound sympathy to my close friend and adopted brother, Dr. Bill Coleman, to whose very special late son *Ready or Not, Here Life Comes* is dedicated.

Writing this book would not have been possible without the skilled assistance of David Taylor, who, while I write and travel the world, helps take meticulous care of the geese, the donkeys, and all the other animals on Sanctuary Farm that I love deeply.

Lastly and mostly, I owe a great deal to my wife, Bambi, who is a constant source of understanding, insight, and brilliant advice. Without her guidance and affection I would still be a startup adult.

PROLOGUE

Dudley Finch's Soliloquy

Somewhere along the way, I guess I must have wandered way off my trail. It's like the whole time I was growing up I was having such a good time kinda doing stuff in the present that there seemed to be no such thing as the future. I never looked back and I never looked ahead.

In high school I was a solid B and C student—nobody special but I never messed up. I must have been pretty smart because I passed all my subjects without having to work my butt off and I had absolutely no interest in anything I ever studied. I wasn't a jock. I wasn't some kind of a nerd either. I guess I didn't make waves, and I didn't cause problems for my family. I also didn't give them a whole lot to be proud of. I spent most of my spare time either with friends just hanging out or in front of the TV or belly up in bed listening to music or maybe playing computer games, but mostly chilling out.

College was a blast. My friends were awesome. I did okay in my classes and I thought I was really finding myself. Anyway, now here I am; I graduated about a year ago from this nothing-special college. I switched majors a few times and ended up studying communications, figuring I didn't have to be a rocket scientist to do communications. I'm having trouble finding a job I really like. Well, at least I have a job; some of my friends don't even have that. Ionic Enterprises mostly has me setting up databases; I know that doesn't have much to do with communications, but that's the story of my life: nothing seems to connect with much else.

My job gets pretty boring, but I really can't say exactly what I'd *rather be doing. The pay's okay, not great. I've gone back to living in New Jersey with Mom and Dad. I guess I'm very lucky because they never hassle me; they have plenty of problems of their own. Me, I'm just, like, wandering around with nowhere to go. I'm almost twenty-three and I have no idea where to go from here. I've had my share of girlfriends but nothing serious. Nothing looks too promising or interesting careerwise. I don't know what I'd do without my friends, my tribe, but they all seem to be getting married or going off somewhere. I sometimes feel as if I'll be the only one left. Down deep inside, I guess I'm unhappy, real unhappy, but I don't show it. Most of all I'm scared, I mean really scared. Like, I feel hollow, and I'm afraid of what will happen if nothing ever happens. No one ever prepared me for what my life would be like at the age of twenty-three. I wasn't ready to feel like this, but now I'm ready to do something about it. I'm ready to take charge of my life and start sticking some real meaning into it. I'm not sure I know how to do that, but I'm definitely ready to get ready. Or am I?*

1
HERE LIFE COMES
How Startup Adults Get Unready for Careers

I do not think I knew what to expect [in the transition from school to work]. I always worked during high school; I always worked and made money. My parents made sure I went to work, but at the same time I was spoiled rotten growing up, so I never really had an idea. It was harsh, a big change to leave the nest and get into the real world and have to take care of everything. I wasn't prepared for what things cost, the value of the dollar, the things you could and could not do.

S.R., age 27

Lives flow with heavy undercurrents, much like the open sea; they undulate through well-timed waves, such as the preschool period, adolescence, and the so-called golden years of late life. Each arriving era brings its special challenges and opportunities, along with its unique stresses and pressures. A person may or may not be equipped to ride the next wave, to manage the requirements—obvious and hidden—of his or her latest time of life.

A particularly challenging period is the opening stages of a life at work, the school-to-career years, a time that, although rarely thought of as distinct, may be one of the roughest to traverse. These are the startup years, a pivotal time that claims more than its share of unsuspecting victims. In fact, most people are better prepared for their retirement than they are for the startup of their working lives! For some the startup years commence at age sixteen or seventeen, upon their dropping out of high school. For others the startup may not begin until age twenty-nine, following a residency in plastic surgery.

Many individuals in and around their twenties come to feel abandoned and anguished. They start to question their own self-worth, and they are prone to some awful mistakes in their choice of career or in the ways they perform as novices on the job. They suffer from an affliction I call work-life unreadiness, which may have its onset right after high school, in college, during the job search, or during the early phases of a job or a career.

The length of the startup period varies from just a few years to a decade or more of uncertainty and justified anguish. Some emerging adults take longer to start up a stable work life than do others. Some never stop starting; they can't move ahead toward a career because of repeated false starts or because they keep changing course. They start up and stall out! Others feel stymied in their work choices, while some of their friends effortlessly and expediently move into job roles that fit them as snugly as their favorite athletic socks.

Clearly, work life is not one's only life! Family life, perhaps spiritual life, sex life, social life, along with assorted other slices of life operate in concert and sometimes in conflict with work life. But work life is the subject of *Ready or Not, Here Life Comes.* To a large extent people are what they do. But we must remember that life at work is influenced by and influences numerous facets of day-to-day existence.

We are in the midst of an epidemic of work-life unreadiness because an alarming number of emerging adults are unable to find a good fit between their minds and their career directions. Like seabirds mired in an oil spill, these fledgling men and women are stuck, unable to take flight toward a suitable career. Some are crippled before they have a chance to beat their wings; others have tumbled downward in the early stages of their trajectories. Because they are not finding their way, they may feel as if they are going nowhere and have nowhere to go.

I have listened to the laments and noticed the moistened eyelids of promising young people who at age eighteen, twenty, twenty-one, or twenty-nine have no idea what they want to make of their work lives. Some may be too accustomed to having their activities explicitly spelled out and scheduled for them and as a result are having trouble making their own significant decisions. Others may have known what goals they wanted to pursue, but then their occupational pot of gold lost its allure; the romance of big business, engine repair, law, or academic life turned out not to be as advertised. Work was no fun; or it was repetitious ("boring"); or it entailed handling heaps of minutiae and menial tasks—grunt work. Maybe it called for far too much playing up to people these young adults did not particularly like or respect. As one person we interviewed put it, "I do not think you can be prepared for the transition. No one can tell you what it is like to get up at eight every day and go to work every day to scratch out a living so you can have forty-eight hours on the weekend to do what you like, when you've had twenty-one years of doing what you want!" Any earlier idealism has given way to disillusionment.

Some anxious junior staffers may have chosen their particular roads for all the wrong reasons. Some embarked upon a career odyssey without fully understanding what that journey was destined to be about. No one told them what dental school or dental practice truly entailed; or if it was explained to them, perhaps they were not ready to hear it. Other young adults find themselves bound to an occupation from which they'd like to bail out, but they feel chained to their entry positions. Perhaps the pay is good, or backtracking would be too hard and risky, or nothing else looks any better. Finally, there are those unqualified for the peculiar rigors and aches of their grown-up work. It may be that their current abilities have failed to match their present interests. You're in for some trouble if whatever you like to do most you do poorly. Some people have strengths they're not interested in exploiting and interests that bring out all their weaknesses.

In all these instances, years of schooling and parenting have entirely missed that elusive target, work-life readiness. Our graduates may well lack the practical skills, the habits, the behaviors, the real-world insights, and the frames of mind pivotal for career startup. Their parents and teachers have unwittingly let them down. Adulthood has ambushed them; its demands have taken them by surprise. Nevertheless, time won't stand still: Ready or not, here life comes!

Their Earlier Lives

Individuals who find themselves gridlocked during the transition to adult work have come to these frustrating impasses from various directions. A lot of them were impressive students, pelted with ego-intoxicating kudos for displaying the dubious but much-revered trait of well-roundedness. These golden girls and boys—ultracool, in the adolescent sense of the word, academically successful, athletic, politically astute, and attractive—were apt to tumble from these pedestals. Their very versatility helped to make it hard for them to commit to the deep and narrow grooves of adult work life. Others suffered with neurodevelopmental dysfunctions that made school a perpetual come-from-behind battle, as they fought to satisfy elusive academic, athletic, or social demands. Many were well behaved and compliant kids, able to meet expectations as long as the demands were explicitly framed. Some were industrious, while others did poorly in school and became accustomed to failure. Whether their earlier life histories were comfortable or difficult, these neophyte adults now feel dazed and understandably apprehensive.

Has this predicament always plagued the members of this age group? Or are we encountering a growing proportion of unhappy wanderers? No doubt, the transition to adult work life is one of life's most daunting periods. But I have a strong sense that our population of career-unready adults is expanding, and doing so at an alarming pace—like a contagious disease.

The Backdrop: Contemporary Influences on Work-Life Readiness

The culture of the modern world affords multiple ways to get lost or ambushed along the work-life trail. More than ever before, young adults are apt to confront job descriptions that are strikingly different from those familiar to elder members of their families. Role models within a family are an endangered species. Even if a young person breaks into the identical occupation as his mother or father, the chances are that its current routines and requirements look nothing like those his parents faced. Practicing medicine or law or tending to the family farm is a whole different ball game these days. Meanwhile, new adults have to face an economic world as unfathomable as it is unpredictable. How does a startup adult go about seeking job security amid today's foggy employment forecasts? Not very well.

We also live in a time when many mothers and fathers are downright fearful of their own kids, especially their adolescent offspring. Adolescents often hold the power in a family because they have so many weapons at their disposal (such as drugs, alcohol, tattoos, anorexia, suicidal thoughts, dropping out). Parents can't help dreading that their relationships with their kids may become increasingly brittle as children grow up. This fear may in part stem from a feeling of guilt that both parents are working and worry that they are not devoting sufficient attention to their children. Some parents may long so desperately for the approval of their children that they go out of their way to make sure their kids are being entertained at all times and sheltered from adversity or hardship of any sort. For example, if their child is having a hard time with a particular teacher, a parent is apt to call the principal or intervene in some other way and solve the messy problem for the child.

Then the student is deprived of the opportunity to learn the strategic skills of conflict resolution, stress management, negotiation, and problem solving, all of which are essential in a career.

Many children and adolescents are not equipped with a durable work temperament, having been submerged in a culture that stresses instant rewards instead of patient, tenacious, sustained mental effort and the ability to delay gratification for the sake of eventual self-fulfillment. Additionally, work life may seem excessively arduous if children have been engorged with rapid-fire computer games, Instant Messaging, and formulaic TV shows suffused with canned laughter and predictable story lines that resolve themselves in an eye blink. In some cases, our society's obsession with sports may also limit a kid's capacity for brain work.

What if, throughout a child's formative life, he has shown precious little interest in the lives of adults? He has never been a student of adulthood. He has identified almost exclusively with other kids, his peers; the only grown-ups he has ever admired have been loud entertainers and oversized athletic idols. He may never have given much thought to later life or to any specific career track, and as a result, he's failed to identify with grown-up role models. I believe that the prevailing tendency in our age is for kids to model themselves mostly after their peers, and it may blind young adults when they need to read career road maps. Adolescence can be a hard act to terminate when a youngster has precious little insight into what ought to follow it. Many youngsters therefore are forced to be opportunistic; they will go for whatever line of work is available to them when they need work. They back into a career.

In their book *Quarterlife Crisis*, Alexandra Robbins and Abby Wilner make the observation, "The whirlwind of new responsibilities, new liberties, and new choices can be entirely overwhelming for someone who has just emerged from the shelter of twenty years of schooling." Startup adults may be totally unprepared for some of the bracing realities of early work life listed below.

BRACING REALITIES

- Startup adults may have trouble making a firm commitment to a single area of interest and a confining work setting when their lives have always offered them a steady flow of diverse attractions and distractions.

- They need to start at the bottom of the work heap, which may be difficult after an ego-inflating senior year.

- Their work involves more drudgery and a lot less fun than they had expected; there are more trivial and menial tasks than they had foreseen. They didn't think work would be so much work.

- They no longer receive test scores and report cards, so it can be tough for them to gauge how well they are doing.

- When the job market is tight, they feel dispensable.

- Competition on the job may be camouflaged, but it bristles beneath a convivial surface. Professional jealousy may be rampant.

- Their closest colleagues also may be their archrivals.

- They may become victims of insidious (or even overt) discrimination on the job; it may be related to race, gender, ethnicity, bodily dimensions, or they may be treated unfairly simply because they are young.

- The initial romantic sheen of their career choice may start wearing thin, and they doubt they want to stick with it for the long haul, but perhaps they're not sure what else they can or should do.

- The actual on-the-job subject matter of the work they are doing is not what they had in mind.

- They are ambivalent about the course they are now pursuing and wonder about all those things they could have done, the opportunities they may have passed up.

- They feel that some people working above them are so smart and accomplished that they doubt if they will ever be like them.

- Their success is less dependent on old standbys: athletic ability, coolness, good looks, rote memory, multiple-choice-test-taking skill, and spelling.

- Expectations on the job are spelled out less explicitly than they were in school.

- They are accustomed to rapid gratification; now they may not be seeing immediate results, the way they did on pop quizzes or during athletic events.

- They have to be politically tuned in and astute—able to figure out how to impress the boss or supervisor without offending their coworkers.

- They were banking on a long-assumed support system called institutional loyalty, and now they realize that the organization they have started working for has no loyalty to them. Life at the company will go on just fine if they quit!

- They may have to cope with new feelings of being lonely, isolated, exploited, unloved, undervalued (perhaps underpaid), and bored.

- They are pretty much on their own; their parents are relegated to the sidelines.

- They feel unprepared; they lack skills that they now need urgently.

A WORLDWIDE EPIDEMIC

Work-life unreadiness can plague an entire society or even a global culture. Individuals who are unemployed, underemployed, or unhappily employed impose a heavy drain on our resources. They are susceptible to long-term underachievement. Every government would be well advised to address an epidemic of such unreadiness, gauging how it might affect its economy, its productivity, and its capacity to resolve perplexing national problems.

Early On, Then Later On

There are dramatic differences between the unwritten rules for growing up and those governing careers. For one thing, a child is encouraged to be well-rounded, while adults are permitted (even required) to commit to specialties. So long as grown-ups are effective within their chosen niches, the world will overlook or even fail to notice their gaping flaws elsewhere. Plans are prepackaged for a kid; expectations arrive in explicit proclamations and are as predictable as they are specific. Parental pressure and support are supposed to keep a child on track. The educational system is set up to teach skills in a rigid sequence to ensure that a child is sufficiently competent in all areas. Are such versatile children at risk? Will they have trouble switching over to a specialty mode? Some may.

A sizable hunk of a child's success is measured by her ability to comply, to learn what she is expected to learn, and to do what she's told to do. An adult must be able to chart her own road maps. The odyssey leading into adulthood can be a lonely and harsh voyage, especially if a startup adult is naïve and uninformed, if he's never learned to be a mapmaker.

Through their years of formal education, students are constantly being prepared for whatever's coming next. First graders assemble the decoding skills they'll need for reading in second grade, while second graders are taught to be increasingly fluent readers so that they can access storybooks in third grade. High school students are primed to get into the best possible colleges or land lucrative jobs. Some institutions even call themselves "college prep schools." The term is most often a euphemism for "college admissions prep." Why not "life prep"? Don't we need to prepare our kids for the tough demands of adult life? I believe so. That's what this book is all about.

Young adults unprepared for their career startups are also not equipped to cope with their disappointment over who they are turning out to be and what they find themselves doing. They may even have to endure long-term maladjustment, emotional instability, spasms of depression, alcoholism, and abysmal self-esteem. Ultimately, their unreadiness to move up and out can thwart not just their effectiveness on the job but, as well, their ability to function as spouses and parents. A precarious, unfulfilling career startup easily undermines family and personal life.

Such pathetic outcomes are almost entirely avoidable. To fortify our kids so they can avert these spirals of failure, we will need to reexamine how we go about equipping them for adulthood.

Of a Mind to Prepare
Rearing and educating children involves establishing some long-range priorities. I believe there is at present a vast gulf between what is taught

in school and what is essential to learn for a gratifying adult work life. We overemphasize a host of facts and skills that will be of little or no use in the workplace. Often such educational practice has been ingrained in schools for generations without being sufficiently reexamined for its present-day relevance. Multiple-choice tests do not prepare a child for anything important in the adult sphere. Making a child feel terrible because his scrawl is barely decipherable is callous and needless; many adequately successful adults (the author included) are hardly paragons of legibility. How accurately a child can spell, how thoroughly he conquers trigonometry, how precise he is at the game of memorizing and regurgitating historical facts, and how athletic he may be are irrelevant to almost any career you can name. On the other hand, the ability to think critically, to brainstorm, to monitor and refine your own performance, to communicate convincingly, and to plan and preview work are among the important skills that could make or break startup adults across countless occupations.

We need to keep asking what we're programming kids for and whether or not our current educational priorities have enduring relevance. I am calling for a major reexamination of our priorities for education and parenting.

As I meet many startup adults, I find myself thinking a lot about the need for change. I have gotten to know them and their parents well, and in many cases, I have met their siblings. In two previous books, *A Mind at a Time* and *The Myth of Laziness,* I drew upon my experiences as a clinician to write about key functions and dysfunctions that impact a child's performance during his school years. From my direct work with children and adolescents as well as my opportunities to find out how they are turning out in their twenties, I have developed a framework for what I believe it takes to negotiate the daunting transition from adolescence into the startup years. Within this framework, I have identified twelve essential areas in which a young mind ought to grow to be ready to take on the demands of work life. I call these the growth processes, and as parents, as educators, as community leaders, and as clinicians, we are obliged to see that they are nurtured in all of our children.

Every parent and all educators want to believe they are preparing kids for the real world. But since that real world keeps changing, it should be obvious that teaching and parenting must keep pace and respond to new demands. But are teaching and parenting keeping pace? I don't think so. It is time to set in motion a system through which we can prevent the devastation of work-life unreadiness. Through a combined campaign conducted by parents and schools, we can meet this challenge.

The twelve vital growth processes that I have identified can be divided into four general areas, conveniently remembered as the four *I*'s: *inner direction, interpretation, instrumentation,* and *interaction.* Each of these four areas contains three of the growth processes (as seen in table 1.1). In this book I will focus on how we can foster these processes in children aged eleven to twenty, although some readers may perceive implications for the teaching and rearing of even younger children.

AN OVERVIEW OF THE GROWTH PROCESSES

A separate chapter of this book will be devoted to each of the four *I*'s:

- *Inner direction:* The cogent adage "Know thyself" deserves the spotlight when it comes to work-life readiness. Inner direction refers to an individual's insight into himself or herself. Often, unready startup adults harbor unrealistic or highly distorted senses of who they are and what they can do. They may have false perceptions of their strengths, weaknesses, and personal values. They may have never developed specific aims and aspirations, or they may have fallen short in sparking the self-motivation and drive needed to achieve their goals. One lofty challenge then for parents and teachers is to help kids know themselves, to teach them to become goal setters, and to show them how to reach short and long-term aims.

- *Interpretation:* If inner direction enables children to understand themselves and where they are headed, interpretation, the second *I,* means getting to know the outside world, acquiring insights into the conditions in which young people live, and understanding the phenomena that surround them. School doesn't always provide for that. There are too many students who memorize their way through their classes without understanding what they are learning. We fail to teach kids how to understand. For example, young children often recite the Pledge of Allegiance without understanding a good portion of the vocabulary it contains. Students' comprehension needs to extend to ideas, issues, expectations, and processes. They need to become proficient at on-the-job learning, interpreting new knowledge and integrating what can be gathered from day-to-day experience. To learn from experience, they have to be good at interpreting that experience! Ultimately, accurate interpretation brings with it good judgment and decision making, along with the ability to evaluate critically opportunities, issues, products, and even people.

- *Instrumentation:* The third of the four *I*'s refers to creating a working tool kit, the skills that foster high-quality thinking and productivity. These include the right kinds of organizational skills, the capacity to harness and allocate one's mental energy, brainstorming power, creativity, and the ability to make sound decisions in a systematic manner. It also takes in academic skills and their adaptation to meet challenging demands.

- *Interaction:* The final set of growth processes encompasses interpersonal skills. This includes the invaluable growth process of communication, which enables an individual to use words and construct sentences that convey personal thoughts accurately, convince others of a point of view, and cement relationships. Alliance formation is a second interaction growth process, fostering the cultivation and maintenance of solid work-life relationships. And finally, interaction includes sophisticated political behavior; that is, sensing or knowing what it will take to make the grade and win the approval of individuals who could have a significant influence on one's future success and happiness. These are the influential people, including those with whom or for whom you work, the power brokers who, whether you know it or not, ultimately will be casting ballots either for or against you.

The twelve growth processes are summarized in table 1.1 and discussed in detail in chapters 7 through 10.

No one achieves a perfect score when it comes to the growth processes; we all lag in some areas. But individuals who are significantly unready for a career startup are likely to be seriously deficient in several or else harbor a cluster of underdeveloped growth processes. Their growth may have been stunted somehow at some point. Or else the processes have never been germinated in the first place, perhaps as a result of a shortcoming in their own brain wiring or in their family or school experience.

TABLE 1.1
THE TWELVE GROWTH PROCESSES

Theme	Growth Process	Description	Career Examples
INNER DIRECTION	Inside insight	Awareness of personal strengths, weaknesses, interests, inclinations, passions, and values	Pursuing work for which one is suited; seeing "the writing on the wall" when job changes are called for
	Foresight	Vision of specific aims and understanding of what it will take to meet the aims; strategic planning	Anticipating and preparing for a particular career or project within that career
	Self-launching	Personal aspiration, motivation, ambition, energy, and optimism; emergence as a rational risk taker, independence	Knowing how and when to aim high and go for major career coups
INTERPRETATION	Comprehension	Understanding of ideas in depth and deciphering explicit and implicit job/life/survival requirements	Being equipped to understand key concepts and figure out what your job entails
	Pattern recognition	Effective reading of recurring themes, precedents, rules/regularity/irregularity	Learning from direct, on-the-job experience during a career, deriving guidance from hindsight
	Evaluative thinking	Ability to evaluate critically (without being excessively judgmental/cynical) issues, opportunities, products, people	Knowing what and whom to believe—avoiding chronic cynicism or naïveté

PLAN OF THE BOOK

Before examining the growth processes, in part two explore some pathways that lead to problems during a person's startup years. Four common scenarios and variations are elaborated: adolescence that won't end, idols who are falling, wrong roads that have been taken, and minds that are in debt. Part two starts by examining the ways in which careers can be chosen appropriately and launched smoothly. It then describes

Theme	Growth Process	Description	Career Examples
INSTRUMENTATION	Skill building and adaptation	Capacity to acquire, access, and apply "hard" and "soft" skills in a versatile manner	Reading technical manuals, writing work plans and proposals
	Work efficiency	Ability to harness and allocate mental energy, delay gratification, persevere, and deploy efficient work and organizational habits	Generating a high level of efficient output and becoming dependable on the job
	Productive thinking	Organized thinking, dilemma-handling tactics, brainstorming and creativity, resolving conflicts, coping with stress and impasses	Coming up with constructive and effective ways to derive solutions and apply new approaches to challenges on the job
INTERACTION	Communication	Skill at expressing ideas, persuading, writing, using your inner voices, accessing alternative communication modes	Selling onself, acquiring credibility on the job; using language and imagery to help channel/regulate your feelings and actions
	Alliance formation and reputation management	Constructive collaboration and positive family/social relationships	Demonstrating interpersonal effectiveness, cooperation, leadership, acceptance in the workplace
	Political behavior	Cultivation of people who could have a significant influence over one's future	Knowing how to please a boss and to establish a good reputation with classmates/ fellow workers

the twelve growth processes and what can be done to assure their optimal development. Part three discusses the roles of the growers, those who need to be concerned with work-life readiness, namely parents, educators, adolescents, and startup adults themselves. These final chapters address the insights and practices these mind growers can use to ensure work-life readiness.

Part One

GETTING UNREADY

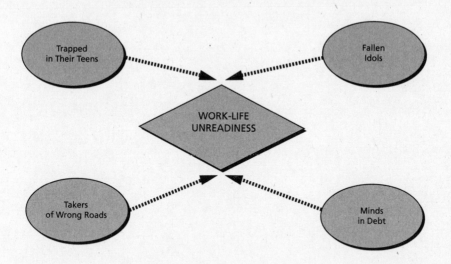

Four predicaments very often set the stage for work-life unreadiness. An individual somehow marooned during the startup years is likely to be caught in one or more of these career binds. There can be many reasons for each of these predicaments, including some destructive forces in our contemporary culture. Certain individual characteristics of emerging adults (and the accuracy of their fit with their work lives), the influences of families, peers, and schools, and the suitability of a young person's preparation for assuming a productive adult role can also be factors. The news is not all gloomy; chapter 6 (in part two) chronicles some triumphant passages into and through the startup years, suggesting reasons why some startup adults are work-life ready.

2

STARTUP ADULTS TRAPPED IN THEIR TEENS

When Adolescents Won't Take Leave

In high school being popular is so based on good looks—you wear the nice clothes—and having a lot of people like you or need you. Now there's a whole different set of criteria. . . . I can't say I'm above the old definition of cool, but it doesn't rule my life.

C.T., age 24

If you continue to try to be cool after school, you are the guy who is thirty-five at the end of the bar in a college town trying to pick up eighteen-year-olds, and you get sloshed every night. These people turn into alcoholics.

D.M., age 28

As I indicated in chapter 1, starting up into adulthood has never been more daunting than it is at present. At the same time, life as a teenager has never been more pleasure filled! The end result is that many adolescents, consciously or unconsciously, seek an extension of their high school and/or college years. They just don't want to pull away from their teens. They may go after more and more education, move back with their parents, postpone tough career choices, and yearn for the intense group companionship that buffered their adolescence. The effects on work-life readiness may be catastrophic.

We live in an era that inflates, celebrates, and consecrates adolescence—the tastes, the mores, the appearances, and the activities of teenagers. Meanwhile, most teens try on various identities as if shopping for stylish shoes, gauging how well their tastes fit with contemporary trends, and revealing their obsessions with images and appearances, with how they are coming across. Young children just can't wait to be teenagers, and countless adults strive, even if in vain, to look and act like seventeen- or eighteen-year-olds. TV shows, magazine ads, pop music, and other media surround us with striking icons of teenage coolness. The result is a steadily growing platoon of startup adults who are not passing through the turnstile of their adolescent years; they are not getting on with their lives.

Charlie is twenty-eight, but you'd never know it. The guy can't stop playing games. He is the younger of two children (the other a girl), the son of Thomas S. Wilson, proprietor of Wilson's Dry Cleaning, a modest but stable business consisting of two moderately profitable shops in an intensely competitive market. Mr. Wilson routinely puts in a twelve-hour day, six days a week. Charlie struggles to make it through his self-assigned five-hour-a-day, five-day week in one of his dad's shops in Southern California, simultaneously detesting and relishing the role of the boss's son. Some days he doesn't show up at all. Tom Wilson, exasperated, goads Charlie to grow up and assume responsibility. But Charlie is on a career carousel; he just keeps going around and around, enticed by fancy trappings but not getting anywhere. His fellow employees criticize Charlie behind his back, as they glimpse the boss's kid feigning work at the front counter or behind the shabby desk in the rear of the shop. He incessantly watches his latest downloaded DVDs, and he still savors video games more than almost any other aspect of his life—with the possible exception of sex and, of course, paintball. He takes to anything on a fast track, especially cars and in-line roller skates. Not surprisingly, Charlie is an avid and deftly acrobatic surfboarder. The man is addicted to what I call visual-motor ecstasy. But after his ultra-high-velocity engagements, he passes endless hours splayed on a couch like jam on a muffin, watching football and basketball games. And he is a serious womanizer, a less passive pursuit!

Whether or not one respects him (and no one seems to), Charlie is hard to dislike. He is generous, outgoing, and as affable as they come. He would do anything for his friends, and nothing matters to him as much as his friends, just as with your typical sixteen-year-old. Much of his seemingly fun-packed existence is devoted to planning weekend and evening escapades. His massive wardrobe of Abercrombie and Banana Republic garb displays the latest in adolescent virile elegance. He trades in his used sports car every eighteen months or so, having put forty or fifty thousand miles on its odometer, and he has had his license suspended twice in the last four years. He is the very model of a modern middle-class teenager—except that his entry into adulthood is ten years overdue, with no end to adolescence in sight. He's a third-decade teenager. Unfortunately, just beneath his ebullient demeanor, Charlie hides abysmal self-esteem. He admits his life has no meaning for him; it's just a potpourri of experiences, and nothing seems to connect or add up to anything else. He is on a pathway to nowhere.

PERSISTENT ADOLESCENCE

In our present culture many teenagers are loitering well beyond adolescence. One can cite numerous reasons, including the potent and immediate gratification experienced by socially sought-after teens, the appearance-obsessed media, and the complex and confused state that can make one's twenties hard to handle. It's a lot simpler to remain eighteen. As in Charlie's case, life for many adolescents has been saturated with pleasures that the banality of the workplace cannot match.

The longing for extended adolescence is not limited to middle-class people like Charlie. One twenty-one-year-old inner-city girl, Bonita, told me that she feels depressed stocking shelves at a pharmacy in New York because she misses all the fun she used to have with her friends at school. "We had much in common. They were all from the Dominican Republic, like me. Now I work with people who are, like, Chinese and from other places; we're not close. I miss the closeness. I miss all that protection and all the laughs you get with real friends all day long. Work doesn't feel good to me now, but I don't know what to do about it." Membership in an intimate, protective clan is one of adolescence's most seductive benefits; it can be nearly impossible to replicate on the job.

The psychologist Erik Erikson characterized adolescence as a period of exploration and experimentation, a time when kids try on different roles, a period of coming to terms with one's personal identity. In our time, increasing numbers of startup adults are still heavily engaged in adolescent-type exploring and experimenting. Such activity is not necessarily hazardous, but some young people seem to be going nowhere or experiencing confusion and chaos. There is, of course, a significant difference between seeking and floundering. A bit of floundering may be healthy, but at some point it can become demoralizing. In many instances indecision about occupational choices plays a major role in the need to prolong adolescence. But sometimes a deeply felt reluctance to leave one's adolescence obstructs the search for an adult identity and career.

COOL DUDESHIP

The mandate to be "cool" may be one of the first adolescent priorities to decay. Coolness is a collection of personal marketing strategies that can be most effective in high school and on into the college years, in some colleges more than others. The word *cool,* which doesn't seem to want to take leave of contemporary culture, has a premium value for those aspiring to peer adulation. Some core manifestations of coolness are identified below.

THE BIG-TEN FEATURES OF ADOLESCENT COOLNESS

Relaxed demeanor
Bravado and confidence
Minor risk taking/taboo breaking
Attire and tastes mirroring current trends
Statuesque and agile body "choreography"
Inner-circle "niceness" and loyalty
Visible acceptance in a clique
Wry sense of humor/mild cynicism
Minor embellishments of norms
Physical attractiveness

Clearly, adolescents are under some pressure to appear relaxed much of the time, projecting a veneer of invulnerability and strength at a time of life when kids feel especially vulnerable and intermittently helpless. They are expected to exude confidence and courage, to take some risks and break a few minor taboos as part of their rite of passage. Cigarettes, alcohol, and compelling tattoos, along with certain hairdos or dyes guaranteed to aggravate adults fill the bill magnificently.

Coolness also involves meticulous posing, choreographing your physical gestures and your facial expressions and then periodically freezing in a vaguely seductive yet ultrarelaxed posture as if awaiting the arrival of the paparazzi. Girls may cross their legs in a slightly risqué manner, while boys daringly expose the upper fringes of their boxer shorts with occasional brief presentations of the vertical hairline extending down from the umbilicus. Smoking, by the way, satisfies two demands at once: it breaks a taboo at the same time that it provides the opportunity for cool body movements. The studied rhythmic gestures and deft movements of a newly recruited adolescent smoker are something to behold, coolness personified.

There is a coolness dress code, a list of acceptable tastes in music, a sharing of heroes, and quite often an allegiance to certain sports (a taste requirement). You can take a few liberties with taste, but they must represent relatively subtle deviations from the code, minor innovations which, if you play your cards right, may be acknowledged as "supercool." Physical attractiveness and a sense of humor add to one's coolness. Finally, you're expected to be kind ("really nice") but that obligation is mainly confined to loyal members of your innermost circle. That means you can bully or verbally attack those on the fringes and still be perceived as cool.

Some startup adults are unable to cool it when it comes to the code of coolness. Symbolically, at age twenty-seven they continue to wear their baseball caps backwards. A colleague of mine, Allan Shedlin, who was headmaster of a school and later director of the Elementary School Center in New York, taught me the word *neoteny.* It refers to older people who persist in acting like teenagers. They may be unable to progress beyond their obedience to the ten features of coolness. I see them posing all the time. During my travels, I look around departure lounges. I might notice a sixty-year-old man wearing blue jeans, a reversed baseball cap, and other teenage accouterments. Is this nothing more than a benign affectation, or is it a serious and disabling arrest of maturation? Sometimes the latter is the case.

I'm reminded of a guy named Buddy. Buddy wanted nothing more than to be everybody's buddy. Fortunately, he was in a position to satisfy this desire. People were his hobby from an early age. He was insatiable when it came to relationships (page 74), and he stuck to friends the way my dog's white hair clings to my navy blue sport jacket. His adolescent years turned out to be, as Buddy would put it, "a ball." There was no doubt about it: he was the very model of a modern majorly cool kid. He exceeded all the criteria in his tastes, in his demeanor, and in his body movements.

Buddy never took school very seriously. He was one of those students who got by. He was not about to be perceived as a nerd or a geek (fatal wounds to a cool guy). He had a younger brother who used to get straight As, and Buddy was ashamed to have any of his friends meet this "nerdy" sibling. Both parents, now social workers, had been hippies in their day and were very permissive, allowing the kids pretty much to live their own lives and become whoever they were destined to become. The parents were not neglectful; they provided well for their children. Buddy's mom and dad enjoyed and admired their son despite his lack of academic honors. They saw him as a terrific people person and felt confident he would find success somewhere someday.

Buddy managed to elevate his social ranking as a loyal fraternity brother in the local state college, the ultimate smooth and nice guy. He majored in sociology after he astutely discovered that most classes in that department were held at eleven a.m. or later. His grades hovered around a "gentleman's C," and he graduated without distinction close to the very top of the bottom fifth of his class.

Buddy hit one land mine after another following college. He had no plans whatsoever. In the past he had lived in or near the present. At the age of twenty, the future for him was Saturday night, and that was all that appeared in his viewfinder. After graduation Buddy strayed like a nomad from job to job, believing that he would be showered with recognition for being so cool. Despite repeated frustration, he persisted in playing his well-rehearsed part. He had firmly typecast himself as the cool dude. He therefore could not appear to be working particularly hard, showing any initiative, seeming ambitious, or dressing like a rising executive (whatever that might entail).

Buddy rapidly became his own worst enemy. His bosses barely knew the meaning of the word *cool*. All around him those dorks and geeks whom he had so disparaged (and often bullied) were making lots more money than he was—the cruel revenge of the nerd. He felt humiliated every time he was asked to go outdoors to smoke a cigarette at work, especially since he was the only one out there on the stoop. But Buddy just could not give up his adolescent ways and values. They had worked too well for him for too long.

Buddy tumbled into a severe depression, for which he underwent treatment with heavy doses of medication. When a psychiatrist colleague of mine related his story to me, I couldn't help but feel that Buddy had urgently needed help as an adolescent. He needed to come to terms with who he was and who he was becoming. He should have been assisted in understanding the unquestionable value of his social talents but also their limitations. Buddy's powerful affinity for people and for relationships should have been explored in detail, and possible career pathways and college courses could have built upon his interpersonal and marketing aptitudes. Most of all, Buddy should have been cured of his naïveté, for he was totally ignorant of what it takes to be a happy adult when the party's over.

In many ways, it is very cool to be cool. Learning to fit in and gain acceptance can be viewed as an important educational goal. The question for any adolescent or startup grownup is, What price are you paying by posing? To what extent is coolness at odds with the image of a person striving to ascend the lower rungs of a career ladder? What are you sacrificing from your family life and education in order to attain and project coolness? To what extent are you overlooking, denying, or stifling your own special strengths and unique individuality so as to fit in and mesh with a group? At what point will you be capable of giving up the coolness campaign in favor of other priorities—a fruitful job, a gratifying marriage, a robust family? These questions must be addressed if ultracool adolescents are to avoid becoming startups stuck in their teens.

LUGGING A BODY INTO THE STARTUP YEARS

Our culture is obsessed with body images. TV shows and music videos that kids watch stress perfect contour and sensuous movement. A relentless barrage of appearance-enhancing products woos teenagers, as well as younger and younger children. Kids are forever adding and subtracting body accessories, experimenting endlessly with their guises and disguises, campaigning relentlessly for physical admiration and acceptance. Adolescents under such intense somatic pressure are at once fascinated and terrified as they observe themselves becoming magically transformed into adults. Many go through periods of self-doubt as they wonder if their bodies are meeting midpubertal and postpubertal standards. At times the experimentation and exploration lead them to sexual adventures or misadventures. As with coolness, the question is, How much preoccupation is appropriate and when does it cross the line? Can intense body obsessions get in the way of intellectual development, career planning, and family relationships?

Jeanette was a pudgy toddler. During elementary school she came across as physically and socially awkward, though she was a very proficient student. She enjoyed mostly As and rave reviews on her report cards. She loved to read, and by fifth grade she was writing poetry laced with rich imagery. Her female classmates sentenced this studious, overweight peer to brutal rejection and exclusion, which made her so profoundly unhappy that her self-esteem was always on the verge of crumbling. She longed for companionship but received very little. She was an only child who had been adopted in infancy by an older couple. She was most often surrounded by adults, all of whom seemed to care about her, but growing up, she had relatively little contact with other children.

Soon after puberty Jeanette lost much of the oval contour of her face. Her fine features seemed to burst forth at age thirteen like a purple crocus blooming out of snow. She even lost some weight and started to become rather attractive and well endowed. As she witnessed in the mirror this metamorphosis, Jeanette became increasingly tuned in to her body image. She started dieting and engaged in heavy exercise. The results were terrific. But her body became an obsession for this girl and remained so for years to come. Suddenly, in eighth grade, she was sought after by everyone.

Jeanette's parents were nonplussed. The telephone wouldn't stop ringing. The sudden surge of social gratification was so totally consuming that Jeanette was unable to think about anything else. Her academic work deteriorated. Her parents began to feel as if they had lost her. By the end of ninth grade, the formerly sweet and docile cherub had become defiant and argumentative, often calling her mother "stupid." Jeanette steadfastly refused to see a therapist. During high school she never stopped asking for money to buy clothes. Sally, Jeanette's mom, always wanting to stay on the good side of her only child, often caved in and collaborated on exorbitant shopping safaris. Together they read fashion magazines voraciously and talked about makeup and hairstyles. They would join each other at the spa to lose weight they really didn't need to lose. I'm always amazed at how often parents will inadvertently play into a child's serious area of weakness, perhaps as part of that all-important quest to gain her favor.

Jeanette spent entire weekends at the mall with her friends or her mom or both. She dated a lot, often strikingly handsome guys whom her father branded "airheads." More than once he accused Jeanette of becoming a tramp. She resented the fact that her parents had no respect for her boyfriends.

Jeanette eventually studied hairdressing at the local community college, but she dropped out in her first year. She said she didn't much like her fellow students. She got married at age nineteen and soon gave birth to a daughter. Her husband was unemployed and had serious drinking and drug problems, but she stood by him like a loyal guard dog. Her mother tended to the baby while Jeanette went to work in the makeup department of a local department store. She felt totally unfulfilled. What ever became of Jeanette the young poet, the writer, the avid reader, the ardent student? Her body had undermined her mind.

All kids, and adults to varying degrees, are concerned about body image and appearances. This is perfectly normal, probably very healthy. But in Jeanette's case and with many other boys and girls, an obsession with appearance overwhelms them. Sometimes social pressures and an unquenchable thirst for peer acceptance fuel this preoccupation. In other cases, teenage athletic triumphs combine with body-image obsessions to crowd out most other values and priorities. Occasionally, disastrous complications set in, scourges such as anorexia nervosa and bulimia as well as serious depression and other mental health catastrophes. More commonly, those who are unable to recover from adolescent bodily concerns may join the wandering ranks of young adults unready to get on with life. In their quest for perfect bodies, they leave behind the preparation of their minds.

UNPLUGGED FROM THE ADULT WORLD

Potent forces in our society distance many adolescents from adults, encouraging kids to select each other as role models in place of adults. How can you emerge as a productive adult when you've hardly ever cared to observe one very closely? How can you preview and prepare for grown-up life when you keep modeling yourself after other kids? The answer is, With great difficulty. A critical factor for all kids is how well they have connected with the adult world. Those who grow up in a culture in which most adults are aliens are far less likely to grow into gratified adults themselves.

Collis, a kid from inner-city Chicago, was fatherless. He lived at home with his mom, who was on public assistance, a brother, and two sisters. All the kids had different fathers. Collis had only a vague suspicion of who his father might be, but he told everyone he didn't much care. He spent his elementary school years attending school sporadically, disenfranchised in the classroom, often wondering what he was doing there. Collis had trouble learning to read and do math. His basic comprehension of literate English was pathetic. He would sit in class in a state of verbal confusion. So Collis often skipped or fled school, for which he was constantly reproached. At home, conditions were at a subsistence level; the family was always locked into a survival mode—having barely enough to eat, facing brutal threats from the landlord, and lacking enough hot water. Collis's mother, a loving and dedicated woman, had all she could do to get through the day, even though she wasn't working. The only extended family was Collis's maternal grandmother, who showed up occasionally to help out. Collis came to resent bitterly his deprived home life, and he dreaded school. There was only one place to turn: the neighborhood and friends.

By age twelve he was an active gang member. He sold drugs (and used them) before his fifteenth birthday. Collis worshipped some of the nineteen- and twenty-year-old gang leaders. He thought they were the coolest people in the world. He loved rap music and proudly wore the uniform of his social militia: braided hair, baggy trousers worn as low as they go, unlaced basketball sneakers, and a dollop of stainless steel attachments, including, oddly enough, a prominent crucifix suspended by a chain necklace—odd because Collis had never set foot in a church.

As you might imagine, Collis dropped out of school and spent much of his day roaming aimlessly with the rest of his clan. He acquired a minor police record that included some shoplifting and gang fighting. Collis had an ominous look about him. He often smirked at the fact that white folks would always cross Michigan Avenue when he and his posse approached them on the sidewalk. By the age of seventeen Collis was alive in a vacuum. He had no values, no plans, no aspirations, no interests. He existed from hour to hour. Most conspicuously, there were no adults to identify with, to be guided by, to cheer him on. There are millions of poor kids like Collis all over the world. Their only role models are each other. They never go forward; they just spin in a lifestyle of redundant thrill seeking. They begin their adolescence before they reach puberty and adopt all the rituals and the tenacious peer bonding that goes with the teenage territory. At age twenty-five or twenty-nine, they remain mostly adolescents.

Collis was in danger of wasting his life or losing it, but he was unusually fortunate. When he was nearly eighteen and on probation, a savvy juvenile judge ordered him to join a mentoring program. He was assigned to Calvin, a gifted twenty-six-year-old social worker. Over a period of months, the two forged a solid alliance. This was the first man Collis could ever identify with—with the exception of rap singers and basketball players (neither of whom embodied attainable goals for him).

Calvin got Collis into a trade school program in heating and air conditioning. Collis rapidly grasped the intricacies of that technology. He could clearly picture things in his mind; he could understand ductwork without having to put it into words. He could bypass the language confusion that had made academic success a seeming impossibility. He felt as if he had something he could do well. It would become his ticket out of adolescence, and it had arrived just in time. The young man's self-esteem took off like a launched satellite. He was ready to gear up for his startup years. Tragically, for every Collis there are hundreds or thousands who never find that crucial adult and so cannot connect to adulthood. They all desperately need mentors.

Inner-city kids often represent an extreme example of disconnection from adult society and value systems, but the phenomenon can be seen up and down the socioeconomic ladder. Some children and adolescents come to feel they can never please their parents no matter what they do. As a result, they unconsciously repudiate the adult world and all its "stupid" values. There's a very common coping tactic: if you can't succeed, denigrate whatever it is you can't succeed at. If you can't satisfy and win the respect of grown-ups, dump them (and dump on them)! Live primarily for your friends, for relationships. The relationships are meant to facilitate a steady supply of immediate happiness. If you're having problems at school and at home, you may seek out other kids who are in the same boat and form a disenfranchised family of peers. In extreme cases, kids may end up following cults or joining gangs. This is a common scenario among members of the Hare Krishna, for example. All such disillusioned kids run the risk of a maturation arrest in adolescence; they may cling to adolescent values and bonds well into their twenties.

Some alienation from adulthood may be associated with actual anger at the world of well-heeled grown-ups. A young waitress at a French restaurant confided how bitterly she resents high-powered business executives. She mentioned that the heads of banks keep raising the interest rates on credit cards so that they can buy expensive cars and join country clubs. She moaned that these executives don't care about people in their twenties who have to skimp and struggle every month to pay off their credit-card debt.

Children and adolescents should be students of adulthood. In the past, grandfathers and grandmothers played influential roles in educating children. Kids gathered around the hearth to absorb the elders' lessons and tales. Every grown-up friend and family member might reveal the secrets of adulthood. There were extended families living in close proximity, allowing for a wide exposure to all kinds of adult minds and stories.

In most cases today, such opportunities are severely limited. Close relatives (perhaps not even encountered very often) and teachers (most of whom students don't get to know personally) are almost the sole adults aside from parents in kids' lives. From an early age children are taught to fear and shun strangers and not to speak to anybody they don't know, so they are further distanced from the world of grown-ups.

When I'm invited to dinner at someone's home, most often the off-spring of the host and hostess broadcast a terse ritual greeting, generally without eye contact, and then they vanish from the social scene. They have no interest whatsoever in my spouse and me. When I was a little boy, when my parents had company, they could not get rid of me (try as they would). Their friends, some of whom seemed so awesome and some so weird, all elicited my curiosity. I studied these people as if I were cramming for a quiz, and I talked to my mother or father about them the next morning. I wanted to know what they did for a living, how they got to be so successful, why they kept arguing. Also, I always talked to grown-up strangers wherever I was—in stores, on trains, in the barbershop. It never occurred to me or my parents that these strangers might injure or abuse me in some manner. I was in career basic training. I was learning how to connect to adulthood.

I think kids desperately need to relate to adult strangers. Maybe our society should screen individuals and certify some of us "safe strangers" for kids to interact with. A child could ask to see my safe stranger certificate before talking to me!

A LONGING TO RETURN

Some startup adults are not striving to resemble teenagers but are sorely missing their adolescent years. The props that supported them from twelve to twenty have been disassembled, and they are having a hard time surviving without them. Here's a familiar scenario:

Fran, at age twenty-two, is chronically depressed. She often feels undervalued and overwhelmed working as a reporter for a city newspaper. A competent journalism major in college, she is not making as much money as she feels she needs. Her parents refuse to support her, saying that she is old enough to fend for herself and that it's time she became independent. Fran realizes that her teenage years were terrific. She grew up an only child in a household where there was a surplus of affection and funding. She had a very loving relationship with her mother, who was always her staunch advocate. Fran's life was highly structured, densely scheduled with extracurricular lessons and orchestrated recreational forays. From time to time Fran complained that she had no time to think. She was always a pretty solid and diligent student, if not heralded for her creativity or analytic insights.

In her present job Fran is compelled to meet tight deadlines, come up with her own ideas for feature stories, and deal with a steady barrage of wounding criticism from her editor. She has been accustomed to unbridled praise from her dance instructor, harp teacher, and parents. She keeps trying to regain or relive that glory—but to no avail. No one seems to be rooting for her, except her parents, and somehow their role feels much less relevant, infinitely more peripheral at this point. Unconsciously she yearns for those bygone high school days. Fran misses the structure and predictability, all the chances she had to gain points simply by being compliant. She has no idea how to cope with the normal stresses and the unspoken rules of the startup years. She feels abandoned. She would like to turn back the clock.

Look Homeward, Angel

It is not unusual for a startup adult who can't quite find his place to head back to the good old days of adolescence. So he goes back to school without any clear posteducation plans, perhaps only a hazy notion that he'd like to get into something having to do with, for instance, telecommunications. He moves back in with his parents, ostensibly to conserve funds, but he won't spurn the laundering services and other domestic perks. Once he's back home, he feels a greater sense of support, though soon he may feel as if he's being spied on and offered more advice than he can use.

Sometimes this seeming regression lets a startup adult recharge his fuel cells and refocus his perspectives. In other cases it is a benign holding pattern—unless it goes on too long. Parents may find their lodger (or freeloader) a bit taxing to have around. They probably need to be careful not to make things too comfortable for him, and they may want to set some terms for the lease. If at all possible, I think they should avoid bankrolling the returning tenant. Subsidization may erode his career motivation while funding an extended rerun of his adolescence.

Several years ago as I was on the way to speaking at a seminar in Copenhagen, a turbaned taxi driver of Sikh descent was telling me his life story en route to the conference center. He explained that he and his wife had their two children, a boy and a girl aged twenty-two and twenty-four, living with them at home. I suggested that this arrangement must get pretty tense. But he vigorously denied this. He went on, "When our son and daughter reached the age of nineteen, we told them very clearly, 'You are no longer our children; from now on you are our friends.' " I asked what that actually meant. He responded, "That means we offer them no advice unless they ask for it. And we give them no money even if they ask for it." He did add that from time to time he and his wife gave their kids modest monetary gifts. I would think that the contract this man held with his kids may be the best of both worlds for some; the kids have a sense of security and connectedness at the same time that they are required to grow up.

The Fate of Programmed Kids

It is not unusual for contemporary teenagers to be as programmed as robots. Their weeks are strategically planned out for them. Structure engulfs them, and they swim in a constant tide of supervision and feedback. Check out Fran's afterschool schedule at age sixteen: band practice three times a week (including Saturday morning), harp lessons Monday and Wednesday evening, religious class Tuesdays and Thursdays and on Sunday mornings, tutoring in math twice a week, modern dance every Friday, plus her community service project and volunteer work at the daycare center. Then there are the more intense but fleeting commitments like the school play, the campaign to raise money for band uniforms, and service on the junior prom decorations committee. In every one of these activities, expectations are well defined: you're told what you need to do. That is in stark contrast to the early stages of a career, when many of the expectations are apt to be less obvious and when it helps to show some initiative and generate some original ideas. For Fran, as for so many others, life was rigidly programmed. The structure was invariably imposed from without; she didn't have to organize herself or assemble her own routines. Nor did she have to demonstrate much initiative or innovative effort. She was always judged by her ability to conform or comply with the demands of a coach or an instructor or of a curriculum. In a way, all that structure was comforting; it made for a busy yet simplified life. But now, as an adult starting to ascend the career ladder, Fran finds that she has to establish her own structure, and she is being evaluated on her ability to come up with original stories. She keeps checking with her boss on everything she does. Maybe her adolescence was not as enriching as it seemed at the time. Fran should have had more hours of free play and more chances to brainstorm, to establish her own priorities, and to organize her time.

BREAKING THROUGH

It may be that no one ever totally outgrows the teenage experience. For most people, the years from twelve to twenty were filled with moments of self-discovery and gratification. Memories of this era can be joyful and energizing, but they are also at times vaguely painful. The trick is to conserve the positive memories and give up the constricting adolescent values—the powerful and potentially paralyzing fixations on appearance, coolness, acceptance, conformity, and experimentation for the sake of experimentation. For those whose teenage lives were tightly structured and supervised, that dependence needs to abate as well (unless they enlist in the military). A startup adult has to bid farewell to adolescence and journey toward becoming all he can become—and savoring the experience. Bidding farewell to adolescence can be one of life's most significant breakthroughs. Yet it must occur if there is to be meaningful forward movement in a work life.

3
ONES WHO WERE ONCE REVERED

When Idols Fall

Coming from the socioeconomic background I did, there was nothing I couldn't do, period. I never had the possibility of being in an underfunded school with an unmotivated teacher. So I see that I had a huge benefit. I also think it may have taken away some of my motivation at a young age.

S.R., age 27

What becomes of all those highly touted kids who were doused with success throughout their formative years? Is it possible to suffer from too much praise too early in life? I think so. A young adult, having vaulted through a decade or more of unfettered fun, awesome personal achievement, and unwavering admiration from bleachers of loyal fans, may suddenly feel bereft, abandoned, painfully undervalued at age twenty or twenty-two or twenty-four. Yes, the party's over. The idol is falling—hard!

TOPPING OUT AND BOTTOMING OUT

Throughout his school years Glen Martin was a sandy blond wonder boy. In elementary school Glen was a determined athlete and a strong student in all subjects. And his early promise developed into a vast mural of childhood and teenage triumphs, trophies, and newspaper clippings. Glen had an equally competent older sister, but his younger brother seemed to drown in the demands of school and endure the life of a social outcast.

Glen, who graduated from high school near the top of his class, was captain of the soccer team and an all-league first baseman. He attended an Ivy League college, which didn't surprise anyone. During his freshman year, however, Glen started to lose ground. Having torn up his knee playing soccer, he pretty much gave up on sports. Academically, he felt overwhelmed and uninspired. He had trouble adjusting to the fact that he was no longer the only smart kid on the block, and over his four years he earned mostly Bs with the occasional C+. For the first time in his life he was nobody special in the eyes of the faculty, and he knew it. He started to gain a lot of weight and lose a lot of self-esteem. With considerable ambivalence, he backed into political science, having no other option that seemed more inviting. Interestingly, during high school Glen did well across the board but never found any subject area that excited him more than the others. In a sense, this kid was too well-rounded for his own good!

During Glen's junior year in college, there were two all-consuming crises: his father was diagnosed with a malignant brain tumor and died within eight months, and Glen broke up with a girl he had been dating since his sophomore year in high school. She said to him that she felt he had changed, that he was not the gracious superstar she had known and loved in high school. He was distraught, but he knew how right she was. Following these two losses he became overtly depressed. He talked of taking off a semester but endured in response to pleas from his mother.

Upon graduation—without honors—Glen had no idea what he wanted to do with his life. He had no particular interests, no obvious passions. As he put it, "I don't know anything and I can't do anything. And you know, I'm not so sure I'm interested in anything special." It seemed as if he had been paralyzed by the events and conditions at college. He remained depressed. He had no strategies to cope with adversity. For the first time in his life Glen had to contend with stress and with self-doubts about his abilities. No one had ever prepared him to deal with setbacks; he had only needed to know how to manage victories and display appropriate modesty! Now he had to handle significant losses. Glen had never been tested, never taught how to negotiate impasses, a skill everyone needs during the startup years. Could he have had too much success and fulfillment too early in life? Was high school his finest hour? Shouldn't he have been prepared for the setbacks he would inevitably encounter during the startup years? Yes, he should have. And so should other kids who stand on pedestals during their adolescent years.

Once I had a memorable lunch discussion with the head of psychiatry in the student health services at a prominent college; he had been a classmate of mine in medical school. I asked him, "Joe, tell me who the students are who seem to fall apart mentally in college. How would you characterize them?" He responded, "Mel, they're not at all who you think they are. They're not the kids who grew up deprived or in dysfunctional families or with lives littered with stress. Most students who crumble during their undergraduate years are the ones who never before had to struggle, the superstars of their prep schools or high schools. Many were hometown heroes, the worshipped jocks, the well-rounded types, the ones who always seemed to do everything right and were revered by throngs of admirers. They were the golden boys and girls. And you know, in reality, those kids actually grew up deprived. They never learned how to deal with feelings of inadequacy. It's a little late to have to do that for the first time when you're twenty years old!"

That was Glen. He had never learned how to deal with feelings of inadequacy and how to rebound from negative beliefs about his own worth. Sooner or later everyone has to meet up with and conquer feelings of inadequacy, and sooner is better.

Glen had no idea what to do when he left college. At first he had no desire to continue his education, proclaiming that he was sick and tired of being a student. He got back in shape and took a job helping out at a health club, having always been interested in physical fitness. Initially he felt comfortable surrounded by people of like mind—and body. Meanwhile, he enrolled in a course to become certified as a personal trainer. Following his certification, he pursued this line of work for about eight months but kept feeling that the day-to-day routine was somehow "gross." He resented the affluent but out-of-shape people in their fifties and sixties whose unsightly bodies he was required to tend to. He was disgusted with the borderline bulimic middle-aged women who would flirt with him while he coached their crunches. Also, he had little respect for his fellow trainers, many of whom struck him as more lost in life than he was. Eventually he decided that human body work was not for him.

Glen decided to return to school. He moved back home with his mother and sought a master's degree in history. Over the next eight years, Glen's life was a mosaic of academic coursework, the aimless pursuit of a PhD in Roman history, a CV bulging with part-time jobs, associate membership in a tribe of rather arty friends, and an assortment of unstable relationships with women. Glen's affairs were always brittle because Glen never could never outgrow his self-image as the wonder boy of his high school, the object of local pubescent female dreams, so he kept seeking the perfect woman, a goddess worthy of the godlike guy he was as a teenager. Nobody he slept with could satisfy those standards.

At age twenty-seven Glen thought he might eventually teach history or maybe start an Internet business or perhaps get a job in state government someday. But mainly he lived in the present.

There are countless variations on Glen's themes among the ranks of those with work-life unreadiness. They share a lack of self-definition and clarity of direction. A subset of these people, aimless in their twenties like Glen, are fallen idols, individuals who coasted unencumbered through childhood and adolescence. They were so successful that they never had to stop to figure out who they were. Maybe they acquired a thick undercoat of hubris and felt that they were destined to excel on automatic pilot, ever upward toward success and glory without even trying particularly hard, sacrificing anything, or fretting about the future. They were somehow born to win. Glen would have been better served to have received fewer awards at graduation, to have developed some passionate interests outside sports, perhaps to have held a job after school. He should have been shielded somewhat from his own success and its damaging long-term side effects. There's something to be said for graduating from the old-fashioned "school of hard knocks." Except when it's too hard, that school can provide a valuable education.

FORMER HEROES

Glen's plight highlights also the critical issue of the positive and negative influences of sports on developing lives. Former athletes are amply represented among the work-life unready.

There are abundant true tales of inner-city kids who were talented athletes, often identified in middle school. Many went on to become star performers in high school. They climbed to positions of high status within their peer group: there's no such thing as a socially rejected juvenile sports star. They became the pride and joy of their families and neighborhoods. Some of these kids go on to attain athletic distinction in college. And, of course, a tiny number of college players become pros. What happens to all the rest?

In many cases these school athletes have been deprived and deceived. They were so adept at sports that other parts of their lives and their minds went underdeveloped. Some barely made passing grades, and they were propped up artificially with heavy tutoring, grade inflation, and gut courses. Some never graduated. Imagine what it must be like to perform before roaring crowds for eight years through high school and college, and then, a year later, pound the pavement alone, desperately hunting for some kind of employment. You had believed that the glory would last forever.

Fortunately, some universities offer sound career counseling to their potentially dispossessed athletes. But not all of these students will benefit significantly from these services. I spoke about realistic planning with Dean Smith, the renowned former coach of the University of North Carolina men's basketball team. Dean has always had a reputation for caring about his players as individuals. He explained to me that early on, he expected each of them to be able to articulate what he calls Plan B, that is, what the player will do if he fails to turn professional after college. Every kid who wants to be a professional athlete needs to approach the future with a Plan B.

Participation in sports can help prepare kids for a work life. Through athletic experiences they learn to collaborate, strategize, self-monitor, and delay gratification. They can acquire resiliency, learning how to bounce back from losses. But here's one more potential side effect of athletics: when a sport is a source of inflated gratification and admiration, a kid may be deprived of the benefits of any intellectual pleasure. I have asked kids what they are interested in and gotten the answer, "Soccer." I respond by saying, "That's a fantastic sport, but I wasn't really asking about what sort of entertainment you like. I was wondering what areas or topics or subjects you're interested in." The answer obviously was none. In such instances, potential mind-building activities are shoved aside as body accomplishments become an obsession. Then one day the game is over. The startup years get going, and that grown-up kid is deficient in some of the mind skills critical for career launches. Every athlete should be helped to develop mind-oriented interests and pursuits alongside his sporting life. I think every kid should have his area of expertise, something he knows more about and feels more passionate about than anyone else in his class or neighborhood. The gradual building of expertise emerges as he amasses focused ideas and a body of knowledge over time; that's what he'll need to do in a career.

On a more modest scale, we sometimes encounter a phenomenon

that has been called the diva syndrome. A child or adolescent takes lessons, say in ballet or horseback riding or skiing, and is constantly told that she or he has extraordinary potential. For instance, thirteen-year-old Meg is told she could be an Olympic medal winner someday. Or an instructor pumps up a pair of parents by letting them know that someday their Chad could well be nationally ranked in tennis. These seductive prophecies can reorder the whole life of a family, particularly that of the future celebrity. False hopes may be raised. The parents may see their kid as a potential trophy, a living testimony to their superior genes and parenting virtuosity. The kid may reach heights of fame the parents themselves were unable to scale. Parents' own egos become richly nourished as they display their child's ribbons and trophies, boasting about her skating prowess or equestrian skills at work and social occasions. But then, at some point, reality reveals its face. How do you pick up the pieces? Did the family invest so much in the prospect of future stardom that no other capacities were valued or cultivated? That happens. Then that person must live the life of a fallen idol.

CHILD-REARING BUBBLES THAT BURST

Nothing is more instinctive for a parent than to idolize a child. It is an ingredient of love, and the love of a parent is irreplaceable. Nothing is more exquisite and poignant. It is the soil and the fertilizer within which a young person takes root. We know that kids deprived of such love and family connectedness are at risk for all sorts of mental illnesses and traumatic breakdowns. But is it possible for parents to convey their caring in ways that might be damaging? Can well-meaning, loving parents inadvertently hurt or obstruct a child's development? I think we see this all the time. The phenomenon is pretty straightforward: life at home becomes an impossible act to follow. To put it another way, it's a bubble that's bound to burst, and it does—most often during the startup years.

There are many ways in which child-rearing practices on the part of conscientious, well-intentioned parents can set up a child for work-life unreadiness. Let's examine some of these.

Perceived Fragility

Out of the goodness of their hearts, some parents treat their child as if she were a delicate crystal goblet. Consequently, the child is shielded from adversity of every sort. This kind of perceived fragility of children has spread throughout our culture and is actually making kids fragile.

The principal of an elementary school in a middle-class suburban community described to me one of her deepest concerns. Far too often when a child is having a problem relating to a teacher or to another child, the parents intervene rapidly and vigorously. They summon the principal and demand an immediate solution to the impasse. The principal felt strongly that parents should let their children play a leading role in resolving their problems. I agree with her. Many heads of schools whom I encounter offer the identical observation, namely, that more and more parents are afraid to let their kids manage their own conflicts or impasses in life. This is risky parenting because these children may never become effective personal problem solvers. A setback in school ought to be considered a vital part of education, but it can't be if it is taken over by parents in an effort to protect (in reality, overprotect) a child. Parents can serve as helpful consultants, but they should avoid actively intervening.

Dispute settlement should be a core part of the growing-up curriculum. When parents intervene, a golden educational opportunity has been squandered. Mothers and fathers need to stay on the sidelines, serving as sounding boards and perhaps offering sage advice, if asked. Settling differences for a kid is one way to put him on a pedestal, possibly making him feel smugly invulnerable. Someday he'll experience the shocking realization that some disputes won't go away unless he actively negotiates settlements.

Highly protective parents also may constrain a child's explorations and experimentations. They may make it hard for a kid to experience a wide range of relationships as well. Fears of kidnapping, abuse, and other horrors may restrict a child's social growth. Such concerns are understandable and wise. But overdoing protectiveness can make a child feel excessively fragile and vulnerable. Ultimately, it can lead to fear of the world the child will have to enter someday. At what point will she be liberated, and how prepared will she be for that moment? Contemporary parenting practices must address this weighty challenge.

Little Princes and Princesses

Most people would agree that it is possible for kids to get too much too soon. Intoxicating levels of gratification and stimulation can drain kids of motivation and ambition. Lives that are mostly fun and games can fan the flames of a potentially self-destructive trait called insatiability (page 74). Parents who seem obsessed with delivering nonstop happiness for their kids may end up with children who, thanks to overindulgence, feel limitlessly entitled. Their feelings ultimately may lead to a sense of invulnerability, a belief that they will always get whatever they want without any effort or self-sacrifice. In other words, they live the lives of little princes or princesses. As parents strive to keep their kids lavishly entertained and in possession of everything advertised on TV, they raise kids who may have gotten too much of everything that's pleasurable too soon in life.

I've had the opportunity to meet many families who have enjoyed well-earned financial success. The parents have been justly rewarded for their entrepreneurialism, executive talents, hard work, and financial genius. Quite naturally, these mothers and fathers want their children to share in the bountiful rewards of their success. They and I often wonder about the effects of such windfalls on their kids.

One patient of mine, Jonathan, was a classic example. His dad made a fortune during the Internet boom, selling his share of his business for close to $150 million. Jonathan, an only child, came to symbolize the family's good fortune. Revered by his parents and four doting grandparents, this black-haired imp with thick expressive eyebrows and delicate facial features could do no wrong. And as you might expect, he was about as indulged as any kid could be. By age eight his bedroom looked like a Disney theme park. He got his first motorbike when he was seven, and he was zooming about on his own all-terrain vehicle (with a helmet) at age ten. The family home boasted its own movie theater, and there was a steady supply of action videos liberally seasoned with high-speed chases, cars tumbling from cliffs, and hemorrhaging combatants. Jonathan, who devoured these vicarious experiences, tended to watch the same films over and over again.

The family went on breathtaking vacations. Dad owned his own Gulfstream aircraft, and they had homes in ski country and at the beach deserving of coverage in *Architectural Digest*. Jonathan's parents took him everywhere, even if it meant springing him from school for a week or more. There were regular trips to Europe, the Far East, and the Caribbean. Jonathan especially enjoyed the two African safaris the family went on with both pairs of grandparents. He benefited from worldly experiences that many parents would love to be able to offer their children. But was Jonathan becoming a victim of too much of a good thing?

Jonathan was not much of a student, and his teachers found him somewhat oppositional. He regularly refused to do what he was told. Although he improved over time, he had trouble acclimating to being just another kid standing in line for his school lunch. At home he was a little prince with a reverent nanny at his beck and call.

When I first saw Jonathan as a patient, he was thirteen and doing poorly on tests and writing assignments. He turned out to have some dysfunctions of memory and attention. Most of his basic academic skills were present but not at all automatized (that is, they were slow and labored). He seemed oblivious to his learning problems and showed little interest when I attempted to explain them to him. I made a series of recommendations for the school and for Jonathan's parents and asked the family to return in three months for a follow-up visit. Their lives were overscheduled with philanthropic activities, country club obligations, and the day-to-day strife of their business dealings, so I wasn't surprised when they skipped their appointment. Shortly thereafter, they sent an email saying that they thought Jonathan was doing a little better so they didn't feel the need to come back. They promised to keep in touch.

When Jonathan was sixteen, he and his parents returned because his school reported he was hopelessly behind in English, geometry, and biology. In talking with Jonathan and examining samples of his writing, I could see that he was being bludgeoned by the memory and attention demands of the rigorous curriculum. Furthermore, Jonathan revealed not a shred of motivation. He radiated a kind of implacable optimism. As he put it, "I'll be okay if everyone stops hassling me. The school sucks; so do all the teachers. Everyone hates them."

At this point his parents were getting fed up with him. He was no longer the adorable little prince but rather an arrogant, overentitled teenager. He blew up in frequent temper tantrums and told his mother more than once how much he hated her. Among other manifestations of unrighteous indignation, he resented his parents for not buying him a Corvette. His father had instituted what he termed "a major crackdown." As he summarized the new policy, "This kid needs to start growing up and assuming some responsibility. We need to stop spoiling him." It is unlikely, though, that you can suddenly pull the rug out from under a kid and expect a radical change for the better in his behavior and outlook.

At one of my very few discussions with him, I posed this question: "Jonathan, you're continuing to have a hard time at school. Your parents are upset with you. They and you too would be a lot happier if things started going better in school. Does any of this matter to you?

You have some genuine learning problems, but you know as well as I that your family is extremely wealthy. A generous trust fund has been set up for you. So you'll never really need to work for money. I guess you could feel that how you do in school is completely unimportant." Jonathan responded unhesitatingly, "Yeah, Dr. Levine, but I have to look at myself in the damned mirror every morning and decide if I'm worth anything or if I'm just a lousy parasite."

Jonathan managed to graduate from prep school scraping the bottom of his class. He went to college—early admission no less, at the school where his dad was an active alumnus—infected with the queasiness you harbor as a legacy kid, knowing deep inside you that you would never have gotten in without your dad's pull. To no one's surprise, he dropped out in his sophomore year, at which point his father canceled his Visa and MasterCard and stopped paying for his car insurance.

Jonathan became a drifter, a depressed vagabond. He must have enjoyed moderate satisfaction in being able to disgrace his parents. He adorned himself with a grotesque tattoo and a fourteen-inch ponytail, semiconsciously aimed at punishing his dad. He survived on a modest allowance, delved into drugs, and managed to accomplish nothing on a daily basis.

I've lost contact with Jonathan. I only wish I or someone else had seen this kid when he was much younger, preferably well before he became a little prince. It's not easy to dethrone juvenile royalty. Currently he is a fallen idol, a guy entirely unready to function on his own during what should be his startup years. He has lots of company. Some people like him live lives of quiet desperation; others go on to turbulent and unstable existences. But there are those who for some reason abdicate their thrones, find themselves, and become productive. They are able to look in the mirror and discern some positive signs.

Overindulged (Whether or Not You Are Rich)

It would be unfair to imply that all affluent people overindulge their kids. I meet many who are adroit at regulating the spigot, ensuring that a child is not so swamped with pleasure that adult life will add very little. It would be misleading to give the impression that it takes heaps of money to overindulge a child. I have seen plenty of working-class families, even some on public assistance, whose kids pretty much run the show.

Alicia Crawford, a single mother who lived with her two teenaged daughters in a single-wide trailer in rural North Carolina, related the following story regarding her fourteen-year-old: "Dr. Levine, I just don't know what to do with that child. She stays out till late at night. Half the time she doesn't hardly do her schoolwork, and she's real smart. She's smoking and she drinks and she runs around. To tell you the truth, I think I'm plain scared of her. So far she's stayed out of trouble. And there's so much bad she could do if she got angry. She could get herself on drugs or she could get pregnant or she could get into trouble with the law or shoplifting or something like that. I love her to death. I've worked so hard over the years to give her everything, and I mean every thing she has ever, ever wanted. Now I have to be careful with her. If I get myself on her wrong side, she can get back at me by hurting herself."

Like Mrs. Crawford, many parents are increasingly fearful of their children, especially their adolescent offspring. As noted earlier in this book, the balance of power seems to have shifted to children. Kids have a wealth of weapons at their disposal and parents have little leverage. A teenager can hurt a parent in so many ways without ever making overt threats. She can become depressed or anorectic, act sexually promiscuous, perhaps get pregnant, threaten suicide, commit petty crimes, become a runaway, drop out or stop studying in school, hang out with the "wrong kids" in town, join a cult, or develop a serious chemical addiction. Often the preventive measures include being extra nice to your kid, trying to keep her or him happy (perhaps even euphoric) as much of the time as possible, ensuring a steady stream of exciting new material acquisitions, avoiding setting limits that might alienate, and lowering expectations for any work output or the assumption of unpleasant responsibilities in life. Parents run the risk of becoming recreation coordinators, caterers to a hedonistic childhood.

What becomes of kids who grow up with such historically unprecedented power over their mothers and fathers? I don't think we know, but it's worth worrying about. I suspect they will have to endure a painfully traumatic adjustment when they have to report to a boss or supervisor who doesn't especially love them and who will evaluate them on the basis of productivity and competence. Such a young person may find out that she cannot manipulate these relative strangers the way she once wrapped her parents around her finger.

Long-Term Feelings of Entitlement

A child who has been overindulged at home and made an icon in school runs the risk of feeling that the world owes him something. While attending college, he may feel that his professors need to be indulgent toward him, entertaining in class, and willing to inflate his grades. He may evaluate his academic courses solely in terms of how much fun they were. As a startup adult he will indeed be fallen idol in a state of shock, as his boss and his fellow workers fail to respond to his sense of entitlement.

PREVENTING FALLS

Parents should recognize and overcome their often hidden fear of their children. It is not in the best interest of an adolescent for her parents to cede power to her because she might become very sad or do bad things to herself and the family. Of course kids need to be loved, but to an extent they crave tough love. All kids want parents to set limits as a way of showing their concern for their kids. Also, mothers and fathers should provide their children with direct experience in the deft handling of frustration, conflict, and loss. They should exercise caution in providing material possessions and exhilarating life experiences that can lead to disappointment during the startup years.

The best way to prevent an idol from falling is to avoid giving a kid idol status in the first place. Childhood and adolescence should contain a healthy blend of victories and defeats, of authoritarian rule and appropriate autonomy, of admiration and criticism, of fun and stress. Kids need to be raised not feared, loved not revered.

4
SOME WHO HAVE GONE ASTRAY
When Wrong Roads Are Taken

I was underprepared for the transition, and money was the biggest thing I screwed up with. I spent a lot of money, more money than I had.

I.F., age 22

My biggest fear is to wake up at age fifty-five hating my job and be, like, "Oh my goodness, what am I doing?" It's scary to me to get to a point and realize you haven't made a difference or done anything that means anything.

S.R., age 27

Robert Frost's poem "The Road Not Taken" offers a near-perfect metaphor for the daunting commitments that have to be made during the startup years.

Two roads diverged in a yellow wood
And sorry I could not travel both
And be one traveler, long I stood
And looked down one as far as I could
To where it bent in the undergrowth; . . .

And both that morning equally lay
In leaves no step had trodden black
Oh, I kept the first for another day!
Yet knowing how way leads on to way
I doubted if I should ever come back.

There comes a time when life's options resemble avenues converging at an intersection; people need to decide which road to take. The choice of routes seems to expand as our society grows in complexity; often there are many more than two roads to choose from. Some individuals are stunned as they face more work-life options than have existed during any other historical period. Ideally, you take the right road the first time, because you may not get a second chance at the choice. But what becomes of those individuals who embark on paths that they can't navigate or that take them places other than where they wanted to go? Where and how did they go astray? They are members of a growing flock of work-life starters in distress. They are victims of an educational system and a culture that has failed to help them come to know themselves and figure out how to choose a productive pathway as a startup adult.

There are several reasons why so many young people start out heading in the wrong direction. First, some folks unwittingly head into a career or job that simply cannot work out for them. Either they fail to comprehend what the work entails or they do not understand their own abilities and limitations, their personal strengths, weaknesses, and stable interests. The latter problem is a sign of the times. Deprived of constructive role models and the guidance needed to "know thyself," far too many unready starters are stymied by a disconnect between who they are and what they are trying to do with their lives. In other cases, a person gets detoured onto the wrong road out of necessity or expediency, such as in response to an immediate need to earn money or a dearth of suitable opportunities amid an economic downturn.

Another wrong road is taken when someone lands a job, gets off to a wobbly start, maybe misconstrues what is expected of him, and keeps traveling in a direction that will not lead to on-the-job success and gratification. As a novice entry-level employee, he may inadvertently get into some dreadful habits and acquire a negative reputation that can be nearly impossible to reverse in the often-unforgiving workplace. Or a person may fail to anticipate and may be lacking in the specific skills required for the job. The road to recovery in such cases can be treacherous, even unnavigable. It may not be feasible to return to where the roads originally diverged and start over.

UNINFORMED CONSENTERS

Work life during the startup years can feel tightly confining compared to schoolwork in high school or even college. Formal education is like a gala buffet banquet: You can have it all! You can sign up for classes in Spanish, advanced algebra, driver's education, Greek philosophy, sex education, and keyboarding. And each weekday after 2:40 p.m. you can pursue badminton, the bassoon, and the trading of baseball cards. Then come the vast evening and weekend smorgasbords offering Instant Messaging, cell phones, DVDs, mall grazing, and TV sitcoms, among countless other mouthwatering side dishes. What's more, you really don't have to choose among these tempting offerings. You can have them all—in small, medium, or mammoth portions. Whenever they feel vaguely bored, teenagers can switch nearly instantaneously to a new channel of excitement. And they can zap whatever they are getting tired of. Life gets regulated by a universal remote control.

Nowadays, luring kids is an industry; in fact, it is a vast collection of industries that tantalize the young with offerings that do nothing to strengthen their minds or help them get a grasp on their lives. Then, wrenchingly, in their twenties they have to make agonizing decisions. They have to limit what they're going to do so that they don't spread themselves thin. They need to commit to an initial career preference, just one spouse (at a time, anyway), and the rudiments of a work life. They can no longer have it all or live it all. The buffet is finished; faced with an unlimited menu, these emerging adults are forced to pick only a few items. This may be rough, especially when they have had little or no practice as long-term committers.

Diane, a middle-class suburban black woman, opted for law school mostly because she was told it would "open plenty of doors" for her. She had excelled at everything she touched in high school and had nabbed a closetload of awards at graduation. Although she was incredibly "well-rounded," she lacked any strong intellectual passions and never gave a whole lot of thought to her future. An economics major, she graduated from an Ivy League college in the top 15 percent of her class but felt she got little or nothing out of the experience; as she put it, "When I finished college, I was ridiculously naïve." She attended an elite law school, where she made law review and joined the cream of the crop of the nation's aspiring legal experts. But Diane despised law school and had no use for her classmates there, feeling they represented raw ambition and "lacked heart."

Presently, at age twenty-eight, she detests the work she is required to slog through as a junior associate in a major law firm. She finds legal matters dry and uninteresting. Her father had been a litigation attorney in solo practice, and from a distance, his life seemed fascinating, a sense she has not been able to recapture in her own career. The kind of practice her dad enjoyed was not feasible for Diane; she has had to toil on the lowest rung of a huge firm's top-heavy career ladder. Diane once mused to her husband, "I think I'm about to burn out. My life has been like an endless mountain-climbing expedition. As soon as I reach a peak, I have to go back to the bottom and start climbing again—over and over. I was beloved by everyone in elementary school, and then we moved and I had to start all over again becoming a big cheese in middle school. I did it, but then I was heaved into a vast dumpster called high school where almost no one knew me, so I had to start that awful climb to the top socially and academically all over again. Then there was college, another exhausting hike to the summit. The next killer mountain was law school, a hell of a climb. And now here I am as low down as you can get at my firm, looking up all over again. I don't know if I can handle it. I don't know if I even want to."

Diane is well paid and married, with two preschool children. Her husband brings in a modest income as a dental practice software salesman. The family has rapidly accustomed itself to her fairly substantial income. They have a new home in a prestigious suburban subdivision with a commensurately upper-end mortgage and hefty car loans on the silver Lexus SUV and the brand-new Dodge Caravan with backseat DVD player and a GPS in the dashboard. Pretty soon her kids will start private school. She can't backtrack. She feels trapped. Is she?

Although she has the ability to succeed in the law, Diane can't tolerate the kind of work she is being asked to do. How did she get into this bind? The answer is that when she decided to enter her profession, she did so without truly informed consent. Even though her father was a lawyer, Diane didn't have any idea what being a young attorney would be like. She had had no exposure to the content of law to any significant degree.

Kids too often blindly pick a pathway for the most superficial reasons, and they don't know what they've gotten into until they're already well into it. I think this represents a significant gap in our educational system, one I will suggest ways to remediate later in the book (chapter 12).

Is Diane really boxed in at this point? I don't think so. Careers are malleable; you can shape them your way if you are resourceful and willing to take some minor risks. Within the law she can hunt for an area that is more intriguing to her. The options are almost unlimited: real estate law, criminal defense, estate planning, sports or entertainment law, teaching law, legal medicine—to name just a few. She can even leave the field of law altogether to go into business, bolstered by her legal background. People in Diane's situation need to examine the career menu and keep reexamining it. Then they should ask around and sniff out current opportunities; they should never call off the search. Sooner or later they will find a pursuit in which they can deploy their educational background in a way that will be fulfilling.

Juanita, now twenty, grew up in a poor neighborhood of Los Angeles. She was raised by her illegal immigrant parents, who never stopped toiling to make ends meet so they could support their children and send funds back to their family near Guadalajara, Mexico. They constantly emphasized the importance of their kids' making something of themselves. Juanita had four siblings; the family was vacuum-packed inside a stifling two-and-a-half-room apartment in a decrepit housing project. There was no such thing as privacy in their home. Juanita never much enjoyed school, or life at home for that matter, but she had a lot of friends and mostly stayed out of trouble. She gave birth to a son at age fifteen and a daughter when she was seventeen—each with a different temporary boyfriend. At her parents' insistence, Juanita managed to finish high school. She enrolled in a community college to become a medical technician but dropped out after four months, saying she felt bored, missed her friends, and had no time for her children.

Juanita eventually landed a job as a supermarket cashier, scanning groceries eight hours a day, five days a week. She took the position because one of her best friends worked at that store. Disappointingly, her friend was fired soon after Juanita came on board. She has been scanning nonstop for about eighteen months. She lives for her breaks and feels "dumb and useless." Juanita says her life is not going anywhere, and it's all too obvious that she's right. Is she supposed to spend the rest of her days sliding bar codes over readers and making believe she is interacting with fellow humans? She offers her "Have a nice day" with an insincere but melodic Mexican lilt, knowing full well she is not having a nice day—and not in the least caring if the customer is having one. Anyway, what's supposed to happen to twenty-year-old checkout clerks who don't even have to calculate change or know the price or even the name of any of the products they slide over their scanners? They don't even recognize customers they see every day. What does that do to their sensibilities? What is their outlook? I see them all the time in supermarkets, and I wonder and I worry about them. I think retailers should be held responsible for what they are doing to the minds of their startup employees.

Maybe it's one thing to have a repetitive, part-time, no-brainer job when you're a sixty-nine-year-old widow seeking added income and a way to escape the monotony and isolation of home. But to have that job when you're young is to be condemned to second-class membership in society. That is, unless some other features are built into the job. First, the work should be thought of as temporary; when it comes to people in their startup years, such employment should be thought of as a holding pattern and, in a sense, a stepping-stone. That person at the scanner should be learning about the supermarket business and getting exposed to managerial positions toward which she can aspire. She should be required to rotate from the scanner to stocking shelves to other jobs. And she should be assigned a mentor, a manager or assistant manager, with whom she meets regularly to discuss her job and where it's leading. In other words, she must be able to see ways up and out.

There's no justification for believing that all repetitious jobs have to entail extended drudgery without relief. All work can be enriched. A school custodian can take pride in the condition of the building he maintains. He can feel like part of a team and establish a network of friends among the teachers and apprentices among the students. A busboy or dishwater can aspire toward advancement and at the same time enjoy on-the-job collegiality. He can derive satisfaction from being good at what he does. He should be able to look ahead to changes in his job description. His bosses need to establish the ambiance and working conditions in which such career benefits are feasible. In the case of startup adults, it is essential that they see possibilities for advancement. Even for young people who come from abject poverty (often as immigrants) or those who are developmentally disabled, a menial position should offer at least a glimmer of light ahead. That's the American way!

CONSERVATIVE NON–RISK TAKERS

Career decisions are nearly always risky, but people have to take chances. I have met many adolescents whom I would characterize as conservative non–risk takers. Not uncommonly these are students who have been burned too frequently in the past. Among my patients, they are kids who have performed poorly in school, academically and/or socially, who have endured overdoses of criticism and public humiliation. They may have been scolded repeatedly for their lack of academic motivation. They are likely to have dealt with more shame in twelve years than most people experience in a lifetime. There's a good chance they have come to feel that they were born to lose, that they are never going to amount to anything. They therefore become pessimistic about their future and, in fact, may make up their minds to write off the future entirely. At the same time, they are apt to stifle any ambition that they once may have felt. They play it safe. If they don't aim at anything, there's no way they can miss. As one young adult confided in me, "I once had a sixth-grade teacher who never stopped putting me down in front of the other kids. She knew I had a terrible time with math, and still she kept making me do problems on the board in front of all the other kids. She would yell whenever I made a mistake—that was a lot of yelling—and the other kids would laugh. I used to have nightmares about that. I would dream that I was up there doing the problems with no clothes on. I still replay that dream once in a while. I never want something like that to happen to me again. So, you know what? I play it safe. I keep a very low profile. I ask for very, very little in life. That way I feel safe."

A former patient of mine, Omar, was a prime example of a conservative non–risk taker. He had endured chronic difficulties with language and with his rapid retrieval memory, dysfunctions that predisposed him to repeated frustration and embarrassment in the classroom. He had undergone years of tutoring, medication, and counseling, none of which succeeded in nudging up his grade point average. His parents, both software engineers, were unswerving in their love and support for Omar. But every time an attempt to help him met with disappointing results, Omar interpreted it as yet another failure.

By the time I first met Omar at the age of almost eighteen, the boy's ego was as smashed as a car that had collided with a train. He was convinced of his own "stupidity" (as he put it) and felt hopelessly lost in eleventh grade; he had already twice repeated grades. But Omar was a talented musician. He played the trumpet and the saxophone and composed some of his own music. His successes in a jazz group and in the marching band were the only sources of affirmation in his diminished life.

It turned out that Omar had had an opportunity to attend a highly respected summer program for players of brass instruments, but he had turned it down. It looked as if he had become his own worst enemy. We discussed possible career avenues that would somehow connect with his passion and ability in music. When I mentioned applying to a music college, he insisted it would be a waste of time, he would never get accepted. When I asked if it would help if he met some composers or other brass players, he said they would never want to help him. When I suggested he might want to teach kids music someday, he barked at me, snarling that it wouldn't pay enough. When I asked him about auditioning for an orchestra or band, he said he could never "in a zillion years" win out over everyone else. When I inquired about whether he might start his own music group someday, he stated that the market was saturated; there were too many ensembles out there already. Omar slammed shut every conceivable door that could open to his future.

At age nineteen, when Omar finished high school, he had such a profound fear of failure that he could not allow himself to take any risks at all. Eventually, after several dozen paralyzing months of inaction and indecision, Omar enrolled in a community college to study music and music teaching for two years. After graduation he landed a job as the band and orchestra director at a middle school. He came to love his work and was a very effective teacher. He had a setback when his girlfriend of two years left him because of his reluctance to marry her and have a family. He said he was not ready to make such a commitment, even though he insisted he loved her. Five years later he was offered a lucrative job as a saxophonist with a very successful rock group. He could still keep his teaching job and play in the band on the side. What a once-in-a-lifetime opportunity! He loved the band's music, but he turned down the offer. He was afraid things might not work out.

Omar struggled and retreated despite coming from a stable family with adequate financial resources. There are many kids, however, who grow up in poverty, shouldering far too many stresses at home and in school, and eventually they risk becoming permanent non–risk takers. It may sound odd, but their lack of risk taking in their career causes them to take risks with other parts of their lives instead. They depart school prematurely. They may get into drugs. They may commit crimes. They set out on roads to oblivion and self-destruction.

MONEY HUNTERS

In our society, as kids' identities become less distinct and they can't differentiate their interests from those of their friends, the acquisition of money may become their dominant aim, rather than personal fulfill-ment. A college senior may auction himself off to the highest-bidding recruiter only to find that he hates what he's doing, as he relishes the overweight paycheck. Sooner or later this quest for money leaves a person feeling unfulfilled. It is not unusual for someone habituated to this pattern of career shortsightedness to change jobs every time a slightly higher-paying prospect crops up. This pattern is fairly common among young adults who have revealed a lifelong tendency toward in-satiability (page 74). Delaying gratification has never been a considera-tion for them.

UNDERSTANDING WORKPLACE REQUIREMENTS

How do you go about succeeding in a job when you don't understand what is demanded of you, when you've never been taught the ground rules for launching a career? What if you've neglected the political reali-ties of the workplace? What if you've been left to your own uninformed wits to figure out how to please your bosses, and you seriously miscal-culate expectations? In such instances, a well-intentioned career starter can get clobbered simply because she or he is naïve.

Irene fell victim to a trap that snags many startup adults. Having graduated from college, she was one of the few members of her soror-ity to land a decent job in a tough economic climate. A successful com-munications major, she beat out the competition and was named an assistant news producer at a local TV station. She couldn't have asked for more, and she was a whiz during her first six months on the job.

Irene worked plenty of extra hours without ever requesting overtime pay. She was aggressive in making contacts and uncovering new sources of information. She performed like a lucrative oil well, gushing forth ter-rific ideas for revealing feature stories, and she offered to organize these special segments on her own. In short, Irene exhibited remarkable ini-tiative and independence. In doing so, she managed to alienate just about all her coworkers. She was too naïve to perceive them as competi-tors as well as colleagues. She often boasted about her successes, some-how assuming that everyone around her was taking pride in her work. Nobody ever told her about office politics. Additionally, in her zeal to showcase and deploy her brilliance, Irene neglected a number of her more mundane responsibilities, thereby infuriating some of the news-casters and senior producers, who expected her to do more for them.

Irene, who was so competent and industrious, was let go after eight months. This was a terrible injustice. No one should be punished for doing a superb job and showing lots of initiative. But Irene needed to do the menial stuff, too, and probably should have given more attention to nurturing her relationships with her fellow workers. She was dumbfounded and crushed, a victim of her job naïveté. It takes more than ability and drive to succeed as a startup adult. You have to be sensitive to the needs and desires of the people you work with and for.

Many startup adults are unable to read between the lines of a job description (either a written one or a looser oral agreement). They are often completely in the dark when it comes to the political realities of a job. As children they never studied these issues. They were deprived of the opportunity to hear grown-ups discuss the ins and outs and the ups and downs of work. No one ever told them how insecure their superiors are likely to be and how important it is not to step on their toes or openly outdo them. Nobody taught them that the employees who work at their level can destroy them by bad-mouthing them if they don't watch their step. A negative reputation shows up vividly on performance reviews.

The conclusion is hard to deny: our kids are not learning in school some vital lessons they need to prepare for the hidden challenges of the real world.

People you work with and for may never level with you; like Irene, a startup adult can incur heaps of hidden resentment without anyone's giving her a clue, that is, until it's too late to repair the damage. In that instance, failure to understand the job requirements means that a wrong approach has been taken. In school, students are the recipients— whether they like it or not—of a steady tide of candid feedback— criticism mixed with praise on report cards, from parents, from friends, and from coaches. In contrast, early in a career, a person may come to the panic-inducing realization that he really does not know how he's doing. I remember when I was a junior faculty member at Harvard Medical School, an associate professor warned me, "Melvin, let me tell you something. Nobody around here will take the time to tell you how you're doing. And if you ask, there's a good chance they'll be evasive. But remember one thing: you're being watched. You're being watched and judged all the time. Never let down your guard."

We have to help students approach their startup years with a lot less naïveté. Well before college, they should be students of careers and career politics. Furthermore, they should learn how to self-monitor, how to examine themselves and pick up the local vibes. Such capabilities will be discussed as we explore the growth processes in part two of this book.

WHEN INTERESTS DON'T MATCH ABILITIES

Merrill hit rock bottom in his late twenties because of the wide gulf between his abilities and his interests. From the time he was a young kid, it was evident that he had a passionate love affair with the outdoors. Most notably, Merrill was a master fort builder. He spent hours on end constructing his pine-shaded fortifications. By the time he was twelve, Merrill was the creator, proprietor, and sometime inhabitant of four amply fortified forts and several baronial tree houses. He and his friends entertained themselves for days in and around these architectural classics. In fact, on many a summer night the edifices resembled fully occupied military barracks. As he grew older, Merrill diversified his product line and started to build rockets, which he and his friends launched from the pasture next door to his house. His missiles were yet another testament to Merrill's extraordinary mechanical-spatial intellect and resourcefulness.

As much as Merrill loved using his hands and his eyes outdoors, he was repulsed by most activities that called for activating his head indoors. He hated to read and couldn't tolerate focusing on small details, a requirement in most of his classes from middle school onward. His worst subject was mathematics. He knew it was hopeless. His academic abrasions were inflamed by conspicuous problems with organization. Although he had no trouble keeping track of his possessions, Merrill couldn't handle time management and was never able to deal with schedules that called for multitasking (page 162). He also could not prioritize, so he would exhaust hours on end accomplishing nothing and then would miss deadlines or not get around to studying for his final examinations. Also, he never was a planner; he did whatever came to mind.

Even when he constructed his fabulous forts, Merrill would work without any set plan; one step just seemed to flow into the next. And the results were super. He seemed to be spontaneously creative when it came to building things. Despite his allergy to details and his malignant disorganization, Merrill made it through high school without failing any subjects—a tribute to his overall intelligence. He had a winning personality and was very much a leader.

Merrill was accepted into the local college that seldom rejected anyone. He succeeded in winging it through two years, during which he concentrated mainly on his social skills, but then elected to take time off to earn some cash. In the summers he had worked in construction, which he enjoyed immensely. At age twenty he became a finishing-work carpenter's apprentice. The man he worked for was nothing short of brilliant when it came to doing the finish work on new homes, and he inspired Merrill. Never before had Merrill been as happy as he felt working alongside this talented artisan. Merrill did not return to college. Instead he did carpentry over the next four years, always employed by his mentor. After only eighteen months on the job, he was no longer an apprentice. He earned pretty good wages and did commendable work. But then Merrill got restless. He was engaged to a lovely girl, who made it clear she wanted to raise a big family. A music major, she was still in college and did not want ever to work. So he made up his mind to make money and lots of it. Moreover, he was tired of working for someone. After all, as a kid he had always been a leader, and he wanted to have people working for him. He thought assuming the boss role would also impress his future wife and her family.

Merrill was always in awe of the contractors who subcontracted out to him and his boss. These guys drove expensive cars, lived in cool homes, and wore eighteen-carat gold Rolexes. They had loyal employees and they had power. So Merrill quit his job and made up his mind to become a contractor, with an eye toward being a major real estate developer some day.

Armed with his seductive charm, excellent communication skills, good looks, and aptitude for leadership, Merrill came across as someone you could trust and work well with. Because mortgage rates were low and the real estate business was thriving in his area of the country, he had no difficulty wooing clients who wanted custom-built homes. A reliable source of clever architectural ideas, he promised his customers the world. People were amazed that he could agree on features of a house and never have to write anything down. He took on quite a few projects, probably many more than he should have. Then suddenly his neurodevelopmental past came back like a ghost to haunt him. He was totally disorganized, unable to coordinate deliveries and the arrival of various plumbers, electricians, and drywall people. He was in over his head. Problems with attention to details, quantitative thinking, and time management had always been like invasive tumors to him. Now they were metastasizing. His carelessness and inability to meet deadlines made his customers irate. There were several lawsuits. Pretty soon most of the good subcontractors refused to work for him.

At the age of twenty-seven, Merrill declared bankruptcy at the same time that his fiancée broke off their engagement. His life was in shambles. What went awry? It is clear that Merrill failed sufficiently to understand himself, a shortfall he shares with many other startup adults who stall out. There was a grievous disconnection between Merrill's ambitions and his abilities. His aversion to mathematics and detail, his organizational problems, were all overlooked in favor of his romantic attraction to the life of a contractor. This was as bad a mismatch between interests and abilities as anyone can endure. Merrill just didn't know who he was.

If Merrill had thought more about his deficits, he could have taken a more suitable road. Perhaps he should have started a modest carpentry business instead of getting strapped with the complex organizational demands of a contractor's work life. Or he might have found a partner or hired someone who relished fine details and was meticulously organized.

André was just as disorganized as Merrill, but on top of his problems with time management, he had difficulty keeping track of things. He spent much of each day searching for lost objects. Like Merrill, he abhorred details and was definitely a big-picture guy. André was determined to be a chef. He always enjoyed cooking, especially coming up with his own versions of his family's dishes. After high school he went to Johnson & Wales, a celebrated cooking school in Rhode Island. There he managed to graduate despite repeated warnings regarding his sloppiness, tardiness, and carelessness. He got a job as a sous chef at a suburban restaurant. He was very successful and went on to be the chef at a busy gourmet restaurant in downtown Philadelphia. André remained totally disorganized in his everyday life. He was often late. He kept losing things. His social life was a mess of forgotten dates and other interpersonal miscues. But in the kitchen André was totally dependable and organized in every way. André demonstrated something called domain-specific function. That is, he shed his deficits when he worked in a highly specific domain. Someone with language problems who loves sports may become surprisingly verbal when talking about basketball. And a guy who is forever at loose ends but loves to cook may get his act together 100 percent when he is in the kitchen. Whenever someone manifests an important kind of deficit, it is always useful to see if there is a domain in which that deficiency is either minimized or eliminated. Discovering such a domain can have immense implications for choosing one's line of work.

Mismatches abound. Many people are attracted to pursuits that fail to mesh with their abilities. Imagine the following familiar scenarios:

- Someone who wants more than anything else to be a dentist but has fine motor problems;
- A person with weak social cognition in a job where she's constantly interacting with other people;
- A highly creative individual who is expected to sit and enter numbers on a spreadsheet all day long;
- A woman who has difficulty expressing herself yet is preparing to be a social studies teacher;
- A budding psychiatrist who has never been able to deal with his own very serious personal problems;
- An untalented guitarist who wants to turn professional;
- A truck driver with attention deficits who gets tired and fidgety when he has to sit in one place for very long.

Are these people entirely misguided in attempting to live lives that may be wrecked by their own shortcomings? When should someone obey the inner callings of his passions and when should he let go of them because of an inability to pursue them successfully? These questions defy global responses. On the one hand, it's a bad idea to stack the odds against personal success as a startup adult. Go with your strengths and sidestep your deficiencies. Try to fit your profile to your passions. There are endless career patterns; no doubt you can find many that would fit your profile. On the other hand, what if you are determined to pursue a goal that will expose your deficits? That may be workable if you know that's what you're doing, if you're not deceiving yourself by denying the existence of your weaknesses. But a person needs to know as quickly as possible when the road taken has reached a dead end. Then it's time for an honest reassessment, a diligent search for ways to blend your passions with your assets.

One patient of mine, Terry, had serious attention control difficulties.

He was all over the place, very impulsive and distractible. In school he was often reprimanded for his hyperactive behavior. He had trouble falling asleep and problems getting out of bed in the morning, the kind of sleep-arousal imbalance that's found in some kids with attention deficits. This boy was always insatiable, constantly yearning for heavy-duty entertainment. Sometimes he caused trouble just to stir up the cauldrons of daily existence.

Luckily, Terry, who had terrific parents, passed through his school years relatively unscathed despite all his problems. Then, at age eighteen, he shocked everyone by enlisting in the army. This was a perfect mismatch. How was this overactive, acting-out, impulsive kid going to conform to the regulations and routines of military life? I've known numerous young adults like Terry who have been discharged summarily. But believe it or not, Terry made it. It was almost as if the army had been his Ritalin. The daily structure and predictability were just what the doctor ordered. That's why I say that there are no global answers. But, like Terry, you have to know your strengths and weaknesses and be prepared to reconcile them within your job.

RIGHT ROADS

In "The Road Not Taken" Frost laments,

> Yet knowing how way leads on to way,
> I doubted if I should ever come back.

In truth, it is possible and often desirable to revisit the spot where roads diverged to renew a work-life choice when it's time to do so— either to affirm the road that was taken or else to opt for a different one. Such a realization could provide comfort to many an unready and once-unwary career starter. It could even rescue a person in midcareer. The trick is in the timing. One shouldn't be a quitter and give up on a road before it has been adequately explored, as some people keep doing. Nor should a person remain stuck on the wrong road. Startup adults should plan on a work life during which they periodically reexamine the road they are taking and the ways in which that road can keep diverging. And that can make all the difference!

5

VICTIMS OF BRAIN NEGLECT

When Minds Fall into Debt

I definitely had an attention problem growing up, to the point where I was eventually medicated for it. But it was not recognized or addressed for a long time because I was considered to have a high IQ and was in the gifted classes. I think if it had been recognized a lot earlier, then school and this transition could have been easier. It was a real struggle in school. If I could have been told that it was okay and here are ways we can go about helping you—if teachers had known ways of presenting things for me—I really think it would have made a big difference. I think that was part of my lack of interest in school, in retrospect.

S.R., age 27

Not all debts are monetary. The mind of a startup adult may be in heavy debt because specific needs of that mind were never met. Most often this problem occurs when a person grows up misunderstood and crippled because crucial capabilities either were weak or never were cultivated during childhood and adolescence.

In our schools and within our homes, we misread and therefore mismanage countless developing minds. Our public policies and short-sightedness encourage these mistakes by assuming universal brain sameness. As a result, the brainpower of many students gets mishandled. To simplify demands on our institutions and lower short-term costs, our policies, practices, and laws presume that all learners can succeed in the same way. That faulty assumption justifies imposing identical standards on all developing minds. In truth, kids' minds are strikingly diverse. To treat and to teach them all the same is to treat and teach them unequally. In particular, the neglect of important weaknesses results in long-term mind debt, debt that causes frustration and failure during the startup years. There are also too many children and adults who have hidden assets, abilities that are being undervalued and underutilized. A young person's creativity, people skills, or extraordinary mechanical aptitude may be decaying from lack of use. Neglected strengths are another form of mind debt.

A mind whose assets and deficits are misunderstood and whose strengths are improperly nurtured may be on the way to long-term faulty function and needless failure during the startup years. The phenomenon is alarmingly common. Our culture has to get over its craving for childhood uniformity.

KNOWING A MIND

To know a mind is to know its specific strengths, weaknesses (dysfunctions), preferences, and traits. These salient individual differences, if accurately perceived, can provide crucial direction to a kid's education, ultimately helping him opt for a life of successful pursuits.

Over many years I have sought to define the specific neurodevelopmental functions that enable children and adolescents to learn and become academically and socially productive. As a clinician, I try to pinpoint breakdowns in learning, so-called neurodevelopmental dysfunctions. Difficulty finding words, a lack of precision in recalling facts, problems with concentration, failure at friendship formation, and trouble forming legible letters are examples of such dysfunctions. I have described many such brain glitches in my book *A Mind at a Time*.

Every child goes to school and every grown-up heads for work armed with his or her neurodevelopmental profile. Someone may possess outstanding language abilities, very poor perception of spatial relationships, remarkable social skills, and adequate memory functioning, while his younger brother is entirely different: a slow, laborious interpreter of language, a spatial genius, a social loner, and a reliably forgetful kind of guy. Nearly infinite combinations of strengths and weaknesses are represented in the population of any community, classroom, or workplace. But are most individuals aware of their profile? Do parents have a sufficiently lucid view of their child's profile? Have a youngster's teachers recognized and taught to his profile?

Many parents and educators do have a handle on children's relative strengths and weaknesses, but have they covered all the important bases? Is their picture complete enough? Often it is not. When a profile is partially defined, misread, or not read at all, a child may be put at risk and can accumulate burdensome developmental debts that will be carried well into the startup years.

EFFECTS OF DEBTS

Joel was a terrific athlete, the son of a bond trader on Wall Street. He attended prestigious private schools and was embraced by peers for his cool appearance, impeccably trendy attire, and buoyant, boyish manner. But Joel was also a tense guy, a person who clung to high expectations for himself, a perfectionist who was easily frustrated whenever he fell short of his own stringent standards. He was an intense competitor, an excellent pole-vaulter, an accomplished lacrosse player, and an acrobatic second baseman. In contrast, academically Joel fared poorly across the board. His greatest frustration erupted with writing, mathematics, and test taking in general, though the boy was a solid reader. Despite recurrent warnings and following a steady volley of accusations of laziness, he was expelled from two New York private schools—one in fifth grade, the other in seventh grade—because of failing grades.

Joel was dispatched to a boarding school for ninth grade. Again he excelled in sports but continued to implode in the classroom. He tolerated heavy doses of tutoring and, of course, medication, but with only meager benefits. In eleventh grade Joel came home for Christmas vacation and announced that he was not about to return to school. He had had it.

On December 30 Joel locked himself in his bedroom and refused to emerge for more than thirty-six hours. He would sneak out to grab some morsels to eat and to use the bathroom but would talk to no one. His parents finally pleaded with Joel to reveal what was distressing him, but he would say either "Nothing" or "I don't know." Joel did not go back to school that semester. In fact, he did not leave the apartment over the next six months. A child psychiatrist who had counseled Joel for six months when he was nine made two house calls and concluded unsurprisingly that the boy was suffering from a severe school phobia.

Joel is now twenty-two. He never returned to school and is not working. He is heavily medicated and does nothing all day except read, watch TV, and listen to music. At night he often takes flight like a bat emerging from its cave and disappears with his close-knit tribe of unemployed friends. Joel hangs out until three or four in the morning and may be into drugs. Occasionally he picks up his guitar and tries to write a little music. He talks to a therapist, an intervention that according to Joel's parents seems to be going nowhere.

Recently Joel's therapist suggested that a neuropsychologist test his cognitive functioning. In the past the emphasis had always been on looking at the emotional aspects of Joel's situation. Surprisingly, Joel consented to this assessment as long as it could be done at his home. The psychologist obliged and made a house call.

The results were striking. Joel was discovered to have outstanding language and spatial aptitudes but significant memory dysfunctions. In particular, he had difficulty filing and retrieving information, trouble with his long-term memory. This explained why writing had been so agonizing for him; nothing in school saps more memory than writing: you have to rapidly and simultaneously recall letter formation, spelling, grammatical rules, punctuation rules, facts, vocabulary, and ideas, as well as a substantial bundle of other details. That's why so many kids with long-term memory dysfunctions seem to wither when it comes to written output. There are heavy memory demands in mathematics, another of Joel's liabilities. Making matters worse were some problems he had recognizing patterns. Pattern recognition, described in greater detail (page 133), allows someone to look at a math problem, know that he's seen that kind of problem in the past, and activate the methods that worked for that kind of problem before. Pattern recognition also enables someone to deal with personal problems and stresses. You encounter a situation and almost unconsciously recall how similar experiences were resolved. For Joel and others like him with weak pattern recognition, much of what occurs in life seems unprecedented. Because there is so little accumulation of wisdom, there is little ability to cope with stress.

Now, at twenty-two, Joel has written himself off, as he remains convinced he is stupid and born to lose. If only years ago someone had explained to Joel that he was experiencing problems with his memory, this young man's educational collapse and career paralysis might well have been prevented. Joel could have been taught memory building and pattern recognition strategies as well as techniques to bypass some of the memory burdens of schoolwork. His teachers would have had options beyond expelling him. Most of all, Joel would have absorbed the energizing and comforting insight that though he was partially handicapped by some memory barriers, he was an intelligent person endowed with very impressive strengths. He needed to know that he has dysfunctions but that most careers place far less stress on memory than classroom learning does. That message would have left Joel optimistic and motivated instead of incapacitated by serious developmental debt. There's still hope for Joel—with the help of career counseling, demystification, and perhaps compensatory education.

By identifying a specific weak function that is crippling learning, it is possible to restore hope in a young person who has given up on himself and blotted out the future. All too often what that individual has come to believe about his mind is far worse than the reality. Children and teenagers often vacillate between denying they have any problems and grossly overrating the severity of their difficulties. I once received a note written by a fourteen-year-old girl I had evaluated at our center. She lived with her unemployed mother. In a marginally legible scrawl she wrote, "When my mom said we were going to see you, I got real angry and told her there was nothing wrong with me. But I was worried inside that there was a whole lot wrong with me. Then when I got there, we did all those tests and talked a lot and stuff. Now I realize I do have a problem, it's not so bad, and I can work on it. Thanks a lot. Your friend, Leslie."

A WIDE SPECTRUM OF NEGLECTED DYSFUNCTIONS

Dysfunctions that are neglected have an eerie way of reappearing like haunting ghosts during the startup years. Their precise manifestations depend a lot upon the nature and severity of the dysfunctions and also the career path and job roles a person finds herself in. Table 5.1 on the following page provides examples of these hidden handicaps and their long-term erosive impacts on a work life.

Some basic principles can be derived from thinking about the mind glitches listed in table 5.1.

SOME PRINCIPLES OF MIND-DEBT MANAGEMENT

- Startup adults (and others) should have some insight into their own neurodevelopmental profiles, and they need to be aware of their dysfunctions as well as the possible work-life impacts of those dysfunctions.

- When a young adult is having trouble getting started or succeeding early in a career, she or he may be harboring a mind debt, a hidden dysfunction that's thwarting success.

- A person can try to select a career pathway that minimizes the effects of his or her dysfunction. (For example, with my conspicuous fine-motor ineptitude, I elected to avoid the surgical subspecialties.)

TABLE 5.1
NEGLECTED AND PERSISTENT MIND DEBTS:
   THEIR POSSIBLE IMPACTS ON WORK LIFE

Mind Debt	Possible Work-Life Impacts
Verbal communication problems	Trouble selling products, ideas, plans; difficulty relating to others; poor understanding of instructions (oral and written)
Fine motor and/or spatial weaknesses	Problems learning manual skills needed on the job
Organizational deficiencies	Difficulty managing time, meeting deadlines, keeping track of materials, prioritizing, multitasking
Production control dysfunctions (often reflecting shortcomings in the function of the prefrontal lobes of the brain)	Trouble planning/implementing projects, weak monitoring of the quality of work, lack of long-term thinking, impulsive decision making and reacting
Processing control dysfunction	Inadequate concentration on work, poor handling of fine details, chronic feelings of boredom at work
Inadequate conceptualization	Difficulty understanding important ideas, tendency to be overly concrete and rigid in thinking
Underdeveloped social thinking	Suboptimal relationships with coworkers, difficulty collaborating, on-the-job political naïveté
Memory limitations	Slow mastery of new skills at work, problems with tasks having many components (using active working memory)
Rate problems	Tendency to accomplish tasks at a very slow pace and therefore fall behind
Persistent academic deficiencies	Reading, writing, or arithmetic skills inadequate to meet work demands

- Alternatively, a person can select within a field a role that minimizes his or her dysfunction. (For example, a young attorney lacking expressive language fluency chooses not to become a trial lawyer.)

- A person can try to collaborate with someone whose strengths counterbalance that person's dysfunctions. (A plumbing contractor with abysmal math skills might work with a more quantitatively skilled partner who can figure out estimates.)

- Finally, a person has the option of trying to fix his or her dysfunctions or skill shortcomings. Can this be done? It's hard to say. It is always possible to take aim at a dysfunction, find ways of practicing the skill (as if engaging in mental muscle building), and observe definite improvement. But it is unclear how fast and how much a person is likely to improve, say in language or motor function or writing ability. If it seems essential for success, it's probably worth a try, especially if there are no available alternatives, such as those mentioned in the previous three principles.

SIMPLISTIC LABELS CREATING MIND DEBTS

In recent decades many clinicians have oversimplified human differences. Too often, if a child's patterns of behavior and learning differ from a preordained stereotype, he is consigned to a rigid category, often one that implies significant abnormality. Clinicians, educators, and many parents appear to have a ravenous appetite for labels for kids who differ, and terms such as ADHD (attention-deficit/hyperactivity disorder), LD (learning disabled), Asperger's syndrome, and a host of others have proliferated like weeds. The labels never take into consideration a young mind's potential, and they imply that all kids within a designated category are basically the same. In reality, there are enormous differences among individuals within each category. The labels are also insidiously pessimistic, implying that any departures from the norm represent a chronic deviancy and therefore prophesy a life of abnormality.

Desperate to come up with a label for a kid, caring adults fail to see what really is occurring within that developing mind. In particular, the glib application of the label ADHD has done more than its share of obscuring and misleading.

I remember Henri, a Haitian-American boy from a single-parent family whose mother was a radiology technician. The boy was a chronic underachiever, late learning to read and never much of a writer or speller. Math was his strong suit, his ability usually hovering close to grade level. His teachers frequently delivered such pronouncements as, "If only Henri would concentrate on what he's doing, he would be a first-rate student." During the early weeks of kindergarten, he would head for the water fountain or the back of the room, where he could be found irrigating his nostrils while his teacher held the other students riveted by a suspense-filled tale. He was a bit more focused at home, although periodic domestic tuneouts and unscheduled excursions were not uncommon. In elementary school, Henri was notorious for taking hikes around the periphery of the classroom.

Henri's wandering ways caused his teachers, parents, and pediatrician to decide that he "was ADHD." So at the ripe old age of eight he was put on Ritalin. The changes were far from dramatic. Henri suffered a loss of appetite and had trouble falling asleep (common side effects of stimulant treatment). The drug was continued with periodic increases in dosage as he grew older and taller (and narrower). He did not take it on weekends or during vacations.

As Henri ascended through middle and high school, his academic woes intensified. In eighth grade he came close to being retained. He was addicted to skateboarding and was a guiding light among a squad of friends.

His mother concluded that his poor school performance was destroying his self-esteem, and she detected gnawing anxiety not far beneath his macho cool veneer. She consulted a psychiatrist, who started him on the first of a long chain of antidepressants.

Over the succeeding years, multiple pharmacological cocktails were prescribed with consistently equivocal results. Meanwhile, Henri's school performance continued to deteriorate. He had trouble distilling usable information from texts, and in most subjects he felt disoriented and, most of the time, overwhelmed. He implemented a work slowdown during much of high school, completing only the bare minimum, and he managed to graduate at the bottom of his class. He went on to a community college to study filmmaking and video. He loved the practical work but struggled with reading, note taking, and examinations in general. He continued to consume pills for his presumed ADHD and depression.

Henri never finished college. Needing money, he got a job selling at an electronics store managed by a friend's father. The opportunity seemed like a blessing. Henri had always enjoyed tinkering with his CD player and other devices, and he had gravitated toward the hands-on high-tech courses in college. He went about his work with greater seriousness of purpose than he had ever displayed before. He was genuinely interested in the products he was selling, and he always enjoyed meeting people. The job seemed tailor-made for him, but after six months, Henri was let go. Despite repeated warnings, he misled customers about products because he had misunderstood some of their key features, details that had been explained repeatedly during weekly staff training and briefing sessions. Henri read over the manuals he was told to take home and study. He had the big picture and thought he could get by without the details. He tended to misinterpret what his customers were asking for, and management decided that his ineptitude was costing the store business. Henri's sales record was well below that of his coworkers. Over the next three years, he had several other jobs, all in the sales of appliances and electronics, all with the same unfortunate outcome.

Looking over samples of his academic work and teachers' comments, I had a chance to splice together the fragments of Henri's history. It was obvious that he was a kid who had trouble processing incoming language with speed and accuracy—an essential skill for achievement in school and success as a salesperson. When he was very young, Henri reacted as many students with language problems do: he tuned out, walked away, and became fidgety and distracted when a teacher was speaking. Also like many others with underdeveloped verbal abilities, Henri exhibited persistent problems with reading comprehension and with spelling. Adults kept focusing on his inattention and his anxiety, both of which were secondary complications of a serious language processing problem. He never received any assistance at improving his language comprehension, so he grew up telling himself and everybody he met, "I'm ADHD." Henri failed to understand how to exploit his dexterity, such as his ability to fix a CD player and operate a video camera. Instead of pursuing his nonverbal thinking strengths, he took selling jobs that called for sharply honed language intake and output as well as accurate reading skills. Far too often, invoking a label like ADHD prevents people from taking a more profound look inside a kid or within themselves. The child gets labeled as if being put in some safe deposit box. Henri had to navigate his startup years shouldering a substantial language debt that he never understood.

When kids struggle, they have a right and a need to know exactly where their breakdowns are occurring and what they can do about them. We can demystify the problems by saying something like this: "Leslie, there are two areas that you need to be working on that are weaknesses for you right now. But they don't have to continue to be problems forever." Such an explanation cultivates optimism and motivation. In the absence of self-knowledge, individuals like Joel and Henri may think the worst and abandon all hope.

UNDERDONE RELATIONSHIPS

Developmental debts need not come to light only with academic failure. The worlds of school and work demand a high level of social prowess, and some kids can't seem to earn passing grades on the interpersonal scene. They lack some highly specific functions needed for acting right, seeming right, and talking right with their peers and sometimes with adults as well. Their classmates may go out of their way to exclude them. Some are bullied. Some become withdrawn and shy. Others display aggression. If their social inappropriateness is overlooked, they can enter the adult world with little or no sense of how to act and interact in ways that gain the respect of coworkers and supervisors. They are in serious mind debt and in work-life jeopardy.

Some individuals with social difficulties have trouble communicating verbally in a constructive way (page 178), while others lack important nonverbal ingredients of relationship building and maintenance. Nonverbal skills include interpreting social feedback (such as reading facial expressions and hand gestures), moving through space without invading other peoples' space, exhibiting socially acceptable behavior, and quelling aggressive tendencies. Individuals with social dysfunctions are especially vulnerable when they enter a profession in which a high level of interaction is a core part of the job. The cultivation of these abilities will be covered in chapter 10.

THE END OF FREE RIDES

Some students get to paddle through their school years with only minimal mental effort. As one mother commented to me, "Nathaniel manages to get good grades without really putting forth much effort. He's not the least bit ambitious or motivated, but you'd never know it looking at his report cards. The kid somehow pulls off decent grades doing hardly any work at all. He does fine on tests; it all comes so naturally to him. I can't really criticize him; the boy isn't failing or anything like that. But there's definitely a piece missing from his education."

I think I know what's missing. Nathaniel isn't learning how to energize his thinking and invest vigor in brain work. That places Nathaniel at risk for all sorts of woes during his startup years. He has not acquired a working capacity, an ability to delay gratification, channel effort, and engage in prolonged work. He has the instincts and intuitions to beat the system in school and take home acceptable report cards. Will that work at a place of work? Can he succeed in business without really trying? Only time will tell. But it's risky to break into a work life without good work habits, work rhythms, and something resembling a work ethic. A lack of working capacity is a costly developmental debt among many startup adults. They want and they expect to surge ahead without having to work very hard. Since they've been able to pull off effort-free feats in the past, they may be hard to convince of the need to plug away while ascending a career ladder. Nathaniel deserves to be warned about this, and he may or may not be able to hear it. Some kids have to hit rock bottom at age twenty-two or twenty-six to realize that there are no free rides in the workplace!

TRAITS IGNORED

An individual's important and durable traits can be neglected despite the fact that they are likely to exert a powerful influence over her or his future. In the field of pediatrics there has been tremendous interest in temperamental patterns, behavioral styles that may be observed in infancy and remain stable over many years. Dr. William Carey and his coworkers describe some babies as withdrawn and shy, others appear slow to warm up, and still others are consistently overreactive and demanding. Such characteristics appear to be wired into people. Shyness, gregariousness, altruism, empathy, and impetuousness are among the range of patterns that may form the basis of a developing personality. An extraordinarily diverse range of these traits can be found within a family. To say, "I really know that kid," in part means you can describe his consistent traits. Over time these traits have tremendous implications for choosing recreational activities, lines of study, and ultimately vocations.

Insatiability, a highly specific lifelong trait of certain people, can illustrate the drama of ignored traits. As a clinician I have encountered numerous patients whose chronic insatiability dates back to the earliest months of their lives. They are likely to manifest some or all of the following tendencies:

> Frequent and extreme restlessness
> Often-recurring feelings of boredom
> Unrelenting need for highly stimulating experiences
> Trouble delaying gratification
> Risk-taking behaviors (especially during adolescence)
> Extreme appetite for material possessions
> Provocative behavior aimed at "stirring things up"
> Trouble performing in unexciting settings (such as
>   many a classroom)

Insatiability is common, and it creates havoc for parents, siblings, educators, the criminal justice system, and, of course, for the victims themselves. Like so many other human traits, insatiability is a two-edged sword. It can evolve into ambition and drive in adult life. In fact, insatiability is a recurring theme in the lives of quite a few highly successful entrepreneurs and self-made people. Yet this trait can also bring with it a bevy of self-destructive behaviors. The problem is that insatiability is seldom identified specifically and dealt with. Parents, in particular, may be too close to it to see it.

Walker is the third son of a house painter and a kindergarten teacher. His mom often described him as the world's most demanding baby and toddler. He cried relentlessly and was colicky throughout his infancy. Often he seemed hungry, but feeding him failed to quell his restlessness. He was an especially terrible two, perpetually whiny, constantly wanting things. As he entered elementary school, Walker developed significant behavior problems. One elementary school teacher described him as a "provocateur" (otherwise known as a troublemaker). He loved stirring things up, especially when the class seemed well settled down. Walker demonstrated a clear distaste for equanimity. He was constantly being admonished and punished. His parents were the numb recipients of a steady influx of notes from school reporting their boy's latest outrageous transgressions. But all Walker's teachers invariably portrayed him as "a very sweet boy," and he was not the least bit hostile or aggressive. His benign intentions, however, never stopped him from firing harmless spitballs, launching paper missiles, blurting out off-color utterances during serious class discussions, or leaping like a kangaroo in front of his classmates on the cafeteria line (he seemed to have an obsession with being first in line). He appeared to relish the fury that followed his unacceptable actions or statements.

Walker carried home respectable report cards in elementary school—no doubt a tribute to his overall intelligence and especially keen verbal abilities. But when he was a teenager, his academic performance took a steep downturn. His provocative behaviors worsened. He got in with a group of antisocial teenagers, became brashly streetwise, pretty much repudiated his family, and developed drug and alcohol problems. Eventually, he underwent rehabilitation and managed to obtain a high school equivalency diploma. He held a succession of jobs, ranging from selling vinyl siding to driving a limo to apprenticing to a pastry chef, but each time he grew bored and restless. His attendance would become erratic and he'd get himself fired. It seemed that whatever he did made him dream up things he'd rather be doing. That was his insatiability coming on strong. His relationships with women were all profoundly intense romances but short-lived. His life was going nowhere.

Walker never once heard the word *insatiability* growing up. If his problems had been demystified, strategies could have been developed to satisfy his appetites in a less self-destructive manner. He could have been given stimulating recreational outlets, maintained collections (of rocks, trading cards, model rocket ships, or whatever) and been taught repeatedly about the need to set some limits on his appetites and practice delaying gratification.

Walker's life follows a fairly extreme but all-too-common script. Insatiable startup adults are forever off on shopping expeditions, craving newer and ever more exhilarating heights of stimulation, unable to fasten themselves into any stable set of goals or intentions.

I believe we are seeing increasing numbers of insatiable children and startup adults because we live in a culture that fosters insatiability by offering kids immense servings of instant gratification. A modern child may not have to endure or wait around for much of anything. Plots on TV resolve themselves in a few minutes, and electronic devices provide rapid-fire satisfaction. Even food is fast. And you don't have to muster much patience and perseverance to appreciate the melodic line of a piece of contemporary popular music: it's short and redundant!

Insatiability takes three basic forms: material (a constant hunger for things, an inability to function until you get what you want), experiential (an intense need for intense stimulation—as in Walker's case), and social (an endless yearning for social interaction). Some kids and adults have all forms; many have only one variety.

Girls and some boys may have less noticeable insatiability. Deanna was such a child. She excelled academically and in sports but was bored and restless in school. In high school she became a stellar gymnast, but at the height of her somersaulting glory, she quit the team and followed the same course in field hockey and in soccer. In tenth grade, elected president of her class, she demonstrated resourceful and innovative leadership. Then she vowed never to run for office again. She received a rare A in honors English in tenth grade but claimed the class was "totally boring" and declined to take any further honors programs. Over and over she would dabble in activities, excel in them, and then tire of them. Deanna maintained no enduring relationships, yet she seemed to love people. It was as if she collected them like seashells. Sometimes Deanna seemed to use friends to have intense life experiences—in speeding cars, later in some heavy drinking binges, and in periodic experiments with risky chemical substances.

Deanna performed exceptionally well on her SATs and was accepted into a top college. During her first two years, she made the dean's list each semester—despite managing far greater gusto for her sorority than for her coursework. But then she was unable to pick a field of concentration; nothing seemed sufficiently exciting to her. With no advance notice whatsoever, shocking her tolerant and supportive parents, she took a leave of absence from college, never to return.

Deanna now works as a bartender in a very upscale hotel, and she is often restless and bored. All of her gratification comes from planning and taking exotic vacations with her friends and partying after work with her urban gang. Lately, she has been following a guru as she seeks what she calls "the highest forms of spirituality." She has become infatuated with his wisdom. She insists things will come together when she discovers authentic truth, the deepest meanings of life. She's on a constant if ill-defined spiritual search. The thought of more schooling or a steady desk job repulses her. Yet, at age twenty-five, she informed her distraught and bewildered parents that her life felt like driving an eighteen-wheeler in the pitch dark with no headlights. Of course, she had to admit that a part of her savored that adventuresome thrill that comes with not knowing where you're headed. Recently Deanna has amassed quite a few heavy financial debts—they often accompany mind debts—never having been able to resist tempting purchases. Spending wads of money has been one of her unconscious self-remedies for insatiability.

Like Walker, Deanna is unaware of her condition, insatiability, and so she has, thus far, missed her chances to bring it under control.

Undernourished Strengths and Affinities

Neglected assets can drag a person down as well. Imagine someone who can't pay his bills because he is unaware of how much money he has. Every child has valuable assets and inclinations. But what if a child possesses neurodevelopmental strengths that are never allowed to flourish and grow? What if a latent talent forever remains untapped? What if a child's naturally strong areas of interest are stifled or deemed illegitimate or devalued by the adult world? The result is likely to be a young person who will endure a seriously delayed takeoff into adult life.

A common example can be found in the swarms of students in every public school who harbor language difficulties and are condemned to struggle to achieve proficient reading comprehension, accurate spelling, and decent writing. Many such students are gifted when it comes to their nonverbal thinking. They are blessed with sharp visual perception and can find order in seemingly chaotic spatial relationships. They may be skilled artists or dexterous craftsmen, or they may be adept at building and repairing gadgets and contraptions. Their grades in school are usually lackluster; some fail. Too many give up on themselves, but most students with these difficulties are at the very least deprived of the opportunity to build on their strong spatial thinking. By the time they arrive at their startup years, an alarming number of them have dropped out of school, lost all motivation, lowered their aspirations, and, in some instances, gotten themselves incarcerated. These individuals suffered from one form of mind debt but never were allowed to cash in their assets. This is definitely a preventable plight. Schools must understand the neurodevelopmental profiles of all their students and ensure that everyone has the opportunity to build up his strengths and take pride in using them. Currently, we seem to be getting farther and farther away from that goal.

As kids grow up, we also need to take very seriously their emerging personal interests, what I call their content affinities. Interests beg for cultivation. It is an essential part of parenting and educating to respond supportively to a kid who consistently shows a strong attraction to a particular subject matter, be it pickup trucks, cats, waterfowl, clothing design, or drama. Affinities should develop into domains of expertise and passion. They can provide a sense of identity and direction as a person marches toward adulthood. They also can enhance skills; the best way to learn how to read and write well is to read and write about something you know and care a lot about.

Too often a child's flaming interests are doused or ignored, often when a child's affinities differ drastically from the tastes or values of her parents. But a mother or father can't completely program a child's affinities. Parents need to respond to what they see in each of their children.

I remember one teenager named Bret who had always been passionate about cars. At age sixteen all he seemed to care about was auto engines, especially those in need of drastic rehabilitation. He would labor for hours on end with his nineteen-year-old neighbor to rejuvenate an over-the-hill Mustang. Bret's dad was the CEO of a North Carolina furniture company, and his mom was a leading philanthropist in the community. Bret's younger sister was a prototypical debutante. Bret, hardly an outstanding student and conspicuously unathletic, was not what his father expected in his sole son. This was not the kind of kid you could proudly buckle into your Mercedes sedan and cart off to the country club: most of the time he was coated in grease and sported an oily wrench.

Bret Sr. had no interest in cars and seemed to shun his son whenever the boy tried to engage him in car talk. Young Bret's feelings were seriously hurt when his dad went out and bought his new Mercedes without even consulting him (an example of extreme insensitivity, I think). In other words, Bret's affinity for cars was never celebrated or accorded the respect it deserved. Indeed, his father stressed to Bret's mother that they should not be encouraging their son to be "a dumb redneck." Bret, on the other hand, refused to take golf, dancing, or saxophone lessons. He tended to socialize with local boys who shared his fervor for cars. All were from working-class families, which no doubt embarrassed Bret's mom and dad.

Bret dropped out of school in twelfth grade despite the vigorous efforts of his parents and the combined manpower of two psychiatrists who endeavored to refashion him pharmacologically. He had become overtly rebellious. But even more tragic was the fact that as he was about to enter his startup years, Bret didn't much like himself. His self-esteem had been all but choked off. This was a mind debtor—big time. His love affair with cars went begging, deprived of the outside affection it so needed for growth, diversification, and then ultimately application.

KEEPING MINDS SOLVENT

Minds in debt are costly. Our society doles out huge amounts of money in the form of unemployment benefits, along with mental health services and adult correctional facilities and staff. Much of this outlay may be a form of repayment for minds in debt. Many adults requiring expensive support are human beings who don't fit in because they have been unable to deal well with their own dysfunctions and exploit their personal strengths constructively. They may have no grip whatsoever on their weaknesses or how to repair or work around them. They may fail to see all the promise of their strengths or fail to know how put them to work.

All minds can be solvent in the business sense of the word. That is, they harbor within them enough of the resources needed to conquer the early challenges of a career startup. At least half the battle is won when we understand fully a child or adolescent's profile and when he and we can set about working out the ways in which his particular kind of mind is most likely to thrive during the startup years and after. Then he can live his authentic life and feel good about the person he is becoming.

Part Two

WAYS TO GROW

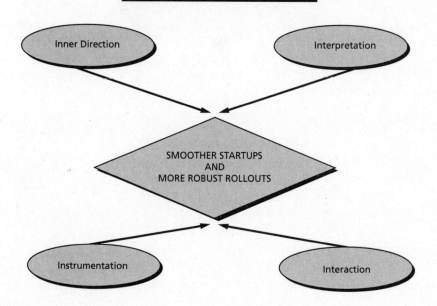

GROWTH PROCESSES:
The Four *I*'s

Inner Direction

Interpretation

SMOOTHER STARTUPS
AND
MORE ROBUST ROLLOUTS

Instrumentation

Interaction

Part two focuses on the building of minds during the formative years that precede and initiate work lives. Chapter 6 details several triumphant passages into and through the startup years, suggesting reasons why some individuals show excellent work-life readiness. The next four chapters examine the twelve growth processes. Each covers three growth processes that constitute one of the four *I*'s—inner direction, interpretation, instrumentation, and interaction.

6

DEFT NOVICES

Achieving a Successful Startup

If you are one of the lucky few who know what you want to do at an early age, then being able to intern earlier and have classes that shape that interest and teach you about that job will be very beneficial. However, that is less than, like, one percent of people between the ages of sixteen and twenty-five.

D.M., age 29

Happily, there is no shortage of people who are off to a very good start during their startup years, those launchers who have deftly navigated the transition from school to work without having their egos bludgeoned. Understanding how they've pulled it off can be invaluable in improving the lot of those with work-life unreadiness.

THE MULTIPLE FACETS OF READINESS

Being ready to perform as a new adult does not guarantee decades of total stability or perfectly smooth sailing. Many people change jobs and revamp their career course multiple times during their startup years (and afterward as well). Some even make fundamental niche switches! These transitions are not all bad. In fact, as long as strategic moves are informative in helping a person realize who he is and is not, they are healthy, life-sculpting experiences. A person can leave a job without having to repudiate or denigrate the immediate past; it was a learning experience contributing interest and color to his biography. On the other hand, there's a problem when work terminations are traumatic, when with each move a person feels she is escaping an incarceration. The startup years can be equally forsaken when someone fails to make needed job changes but feels marooned in an untenable position or unwittingly takes part in a career drama destined to have an unhappy ending.

What, then, makes for a successful career launch, whether it follows a straight path or meanders through the startup years? Let's examine laudable launcher Benny.

Benny was born to be the consummate plugger. He worked in school with the fervor of a carpenter ant and seemed powerfully driven to please his parents, who showered him with effusive praise when he was successful on a test. They were his exultant cheerleaders. Benny was not much of a verbalist and therefore not a top student, but throughout his childhood, he was conscientious and resilient. He loved to go all-out. He continues to harbor some problems with reading and spelling (due to a little trouble with phonology—his processing of language sounds—and also some difficulty acquiring vocabulary), but Benny was a solid performer in math. When he met with trouble in English or history or other highly verbal subjects, he was always willing to ask for help. He knew how to get his teachers to like and support him. He was very popular with adults and he savored their company. Benny always had a throng of friends, but he seemed able to take them or leave them; he was equally content to be fooling around by himself.

Benny was a brilliant cartoonist, and by age eleven he was creating his own whimsical comic books. He only halfheartedly played sports, but he was a good athlete. Most notably, he could repair just about anything that malfunctioned in or around his house. He had remarkable spatial and mechanical aptitudes. Benny's dad, an auto mechanic, fed his son's interests: his cartoons papered the walls of their double-wide modular home in rural Alabama. On weekends they would work together in bliss on an old heap of a car Benny's father was reincarnating.

Benny had steadfast parents who never gave up on him, and they constantly kindled his love affairs with art and mechanical devices. Although they could barely afford to so do, over several years they signed up Benny for weekend art classes.

From the time he was fourteen, partly at the insistence of his parents, Benny held a job after school in a construction-related activity; he saved the bulk of his wages to purchase his lusted-after GMC pickup truck. Benny had always revered his uncle Bert, a very successful contractor (with a mighty and alluring 375-horsepower GMC turbo pickup with four-wheel drive). Bert, who was unmarried, took Benny under his wing. The boy got to work alongside his uncle at construction sites. He was plainly awestruck as he watched buildings emerge from the earth. Benny's dad frequently told Bert to work his son hard, insisting that life shouldn't be offering the boy a free ride.

Benny never attended college but instead took courses in plumbing and managed to pass his state's certifying examination on his first try. Now, at age twenty-three, Benny is a winner. Having passed on an opportunity to work for Uncle Bert, he is an independent plumber who employs three others in his company, which specializes in plumbing in commercial construction. He remains a marginal reader and speller, but that's not stopping him from installing the most cost-effective plumbing in a new office building. As he went through school, Benny had his trouble with the three Rs, but he managed to learn the critical "soft skills." He emerged as a strong decision maker (page 166), an effective collaborator, a hard worker, and a true leader. Most likely he would have trouble passing the current end-of-grade academic testing requirements in many states, but so be it!

Benny was a dreamer who enjoyed speculating about his future. He had parents who loved him but were strict taskmasters. Benny's youthful reverie and ambition blossomed into entrepreneurialism. He still likes to draw cartoons on weekends and is soon to wed his high school sweetheart. He was more than ready to meet the calling of the startup years.

Throughout his life Benny did a lot of things right; so did his parents and teachers. They knew his strengths and weaknesses. They made sure that his dysfunctions did not annihilate his self-esteem and his motivation. They cultivated his strengths and his passions. They built his working capacity. They were his cheering squad, so Benny relished every opportunity to give them something to cheer about. Benny himself was resilient. He understood his learning problems and handled them well. He was unashamed and resourceful in recruiting help. Although he had friends and was good at sports, he never let himself get sidetracked with either of these. As a kid he kept exploring his feasible futures and forged numerous constructive connections with the adult world.

CRAFTING WORK-LIFE DECISIONS

Deciding what to do with your life requires assembling a puzzle from lots of odd-shaped pieces. First of all, a person has to decide to decide.

I've known kids who opt out of this decision making. They want to go with the flow. They may anticipate experiencing the bulk of their plea- sure and gratification from their leisure activities. The guys might look forward to playing some golf, watching football on Sunday afternoons, going out for a few drinks after work, and having a fun marriage. The girls may think exclusively about maintaining a gaggle of close friends, raising neat, lovable kids, having a pristine home, and saving to help send the children to college. These folks expect to get some kind of job somewhere, depending upon what's available. They want enough money to live on and a decent family to live with. They have no pre- tenses regarding wealth, power, or fame. I routinely ask my adolescent patients (not a random sample, since all are doing poorly in school), "Are you ambitious?" Most exclaim almost proudly that they are not. If they really mean it, they are committing to opportunistic rather than strategic career evolution. Others feel they need to buy more time to think about themselves and their future directions. They may see their startup years as a way station, a time to reflect and sustain themselves while considering their possibilities. Some with work-life unreadiness never emerge from this holding pattern.

When someone decides to commit to a career or a strategically cho- sen job, he initiates the complicated process of custom fitting himself to a realistic line of work. Some kids begin the process at a very early age and some never do. I decided to be a physician when I was eight years old, following a two-year period when I envisioned becoming a veterinarian. Propelling oneself toward a career by early decision has its advantages and drawbacks. If you make up your mind at a tender age, it becomes harder and harder to imagine yourself doing anything else; there goes your freedom of choice! On the other hand, it is somewhat comforting to know when you're nine what you'll be doing at thirty- nine.

Interests, Passions, and Callings

First, and it is almost trite to say it, people should follow their passions, so that they feel during their startup years that they are doing or on the way to doing something exciting. This may be easier said than accom- plished, since not everyone has a clear idea of what he is interested in. I know many teenagers who acquire a brand-new interest every five days. Others haven't had a discernible interest in five years. Still others are only interested in sex (not so easy to make a living on that one).

In his book *What Should I Do with My Life?*, Po Bronson puts it this way: "The true search is for what you believe in. When your heart's engaged, the inevitable headaches and daily annoyances become tolerable and don't derail your commitment. Let your brain be your heart's soldier." In other words, it helps to have a calling that makes you feel compelled to act. The cause might be to improve the economy, to build more fuel-efficient automobiles, to stamp out obesity, to combat crime, or to discover a cure for AIDS. Having a cause fuels momentum during the startup years, especially when it's combined with some self-discipline and well-honed work habits. Unfortunately, some startup adults convince themselves that feeling strongly about a topic or a cause is all it takes to be a leading authority on the subject. I remember one twenty-two-year-old lad dressed in massive hiking shoes, explicitly unshowered and sweaty in a nice, mountaineering sense, and shouldering an eighty-pound knapsack, who let me know he was "heavy into the environment—big time." I expressed my unreserved admiration for his cause but had the audacity to ask him if he had studied ecology or geology or perhaps oceanography. I elicited a confused and perturbed facial expression. I think he thought I was really out of it. He had studied nothing except the guitar and bodybuilding. He saw himself qualified to save our natural resources because he had such powerful sentiments and righteous indignation about the cause. He was missing the requirements, all those skills and credentials that empower an individual to effect the changes he so believes in. This step is often perceived as boring, time-consuming, and needless. Some startup adults become stranded because they decide to skip it.

Figuring out what you like or what you feel strongly about is not always a piece of cake. Some passions and causes are more conspicuous than others. I have encouraged many kids to think back over their lives and search for the themes or patterns that keep popping up: "As long as I can remember, I've loved animals." "I'm happiest when I'm doing things outdoors." "I've always been adamant about cruelty to animals." "I used to be the kid other kids would turn to when they were having a problem." "Since I was real little, I have had to be performing in front of an audience all the time. I'm a born show-off; I just eat up all the attention."

Whether it's tropical fish, ceramics, concocting pastries, reading newspapers, or helping out in a day care center, there's bound to be one or more leitmotifs. I remember when I took American literature as an undergraduate, Barry Marks, the professor, told us, "If you want to know what a novel is really about, you have to look for themes that keep coming back in each chapter. Those recurring themes give away the author's intention." It's the same when you go on a passion hunt: uncover the recurring themes.

Job Values

Finding work that fits one's passions and callings is only part of the mission. Researchers in vocational education and psychology have studied what they call job values, the elements that a person would like to derive from her or his work. Here are some of the most commonly cited job values.

SOME MAJOR JOB VALUES

Image

Potential for advancement
Opportunity to be respected on the job
Chance to be doing something prestigious

Independence

Likelihood of making plenty of money
Being my own boss
Setting my own hours

Work Qualities

Doing work that interests me
Making good use of my skills
Seeing results from my efforts
Doing work where my skills won't go out of date
Continually learning new things
Being creative

Outreach

Chance to serve others and be helpful
Opportunities to do things that feel worthwhile
Chance to teach or train others

Social Aspects

Opportunities to make new friends
Meeting a lot of people
Chance to work competitively

Workload and Work Style

A job in which I don't have to work very hard
Chance to do a lot of work at home
Work I can forget about nights and weekends
A job that involves traveling
Work that doesn't require sitting at a desk

Beginning in the adolescent years or perhaps even sooner, a kid can scan a list like this one, ask himself what will really matter to him in a career or a job, and rank these priorities.

The analysis of job values can help a kid or young adult come to terms with a key aspect of work, namely how someone frames his career within a certain field. If you decide to study pharmacy, you might own your own drug store, test antibiotics at a pharmaceutical firm, work as a pharmacist at Wal-Mart, teach pharmacy, add an MBA to your credentials and then work your way up the corporate ladder at Pfizer or Merck. As I mentioned earlier, when you're a kid you can study and pursue a wider range of things at the same time than you can as an adult in a career. But as a grown-up you can do a lot sequentially. For example, you could start out teaching pharmacy, then buy a drug store, then sell it and go to work for Wal-Mart while enrolling in an evening executive MBA program, and end up running the antidepressant division of a pharmaceutical giant.

Adolescents need insight into the sequential flow of careers. That can reassure them that their early commitments to a career frame are just a start. It can help them overcome the paralyzing effects of career ambivalence (page 7). Kids usually have an absurdly static view of what it will be like to be an adult. I remember Beau, a teenager whose passion was Arabian horses. A decidedly unconscientious student, he spent all his spare time at a North Carolina stable assisting a trainer. Both parents were college professors, one in history, the other in sociology. They were fairly prominent in their community; his mother had served several terms on the school board. As sometimes happens, these intellectual folks, who had never handled a horse whip or shoveled muck, were ironically mismatched with their son, and it was no one's fault. His father once referred to Beau as a throwback to some earlier generation, the ultimate eighteenth- or nineteenth-century farm boy. Beau wanted nothing more than to work on a farm or a ranch, but he also loved eating in fine gourmet restaurants. He was somewhat conflicted over this but confessed to me, "You know, Dr. Levine, I love working with horses more than anything else I do, but I don't want to be cleaning stalls all my life." I assured him he could and should follow his passion without having to spend his whole life scraping manure off his boots. Someone needs to run the stable—or own the local John Deere franchise or teach at the state agricultural school. Life is all about growing, changing, and adapting.

PREVIEWING THINGS TO COME

A career trajectory can be divided into six distinct stages that ought to be thought through before any startup. The stages are generic; they exist in every occupation. All kids need to learn about and think about the first four stages. They should get practice in studying how these stages unfold in different careers.

THE STAGES OF A CAREER

---

1. Preparatory
2. Startup
3. Midcareer
4. Main Act
5. Tapering Off
6. Retirement

Three big questions should be posed regarding each of those first four stages: What will it require of me? How will it feel? And will I be able to handle it? (Stages 5 and 6 are important to many of us, but not germane to startup adults.)

Stage 1—Preparatory
Way back when I was a highly impressionable premedical student at Brown, several of my science instructors sternly warned me, "If you

can't hack organic chemistry, there's no way you're going to make it as a physician. First of all, you're unlikely to get in or through medical school, and if you do, you'll hate medicine." As it turned out, I did not enjoy organic chemistry and I love my work as a physician. I'm so glad I ignored their false prophecies. I remember several of my classmates who would have made wonderfully compassionate doctors but who, unfortunately, dropped out of premed because of such ill-conceived warnings. I also knew of several classmates who were mesmerized by acids, bases, esters, and isomers, yet I didn't think they were particularly cut out to care for the sick. The narrow scholars promoting such ill wisdom had no understanding of career stages and how they work. Who says you have to find basic training a lot of fun to become a valiant soldier?

Adolescents looking ahead toward work life need a fairly clear image of what the preparatory stage will feel like. They should observe the process firsthand, read about it, talk about it, and think about it. In the best of all worlds, getting there is half the fun! But for any given career, it may not be. If a student yearns to be a psychiatrist, should she abandon her plans because she can't stand the prospect of all those afternoons in college biology labs? What if a nineteen-year-old gave up his dream of driving an eighteen-wheel rig back and forth across the country because he might fail his truck driver training program? Sadly, such fatalistic thinking occurs all the time. Young people often have apocalyptic apprehension regarding stage 1. Fears of hard work and possible failure overtake some kids. Adults should be cheering them on, helping them recognize that stage 1 is of very short duration compared to the span of a career. It should be thought of as an initiation rite, perhaps a hazing process, or even a vocational boot camp.

Stage 2—Startup

Everything that went before it converges on the startup stage, the period that is the focus of this book. A person's updated profile of strengths and weaknesses, his educational background, the dividends from years of accumulating wisdom, kindling passion, and building skills and insight flow together during this watershed period. This is when startup adults are compelled to submit to some rigorous testing of their work-life readiness—whether they realize it or not.

Startup adults who get off to a running start in their work lives are the ones with the clearest understanding of what they'll need to make the grade, to impress their superiors, to get ahead, and to find enjoyment in what they do. It has been said that many successful high school students excel because they have mastered the "hidden curriculum." They have been able to "psych out" their teachers, knowing what it will take to win each one's respect and extract good grades. Without any question, every job, much like school, has a hidden curriculum, some unspoken rules about how to succeed.

Successful career launchers work hard, relate well, show intiative, have a beginning grasp on the politics of their organization, and radiate enthusiasm for what they're engaged in. They emerge as people anyone would like to work with anywhere on the job hierarchy. As well, these are individuals who seem to fit with what they are doing. They are in the right place at the right time, doing their thing.

Stage 2 also requires some self-pacing. The rewards of a career are likely to arrive slowly, and there are limits to how much you can rush things. I encounter ever-increasing numbers of kids who want to skip the first three stages entirely and get right to the main act. They are unwilling to start at the bottom and work their way up. They are as presumptuous as they are ambitious. At age twenty-one they may turn down job opportunities because the work seems too menial, even though the organization they would work for would offer exciting opportunities for advancement—in due time. They may not be aware of all they could learn about a business or other institution in looking from the bottom up. Maybe it's because they are part of a generation accustomed to instant gratification. Maybe it's because they have groomed themselves on role models who started at the top, twenty-year-old rock singers tattooed with dollar signs and basking in fame or twenty-three-year-old multimillionaire halfbacks. During the Internet boom of the 1990s, some startup adults created their own companies with little or no experience running a business. Most failed. The model of Bill Gates is not readily replicated. A willingness to start way down and climb way up is, of course, the American dream.

In my book *The Myth of Laziness* I related a true story that bears retelling in this context. It concerned a man named Bill Charette, who was a cameraman I worked with while creating a video library on learning with public TV station WGBH in Boston. Throughout his childhood Bill had an affinity for television. He left school early and worked in shoe stores without a lot of satisfaction. But he kept aspiring to a career as a TV cameraman, specifically one in public television. So he took some courses and became certified. Alas, there were no jobs for a cameraman at any station. Somewhat dismayed, Bill continued to stock and stack shoe boxes, until one day a buddy showed him a classified advertisement in the *Boston Globe.* WGBH was seeking someone to work in the mail room. Bill applied for and got this low-level, low-paying job. He then went on to become the hardest-working, most personable, and most resourceful mail room guy any company could imagine! About six months later, WGBH had an opening for a cameraman. Bill, beloved by everyone at the station, applied for this slot and got it. Now, years later, he is one of the most successful and highly respected documentary cameramen in the United States. Bill was willing to start at the bottom. He was prepared to delay gratification, to endure the rigors of stage 2.

Stage 3—Midcareer

Many startup adults get worked up over what life will be like in the middle of a career. Will I be bored out of my mind? Will I plod through the same dull routines day after day after day? Once I'm well into my work, will all the fun evaporate? Will I be trapped behind a desk or in the cab of my truck? Am I going to be working under people who are not as smart or competent as I am? Will I be perpetually underpaid and undervalued? Will I be discriminated against because of my gender, religion, race, or physical appearance? The angst expended over such perceptions may be justified. Midlife crises are all too common. People do become disillusioned or burned out or have their feelings hurt brutally during the extended midcareer stage. Who knows, maybe that's a normal occurrence, a benign signal that it's time for a change.

Adolescents and startup adults need to be told truthfully that after ten or fifteen years, any job or occupation may seem stale and empty. That's not the end of the world. Workers in midcareer can and often do make some new decisions at that point almost as if they were back in high school or college. One's biography is enriched if it has chapters in it—the Dallas years, the years in high tech, the years in business for myself, and so on. So startup adults should never fear stage 3, but instead be aware of the unique challenges and opportunities it offers.

Stage 4—Main Act

What do you see as your highest level of attainment in life? What will you consider your ultimate emblems of success and happiness? Would you be apt to be wealthy, well known, a leader, a charitable person, someone who has touched and reached out to many others? What will your daily life be like during the main act? In planning their lives, I believe kids should ask themselves these questions. They should preview the main act and what they hope it will feature. Ambition is all about previewing stage 4.

I think people can tell when they're in stage 4. The author is one such beleaguered fourth stager. This is a time of life when you're fulfilling your promise. You are going about as far as you can (or will) go. This is a last chance to show what you can do. It is often an era during which egos become inflated and fragile. Status anxiety may reach its peak (De Botton, 2004a). Startup adults have to be careful not to cross bosses or supervisors in stage 4; they have power and they can be vengeful. This can also be a time of unrealistic hubris, a moment when people get in trouble for cheating on their taxes or their spouses.

Just as I stressed the importance of young people's previewing the disquietude of stage 3, they need to look ahead to stage 4 with an upbeat view and decide what that period ought to be like in their lives. The decision obviously is not binding, but it is still helpful and healthy to take aim. Looking ahead to stage 4 is the same as setting long-range goals, establishing priorities that will guide you through your career, putting light at the end of the tunnel. It involves making sure that the coming attractions look sufficiently attractive. A clear vision for this stage can propel you through stages 1 to 3.

A PERSONAL CASE STUDY

I would like to segue into part two by volunteering myself as a case study and presenting a brief chronicle of my evolution as a pediatrician. During the earliest years of my life, I had a deep love, a true affinity for animals, and I found out that they were attracted to me as well. So at age six I decided to become a dog doctor when I grew up (the word *veterinarian* encompassing too big a phonological sequence for this average first grader). On a daily basis my mother would chase me down the street when I brought home snakes, tortoises, and other injured patients. I let her know that when I grew up I would have all the animals I wanted, to which she reacted skeptically.

When I approached nine, my older sister met, fell in love with, and married Keith, who was studying to become a pediatric surgeon. I clung to my new brother-in-law like a plaster cast; I worshipped the man. As a result, I decided to forgo animal care and head toward medical school.

I loved reading biographies. I had a voyeur's fascination with people, especially with what becomes of them over time, the plots of their lives, so to speak. It seemed as if I read every biography I could find. Also, I found that I loved writing, and I eventually became editor in chief of my high school newspaper (in part because I was so abysmal at sports). As a premedical student I took courses mainly in the humanities, lots of literature and philosophy with a bare minimum of science courses.

Throughout much of high school and into college, I worked during the summers as a camp counselor; my specialty was taking boys and girls on mountain-climbing expeditions in New Hampshire. I was fascinated by the different ways individual kids handled the physical and emotional stress of their upward treks—my first exposure to all kinds of minds. In college I ran a large social service organization called Brown Youth Guidance, where we worked with kids at neighborhood settlement houses and in a hospital for emotionally disturbed children. Sometimes we climbed mountains with those underprivileged children as well.

I was fortunate enough to win a Rhodes Scholarship, and while at Oxford I became immersed in philosophy—a hot subject there at the time. I was attracted to ethics and epistemology (the study of knowledge—how we know what we know is right, and so forth). When I returned to Harvard Medical School, my long-standing interest in school-age children pointed me toward pediatrics, and a chronic history of severe fine motor ineptitude ruled out any thoughts of a surgical subspecialty. I had to exploit my neurodevelopmental strength in the language realm in a field where you mainly observe, talk, and listen. I also found that I was far more oriented to vertical than to horizontal patients, so I most enjoyed working in the outpatient department during medical school and then as an intern and resident in Boston. I was most fascinated by people in the contexts of families, schools, and communities rather than those lying supine in hospital beds.

During the Vietnam War, I was obliged to enter the United States Air Force as a pediatrician stationed at Clark Air Base in the Philippines. While in the air force I became the school doctor: I think we had nearly 15,000 children on Clark. I really loved working with the schools and saw the need for much more close cooperation between the fields of pediatrics and education. After my two-year stint overseas (they called our bunch of medical draftees "the Christmas help"), I returned to Children's Hospital Boston, ultimately to run the medical outpatient department. I discovered there that most of our truly challenging cases were not kids with traditional diseases but children and adolescents who were not functioning well. They suffered from dysfunctions rather than diseases. Often they were accused of being lazy or poorly motivated or else just written off as slow or disturbed. I became indignant over the ways they were regarded and the way their parents were unfairly blamed for their children's plight. I saw them all as innocent victims. I could discern my calling. It was like an exquisite sunrise.

At about that time I was asked to help frame and implement a special education law (Chapter 766) in Massachusetts. That opportunity further involved me with schools, my first love. Among other things, the law prohibited the use of labels and required that children with developmental problems be described by their needs rather than being forced into a simplistic category. The rest is history: I plunged deeper and deeper into issues at the interface between education and pediatrics. I went with my passion and have grown to feel more passionate about it than ever!

So what is there to learn from the Mel Levine case study? Primarily it reveals how many strands can be interwoven into a rich and rewarding life. My interest in biographies evolved into a commitment to child development. In fact, whenever I evaluate a kid, I feel as if I am exerting some influence on chapter 2 of her biography ("The School Years"). As a pediatrician, I have tended to focus on school-age children rather than babies and toddlers. In other words, consistent with my past, I became a high-paid camp counselor. As I dealt increasingly with learning disorders, I fulfilled my fantasy of helping to narrow the gulf between medicine and education. Also, my interest in philosophy proved to be entirely relevant; the kids I encounter raise many complex ethical and epistemological issues, including: Is it fair to label a person or is this an unethical means of reducing him? What does it mean to be called normal or abnormal? When is a variation a deviation? Should someone be forced to do things he is not wired to do? Under what circumstances can we punish someone for actions he can't help because they're part of his wiring? The questions go on and on. To this day, much of what I do might be characterized as clinical philosophy.

My career also enabled me to sustain my affinity for writing. I have discovered that writing is my way of thinking and exploring.

What, then, ever happened to my other first love, animals? I now live on Sanctuary Farm in North Carolina, where Bambi and I are parents to more than two hundred geese, about a dozen swans, twelve or so peacocks, roughly twenty kinds of pheasants and related species, sixteen mammoth donkeys, one mule, one horse, six dogs, and six cats. I find I am most interested in the behavioral and developmental features of all of these creatures. I work hard on my relationships with them and on helping each of them fulfill its promise as an individual member of the menagerie. I have discovered that no two geese have the same neuro-developmental profiles, so I do not expect them all to find fulfillment in the same ways.

A GENERATION'S NATURAL RESOURCES

Throughout this book I describe shortcomings that result in work-life unreadiness and what can be done to prevent and fill these gaps. But it is important to acknowledge that there are numerous individuals out there, much like Benny, representing terrific success stories. The newest generation of startup adults boasts abundant assets. Most possess remarkable technological virtuosity, a sophisticated facility with computers and related technology that is so much in demand. In addition, today's college and high school students display deep loyalty and respect for each other. Most are profoundly ethical in their values and staunchly committed to supporting human rights and respecting differences between people. I have noticed how many of them form strong alliances with one another; they are likely to become proficient at collaborating to achieve important goals. The adult work world, with its overwhelming project orientation, is in desperate need of true team players. This generation has so much it can donate to society.

There has to be a way to prepare children and adolescents so that they do not endure work-life unreadiness when their formal schooling ends but rather experience their personal startup and rollout in a way that is productive and satisfying, a way that leads them somewhere—on a road well chosen. No one expects the startup years to be a period of unfettered joy and triumph. Minor setbacks are inevitable, and they can become a source of strength and resiliency, but during these years startup adults should not endure unneeded suffering and potentially irreversible self-destruction. How do we maximize the likelihood of successful startups? In the chapters that follow I will explore the growth processes that must be active well before kids arrive at the demanding threshold of career entry.

7
INNER DIRECTION
Deepening Self-Knowledge

I like to think that I would much rather measure my success against my own personal goals rather than against what my peers are doing.

C.T., age 24

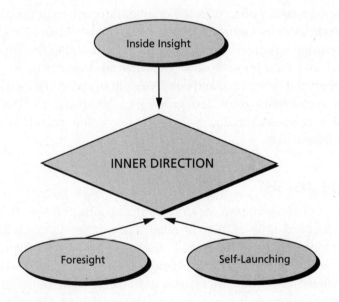

"Who am I anyway?" "What am I turning into?" "Where do I go from here?" Those probing questions are worth pondering even if they can't be answered with much certainty. Yet too few individuals ask themselves such things before entering their startup years. A sixteen-year-old patient once told me, "You know somethin', Doc, I think I can say I really know myself." After chatting with him for a few minutes, I could see how wrong Carson was. He thought he had good social skills when in fact he was very much a loner, regularly excluded from activities by his classmates. He also clung to the belief that he was an excellent science student, something equally untrue. He had an unimpressive seventy-two average in biology.

The sociologist David Riesman once defined a portion of our society as "inner-directed." These people possess an internal gyroscope; they keep looking within themselves for guidance in life. They base much of their judgment and direction on their self-knowledge and personal values rather than imitating or performing for others in their social and family milieu; such audience-oriented behavior Riesman called "other-directed."

No one is totally other-directed or inner-directed; most people read both compasses in making life decisions. But I know many kids who are driven mainly to impress. In the process they may fail to find their own identity and then go on to live lives that are inauthentic for them. Therefore, the emergence and enhancement of influential inner direction is an essential ingredient of growing up. The building of that inner direction relies on three growth processes: inside insight, foresight, and self-launching.

INSIDE INSIGHT

There is no one harder to get to know than yourself. The work of personal discovery is never quite finished; a person always needs to keep learning new things about himself. Some startup adults—falling idols and those trapped in adolescence among them—barely know who they are. When I asked one twenty-year-old college sophomore what he thought he could do best in this world, he responded, "To tell you the truth, I haven't given it much thought." Then I asked politely, "Tom, do you think you need to think about it?" His answer was "Yeah, probably, sometime, I guess." This student had a led a peer-centered life and spent almost no time by himself. It was as if he feared being alone with his thoughts, so he was forever performing. During the few moments he had to himself, he would immediately turn on loud music and start his body in rhythmic motion, as if the sound was insulation from the strains and sometimes pains of looking inward, of thinking about who he is and where he's headed. The music keeps flowing; it has direction and structure, even when life doesn't feel as if it's going anywhere. I see many adolescents like this. It is a common pattern in a culture preoccupied with outward appearances and with entertainment that caulks the intervals between social performances—no time, no place, no desire for introspection.

Numerous unready startup adults carry around incomplete, fragmentary, or fantasized images of themselves, unrealistic assessments of what they can and cannot accomplish given their personal repertoire of abilities, skills, and consistent traits.

Becoming Aware of an Evolving Profile

A child's understanding of himself depends on his awareness of many facets of his being. The experience of school should be used as one means of understanding one's strengths and weaknesses. A report card, examinations in school, and other forms of feedback from teachers can be revealing mirrors. A student should be helped to analyze these results for what they say about his or her neurodevelopmental strengths and weaknesses: "Eva, you do so well in all your English and history classes, while you struggle in science and math. It sure looks as if you are becoming a person who handles challenges best when they involve a lot of language."

Getting in Touch with Feelings and Moods

Kids also should assess their patterns of moods and feelings. A teenager might observe, "I think I overreact to a lot of things" or "I am a real worrier" or "I am horribly nasty when I first get up in the morning" or "I'm the kind of person who feels sorry for anybody—or even any animal— who is suffering" or, tragically, "I keep on wondering if my life is worth living." Inside insight takes a willingness to be self-critical. Being able to talk about these patterns may help kids decide which ones they want to preserve and which of them they need to change. The important thing is to have an opportunity to discuss these issues rather than avoid them or keep them locked up inside.

Perceiving Environmental Influences and Personal Values

A developing mind also has to gain some insight into the continuing influence of its surroundings. "How are my family and my neighborhood affecting what I am becoming?" "What does my family value and how

has that shaped my own values?" Kids should realize that these influences can be negative or positive. As one student told me, "All my parents care about is their money and their social status. I'm interested in
neither of these; I love playing music and making other people happy.
That's what I value." One girl informed me that her family's religious
devotion was the single most important influence in her life. She said
that strong religious values were going to play a major role in whatever
she did with her life. A child picks up these inside insights through daily
osmosis, via the direct or indirect teachings of his parents, and by comparing and contrasting himself with others.

Active Self-Assessment

Knowledge of one's background, personal strengths, weaknesses,
tastes, and disinclinations helps immeasurably in charting a course for
the startup years. Knowing who you are makes knowing what to do a
whole lot easier and more satisfying. It's important for that insight to be
explicit and acknowledged, rather than submerged or semiconscious.
Parents and teachers have to encourage this line of thinking and talking, since so many kids never experience it. Class discussions, talks in
the car, and chats at bedtime can reveal what a child or teenager is
learning about herself and what that might mean for the future. At the
Highland Park School in Austin, Texas, every third and fourth grader
creates a poster exhibit about his own neurodevelopmental profile.
The kids illustrate their displays with images of their strengths, their
affinities, and what they called their "challenges," their areas of weakness. I believe activities of this type should take place on a regular basis
in schools.

Like those children in Austin, kids rising through grades six to nine
and on into high school should begin the lifelong job of assembling
their self-awareness by thinking about their strengths, their weaknesses, their preferences, and what these characteristics may have in
common. They should also be alert for trends, for instance, "I seem to
be getting more and more interested in the way people treat each
other." That thought process can be switched on without submitting to
formal aptitude tests, and a kid's inside insights should undergo revision as he strides through adolescence. The mission is simple: "I'm getting to know me, getting to know all about me." With increased inside
insight, far fewer young adults will take the wrong roads. I would
launch all kids on an informal process of self-description during ele-

mentary school, though some early educators prefer to introduce such exploration even earlier.

Table 7.1 is a simple mechanism for getting kids and parents to talk from time to time about where a child or adolescent seems to be heading in life.

TABLE 7.1
INSIDE INSIGHTS: STRENGTHS AND INTERESTS LISTS

STRENGTHS

Things I Do Well in School	Things I Do Well Outside School

WEAKNESSES

Things or Kinds of Things I'm Not So Good At

(continued on next page)

INTERESTS
(including *both* recreational interests and knowledge interests)

Kinds of Recreation/Entertainment I Enjoy	Kinds of Knowledge I Like Learning About

POSSIBLE COMMON THREADS (INTERESTS THAT STICK OR KEEP COMING BACK)

Possible Common Threads	Strong	Medium	Slight	None
Doing things with other kids				
Spending time with grown-ups				
Leading others				
Working with others				
Outdoor activities				
Competing				
Sports				
Music/dance/theater				
Design/graphics/cartooning/other artwork				
Crafts/construction/repairing things				
Technology				
Reading				

Possible Common Threads	Strong	Medium	Slight	None
Writing				
Doing math				
Hands-on activities				
Having a busy social life				
Religion/philosophy				
Politics/government/current events				
Historical events				
People's problems/behavior/emotions				
Animals/nature				
Caring for younger children				
Science				
Fantasy/science fiction/comics				

Additional threads:

_____

_____

_____

_____

PERSONAL TRAITS AND VALUES

Trait	Very Important to Me	Important to Me	A Little Important to Me	Unimportant to Me
Being a religious person				
Having close friends				
Being popular				

(continued on next page)

PERSONAL TRAITS AND VALUES

Trait	Very Important to Me	Important to Me	A Little Important to Me	Unimportant to Me
Working with other people				
Being alone				
Helping others				
Having plenty of money to spend				
Having a close family				
Feeling happy most of the time				
Being ambitious				
Getting excellent grades				

Other traits and values:

_____

_____

_____

_____

_____

I believe this inventory or one like it should be revisited two or three times a year, especially as a student passes through middle and high school. A parent or teacher can help a child or teenager engage in what I referred to earlier as the search for recurring themes, the biographical trends. In doing so, it is important not to pigeonhole a person; it is most helpful to describe someone vividly rather than subject him or her to some constraining classification (such as "a visual learner" or "a kid with Asperger's syndrome"). What does this mind keep trying to tell us about itself?

In the inventory, it is important to note the distinction between recreational and knowledge interests; all kids should be encouraged to cultivate both. A recreational interest might be a love of acrobatics, computer games, or swimming. A knowledge interest might be rocks and minerals or reptiles or aviation. It may involve building collections of things and learning about them or enjoying specific activities, such as planting a garden or viewing the planets. Whenever possible, these interests should evolve into domains of expertise and passion. All kids should cultivate one or more knowledge interests that grow, enduring themes or subject areas they keep coming back to and continually learn more about. Too often in our society, when asked what interests him, a child cites only a form of entertainment. That child can accumulate some serious mind debts (chapter 5), missing out on the intellectual power that comes from amassing knowledge in depth within an area of continuing interest. A developing mind should sop up both knowledge and entertainment interests. Of course, while searching for these, it is important that minds evolve, building on their preferences and sources of excitement over time. But for many highly fertile minds, the turnover rate is relatively slow, and passions have a worthwhile way of building on earlier interests.

FORESIGHT

To what extent should thoughts about a child's future occupy his present life? Is there a danger in overemphasizing plans for college and careers at the expense of enjoyment and personal gratification as a kid? Everybody would agree that youth should have its own rewards, that childhood and the adolescent years should be far more than pipelines yielding barrels of grown-ups. Nevertheless, kids should have some sense of direction, a preview of what lies ahead. Such foresight is a critical part of taking the right roads in life. Short on foresight, young people become prime candidates for work-life unreadiness.

Taking Headings

Just as a conscientious steamship navigator takes headings while traversing the river, we should see to it that kids regularly examine the directions in which their minds are taking them. Where you think you're going reflects who you think you are. When kids peer within themselves, all too often they see a highly distorted image. Commonly, their notions of who they are derive from skewed, other-directed comparisons with their friends or siblings. In fact, many potent influences in our society may be conditioning kids to live entirely in the present. These include the following factors:

- Such intense gratification is available from sports, shopping mall excursions, and music videos and games that kids hope the party will never end. "I'm having so much fun right now, why should I look at what's ahead?"

- So much rich pleasure may derive from material possessions that acquiring them becomes the core quest in life. In that case, the future is perceived as a pure and simple money chase, the hunt for the resources needed to maintain the unimpeded flow of novel paraphernalia.

- There may be such a tremendous stress on getting into college that kids begin to perceive this rite of passage as an end in itself; they need not look beyond the precious moment when they open up a letter of acceptance. And of course, you don't need substantial insight into yourself to get into college.

- Kids may harbor a tremendous fear of being different. The media bombard kids with images of what's considered cool and what's deemed nerdy. In their desire to follow the mores of coolness, kids may never look inside. They may worry that their personal traits will thwart their acceptance by peers, and for many of them, nothing is more important than acceptance.

Children and adolescents should be coaxed to engage in future gazing, to realize that it's fun and rewarding to visit the decades to come. They should see that by playing their cards right, when the time comes, they can actually get paid for doing things that are fun!

Once kids have sharpened their inside insights, discussions can focus on what their self-descriptions foretell about their futures. This discussion can take place in school or at home—ideally in both settings. Of course, no one is committing anyone to a specific career track; pursuing their present inclinations should not be thought of as a highway with no exits. At any time they can pull off and head in a different direction, perhaps responding to a new passion. Taking headings is intended to provide kids with much-needed practice in looking ahead from a position of sound self-knowledge: "Here's who I am and here's where it looks as if I should be heading—but that's just for now."

I've seen some good examples of kids who have been helped to know themselves and then pursue activities that are fitting. One boy named Tyrone was always fooling around and getting into some trouble for it in school. But one of his seventh grade teachers felt that his zany displays in class were actually a strength. She helped him start a humor magazine and develop a comedy routine as part of the yearly school show. When I met him in eighth grade, Tyrone explained that he was thinking seriously about becoming an entertainer someday. A girl named Kate was, like many other eleven-year-olds, preoccupied with her friends and her body, only she was an extreme case; those things were all she could think about. In school she was at her best in art classes. Her mother got Kate interested in dress design, and she really took to it. When I met Kate a couple of years later, she told me she was studying much harder than she used to so she could go to an art school and learn how to design women's clothing. Kate and Tyrone have both acquired foresight, which will motivate them, even if they end up in fields that differ from their current visions. They've gotten practice in thinking about the future and where they fit in.

I once suggested to an English teacher that she ask her ninth graders to compose an essay on "How Who I Am and Who I've Been Might Tell Me Who I'll Be." That's an essay that all students should write from time to time. The "Who I've Been" segment should represent a blend of influential life events, consistent interests, strengths (and gaps), and personal priorities. The search for recurring life themes and speculation on their present and future significance can help to incubate readiness for work life. It is helpful for kids not just to look for the themes but also to state the possible past-present-future connections in their own words. As one thirteen-year-old girl told me, "Well, I used to like mostly cats; then I got into horses. I really love horses. I also enjoy helping my mom with her vegetable garden and stuff like that. And I really, really like our science class this year. We've been studying insect life. Come to think of it, I guess you could say I'm into nature. Maybe I'll be a biology teacher someday or else I'd like to work in a zoo or it could be I'll train horses."

A brain process called "previewing" plays a major role in linking the kind of person you are to the work you might pursue. The prefrontal lobes of the brain are the principal headquarters for previewing, for thinking ahead (page 172). Undergoing very rapid development during the adolescent and startup years, they help you look ahead, anticipate outcomes, and predict likely consequences, including, crucially, the possible consequences of your choices. Previewing helps you answer the important "what if?" questions. "If I say this, what will people think of me?" "If I act like this, will I get in trouble?" "What will my life be like if I become a chemist?" Many startup adults have never previewed the realistic consequences of their work choices and, as a result, have taken the wrong roads.

The Alignment of Strengths with Interests

In chapter 4, I described young adults who may have taken those wrong roads into their futures because of gaping disparities between their abilities and their interests. What if a child or adolescent likes things he's not good at or else is good at things he doesn't like to do? If a person pursues a career she likes but is not good at, she is inviting disaster. Such a misalignment of inclinations and abilities is not unusual in my experience. I've seen countless kids who have been shortchanged when it comes to their motor gifts but who love sports and dream of a major league contract. Others are wonderfully creative writers but detest having to write.

As children travel through their adolescent years, they will experience their greatest satisfaction and sense of direction if they can come to a tentative accommodation between their skills and their desires or tastes. Of course, you can love playing sports without being a football star or pound on drums without being actively recruited by your local band. But optimally, you ought to pursue some interests that you both savor and excel at. And some activities should contain a few life-defining options, meaning it would be good if certain endeavors held possible implications for what you might do with your work life.

Discovering and Planning the Use of Competitive Advantages

Adolescents feel the need to compare themselves to others, especially other teenagers. Often these comparisons are done so kids can fit snugly within their peer group. But more important, adolescents should address a critical question, "What are my competitive advantages?" They need to consider what they will be able to do or offer that most others can't. Below is a sample inventory completed by a student exploring his competitive advantages and their future applications. The simple exercise of creating such an inventory can benefit all kids at all ages.

MY COMPETITIVE ADVANTAGES AND HOW I MIGHT USE THEM

I'm Better Than Most Other Kids at:

1. getting along with lots of different kinds of people
2. talking well and expressing my ideas
3. playing most sports
4. science
5. showing people how to do things

I'm More Interested Than Most Other Kids in:

1. little kids
2. people with disabilities or other problems
3. biology and health
4. sports

I Might Be Able to Use My Competitive Advantages by:

1. becoming a coach and a health teacher
2. becoming a physical education instructor in a college
3. getting into sports medicine or becoming a trainer
4. teaching sports to handicapped children
5. starting a school for young children with physical problems

I recently read about a man who ran a profitable nursery. As a teenager he gardened with his landscaper father. He discovered that he was fascinated by living things, romantically attracted to the phases and stages that so vividly and repeatedly played out in his mother's perennial garden. By the age of sixteen he believed that with his ability, his well-grounded knowledge, and his frontline experience, he could beat out the competition as a landscape architect, a botanist, the manager of a botanical garden, or a nurseryman. He could discern his competitive advantage. He knew that no other kids shared his background, which led Jackson Stone eventually to believe that he could run a nursery better than anyone else in town, a conclusion that was part hubris (not such a bad thing), part ambition, and part reality—a winning blend of career ingredients. Mr. Stone, by the way, never did manifest work-life unreadiness. He majored in horticulture, got his MBA, and became assistant manager of a nursery that he eventually bought and expanded.

Far too few kids articulate their competitive advantages, but they ought to. Certainly, beginning in elementary school, they should set out on an exploration of the potential pathways in which they are likely to excel and contribute. Uncovering a competitive advantage may sound cutthroat, but it can initiate a habit of self-examination that may immunize someone against work-life unreadiness. Sooner or later such an examination must take place, and better at age seventeen than at twenty-three or twenty-four.

Deploying Some Short-Term Aiming

Foresight is not just about long-range aspirations. I believe kids need to get into the habit of setting short-term goals and objectives as well. Taking aim at specific results within a specified time is terrific practice for any adult career. On a football team, in the school orchestra, and in history class, students from time to time should engage in specific short-term goal setting. It would be comforting to hear an eleventh grade kid say, "Writing is not my strength, but I'm setting a goal this semester to become a better writer. I want to be able to feel good comparing things I've written in February to the stuff I wrote in October. And I'm planning to see a difference." Setting and reaching attainable short-term goals boosts self-esteem while helping an individual feel greater personal control over his destiny. It can teach kids and young adults about the value of incremental gains; it can show them that although you can't achieve all you want as soon as you want it, with patience and persistence you can reach your goals.

SELF-LAUNCHING

Life inevitably contains launches. Entering a new job, getting married, having a child, or starting a small business are common examples. Self-launching opens a chapter in a life story, a process through which we gather the tools we need and set off to do something more or less on our own. No period of life demands more concerted self-launching than the startup years. How then do we ensure self-launching abilities are in place on time?

In fostering the self-launching growth process, we need to start by teasing apart some of its major ingredients: motivation, aspiration, optimism, and ignition.

Finding the Motivation

Here's an all-too-common parental wail: "My child just isn't motivated. If only he would start caring and begin to put in the effort, he would realize his true potential. We just don't know how to get him motivated." Motivation takes courage, and courage takes encouragement. Every kid needs a cheering squad, a sense that others are his allies and supporters rather than his stern evaluators.

It has been demonstrated that motivation is most likely to rise when three conditions are met: when the goal is sufficiently attractive, when the goal feels attainable, and when the goal can be reached without exhausting effort. If you want more than anything else to be an actress, and you believe you have the talent to star in a Broadway musical, and you sense you could attain that level of acclaim without wiping yourself out, motivation surges inside you, and you go for it. If, on the other hand, you would love to get a B in Spanish so you can please your parents, but you believe it could never happen because the subject is too hard or because nothing ever seems to please your parents for long, or else you sense that it would be so hard to do that it would wreck your social life, motivation evaporates.

Numerous teenagers and young adults are sapped of motivation out of a fear of failure. All people, especially young ones, have limited tolerance for failure and so go out of their way to avoid it. Whenever we are tempted to assert that someone would do better if only he'd try, we have to consider that he may not be trying because he is not doing well. As we try to light a fire under a languishing kid, we need to temper expectations and seek clearly attainable, even modest gains. Fortunately, motivation has a way of snowballing; when you get motivated and go on to succeed, you keep on getting more and more motivated. Modest triumphs can pave the way for major victories.

One mother told her thirteen-year-old son, "Our one goal for this marking period is for you to hand in every single assignment in English and in social studies. That will help your writing ability kick in." She offered him modest rewards—we should not underestimate the value of incentives—and the recognition of accomplishments. Her son reached his goal, and then she gradually raised the bar to include getting positive feedback from his teachers on the quality of his reports. Because he had very poor handwriting, legibility was never a goal; he wrote his essays on the computer.

Getting motivated to accomplish small feats is an essential part of preparation for the startup years. Early in a career, major triumphs are less likely than minor ones. Getting motivated to go after little gains is a crucial ingredient for success and cannot be dismissed by a startup adult. Those modest gains lead to bigger and better things.

Calibrating Aspiration Levels

Aspiration unearths some tough questions, such as, What do you want to become? Are you ambitious? What would you like to be doing ten years from now? Do you have any desire to be powerful, rich, a leader, a person at the top of your field, or do you have other kinds of hopes for yourself?

Here are a few typical answers harvested from some of my teenage patients:

- "I have no need, no drive to be a huge success in life. I just want to get by. I just want to be a happy person living with a happy family, and I want to be a good mom, and that's good enough for me."

- "I don't know why my parents keep bugging me about my grades. I don't see what's wrong with getting Cs. That's all I want. As long as I pass, that's okay by me."

- "There's plenty of people who are real ambitious and have gobs of money but they're never happy. And there's folks who are very famous but they're miserable. I want to have a nice family and make just enough money to live on; that would be cool."

How high should a kid set the bar? Is it okay to live from day to day, take advantage of opportunities that come your way, and not try to have higher aspirations? Whether an adolescent has lofty aspirations or not, he should think seriously about the decision and its ramifications. These weighty questions have to be addressed and readdressed in school and at home.

When a teenager proclaims, "I just want to get by in life," there are at least two plausible explanations for his modest policy statement. The first is that he's stating a truly felt value. He really wants and needs very little when it comes to career success and adulation. He feels he can be content without much of a return on his investment and perhaps without much of an investment either! He may believe that happiness and the vigorous quest for achievement in life are incompatible. It's his honest statement of how he sees himself and the life he hopes to be leading. A quiet modest life may be his idea of success. Is there anything wrong with that? Probably not.

A second possibility is that a kid who has endured excessive frustration, especially in school, becomes a conservative non–risk taker. This happened to Omar in chapter 4 (page 53). Someone who has been burned too often in the past lowers his level of aspiration because he simply doesn't want to risk any more failures or setbacks. He may have some suppressed inner yearnings to be ambitious, but they are blanketed in feelings of futility. Many teenagers caught in this predicament are actually depressed and are struggling with their self-esteem. When you don't feel very good about yourself, it's hard to aim high or take risks.

I have seen many a young conservative non–risk taker emerge from a family that is a virtual bookshelf of success sagas. His parents, grandparents, or siblings have achieved magnificently. Can you sustain high aspirations when your dad was the founder of a company listed on the New York Stock Exchange or when your mom is principal of the high school you attend? What hard acts to follow! Should you try to make a contribution of your own, or should you retreat into your shell or into a life of accessible pleasure and heavy socialization? And what about kids whose brothers or sisters are superstars academically, athletically, or socially? In too many cases, they decide to aim low so that they don't come up short in comparison with their golden siblings. In all such scenarios, kids need to find constructive ways of aspiring, because developing, holding, and understanding your aspirations is an essential growth process. Each kid needs a specialty, a potential niche in which he can feel justified in aiming high. I believe he needs to have great expectations for himself, and some need our continuing help in defining those expectations.

When the pursuit of happiness becomes the overriding aspiration of a teenager or a startup adult, he is unwilling to endure a period of relative unhappiness to arrive at a state of stable happiness in his work life. Therefore, a kid may decide not to go to trade school or graduate school or start at the very bottom of the company's employment ladder because it "looks like a real drag." When you're used to a life of steady entertainment and immediate gratification during your teenage years, you may lower your aspiration level, give up on preparation, and persist as an adolescent into your twenties (as described in chapter 2). I think the numerous contemporary kids who have fallen into this pattern need some frank counseling from someone outside of the family, advice that can show them the possible trade-off of fun now versus long-term happiness. They need to know what's at stake when they decide which road to follow.

The writer Alain de Botton in his book *Status Anxiety* describes what he points out as a relatively new trend in human history. He depicts our modern-day meritocracy as a milieu in which people are obsessively engaged in a struggle to attain high status in society and among peers. As he notes, "however unpleasant anxieties over status may be, it is difficult to imagine a good life entirely free of them, for the fear of failing and disgracing oneself in the eyes of others is an inevitable consequence of harboring ambitions." Status anxiety is likely to be contagious. In particular, it can be transmitted from parents to their children, making some of them afraid to take the risks that go along with ambition out of dread they might fail. Some kids lower their aspirations because they have come down with a bad case of status anxiety.

I learned a vital aspiration lesson as a college senior. Early in the first semester Dean Charles Watts called me to his office to let me know that Brown University was about to nominate me for a Rhodes scholarship. I smiled graciously and gratefully, then informed the dean that, as an avowed and proven nonathlete, I had no chance whatsoever of winning. He said, "Mel, if you keep trying for things you can't possibly get, you'll end up getting sixty or seventy percent of them. That's because most people are afraid to try." So, what the heck, with nothing to lose but my pride, I went ahead, I tried, and I won. I never forgot that lesson. More often than not, when you aim high, there's less to lose than you think.

What if a person's expectations are clearly unrealistic? In most cases, it's an entirely benign condition, especially if he knows he's a long shot and has some solid options to fall back on. So when a conspicuously undersized thirteen-year-old boy lets me know he intends to play in the National Basketball Association, I don't stifle that aspiration. Instead, I discuss the odds with him and the various wonderful fallbacks. I say, "You could always become a basketball coach or a sports writer, or you could own a sporting goods store or run a basketball camp for kids." I think it's healthier to have unrealistically high aspirations (with backup options) than to have none at all.

Fueling Optimism

Children and adolescents show tremendous variation in their levels of optimism about the future, ranging from the regularly uttered "I guess I was born to lose. My dad says I'll never amount to anything" to "I know I can succeed at anything if I want to." Both extremes can be setups for disappointment and failure.

As a clinician I often have to try to induce optimism in the kids who have been overburdened with personal failures, a common need among students with school problems. I try to boost their sense of self-worth by discussing their strengths with them and pointing out the array of career possibilities that would fit them. I might say something like this: "You know, with your great people skills and your awesome creativity and the way you love to travel, you would make a wonderful tour guide. You could take people on African safaris and think up all kinds of new trips folks would enjoy." Downtrodden kids, in particular, need to know that many adults find it easier to be a grown-up than it was to be a kid. As I've said, when you grow up, you no longer are expected to be good at everything; you're allowed to practice your specialty. You can even get paid for it!

Whenever possible, parents should describe to kids instances in their own lives where their optimism paid off. One father told me, "Every time I make a good investment in the stock market, I go back over it with my daughter, Ann. I want her to see how successful someone can be by betting on his own judgment. And I want her to learn how optimism about the future pays dividends. I want her never to be inhibited by pessimistic feelings. My investments have been a great way to teach her this lesson." Teachers too should emphasize an upbeat attitude about the future. Athletic coaches often do the best job of this by encouraging their players to believe in themselves and their chances of winning the big tournament.

As noted above, too much optimism about the future may be just as thorny a problem as pessimism. If kids come to feel invincible, they may become fallen idols like those described in chapter 3. When they manage to achieve success with minimal effort and endure few, if any, roadblocks, they develop an unhealthy belief that they are meant to live a charmed life, that the agonies that plague other people will not affect them. These individuals are at risk because they fail to develop the coping skills needed to deal with life's impasses. I remember one boy for whom almost everything had come easily. When he obtained his driver's license, his feelings of invulnerability got out of control. He harbored a sense that the laws were not written for him; he was special. He received several speeding and reckless driving tickets. At age nineteen he totaled his parent's Volvo station wagon. His girlfriend perished in the accident and he spent several months in traction. He still walks with a limp. The boy was a classic fallen idol.

Getting the Ball Rolling

Parents need to be the stimulators or instigators of self-launching. Getting a kid who enjoys photography off the couch and encouraging him to take pictures of his neighborhood, prompting a child to set up a lemonade stand, suggesting that a kid get a job delivering newspapers or mowing lawns are examples of little parental jolts that can set the expectation for self-launching. If kids never initiate their own ventures, it can be nearly impossible for them to know how to begin a career or an important project. Childhood entrepreneurialism may be one of the clearest predictors of adult productivity. Some children are natural self-starters; others need some gentle coercion. A parent has every right to ask a kid which activities and projects he's launched on his own over the last twelve months.

One mother observed, "Jessica always seems to need a jump start. She can't figure out how to get going with her homework. She can't get out of bed in the morning. She's stymied when she has a report or project in school. If you can get her going, Jessica can keep going, but getting her going is never easy." I suggested that the mother continue to help Jessica get started and gradually encourage her teenager to undertake "step one" with maternal consultation available as needed.

We encounter quite a few students like Jessica. Their ignition problems need to be addressed explicitly. They need to be helped to stop and think and come up with a multistep plan before engaging in any complex or extended activity. Very often students have trouble knowing where and how to begin because they cannot seem to foresee steps two, three, and four. They have trouble with a process I call "step-wisdom." These kids need a mentor or coach to help them map out a strategic plan, a set of manageable steps or phases that will lead to any important goal. Being competent at staging is a key part of self-launching. Kids need strenuous practice sessions working through the steps described later in table 9.4.

If a child loves goats and sheep and desperately wants to be a large animal veterinarian, how does she begin to set the proper career wheels in motion? To preach to that girl about how she must study hard and obtain honor grades so she can attend a prestigious college and veterinary school, the age-old pyramid approach to educational motivation (good grades → good college → good graduate school → good job), does little more than foment anxiety. Besides, it's not altogether accurate and it's mostly unhelpful. It would be far more energizing to fortify with direct experience her desire to become increasingly knowledgeable and skilled about animals. She might work during the summers in a zoo or an animal hospital. She could become a research assistant in a biology laboratory. To focus solely on her grades in school could convert her entire school career into a horribly threatening experience. You ignite a career by helping a kid accumulate expertise, enthusiasm, and direct, hands-on experience—not with threats. In college some students are helped to find their way to a career through summer internships.

Initial ignition often entails a willingness to start at the bottom and work up. As described in chapter 3, far too many startup adults have serious trouble getting started because they will accept nothing less than starting at the top. Fallen idols who have long been leaders, honor students, and revered athletes may find it nearly impossible to start on the bottom rung of a business, a military career, or an academic ladder. Fun-loving adolescents may have trouble adjusting to the plodding lifestyle of a low-level worker. Overexposure to people in their twenties who are music icons, sports stars, and instant millionaires may convey the impression that effortless instant success is available to any eager twenty-three-year-old. Those with mind debts may find that their weaknesses become exposed under the close scrutiny of a supervisor at work. Out of fear of such exposure they may venture out on their own—with dire results. Kids need ample previewing and preparation for this modest phase of their lives. This can be achieved through more specific career education (see chapter 12), including the study of biographies of people who worked their way up.

Reality Checks

From time to time during self-launching, kids have to stand face-to-face with the real world and ask whether their goals are realistic, impractical, or impossible. Nonetheless, many people who have made an enormous contribution to society have launched themselves with seemingly unrealistic goals and have masterfully defied the odds. Knowing this, should we extend the borders of realism for our kids? I believe so.

There's much to be said for being highly idealistic, extravagant about one's future. In fact, when an adolescent or startup adult feels too hemmed in by realistic considerations, we should do what we can to elevate her expectations by helping her list some of her real possibilities. Then we should assist her in mapping out her launch and what follows.

Taking Directions from Inner Direction

The components of inner direction translate into a three-step operation that makes use of a child's uniquely developing identity to help him or her navigate toward life's startup years. The steps are recapitulated below.

ESTABLISHING AND MOBILIZING INNER DIRECTION

Acquiring Inside Insights

Using active self-assessment and discussion to understand
- evolving strengths and weaknesses
- patterns of feelings and moods
- environmental/family influences and values
- consistent interests—both recreational and knowledge-based

Acquiring Foresights

Thinking and talking about where one's life seems to be going by
- taking headings
- previewing suitable pathways
- lining up strengths and interests
- planning ways to use competitive advantages
- setting short-term goals to help meet long-term goals

Self-Launching

Getting going by
- becoming motivated
- setting levels of aspiration
- acquiring optimism regarding the future
- engaging in self-starting
- performing reality checks

8
INTERPRETATION
Sharpening Outside Insights

I find myself comparing myself with my classmates and friends, absolutely, though I try not to. I try to take a step back and realize that we are all on different paths. I have made choices that have taken me off the traditional path for people my age, so it is difficult for me at times to compare myself, because they are more established in their careers and farther along. I do compare myself, but I try not to.

S.R., age 27

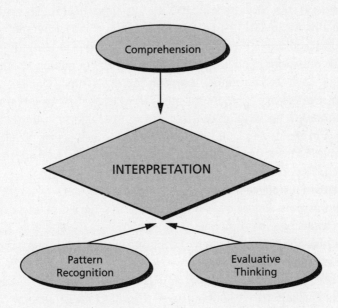

In the last chapter we explored self-awareness, a person's inside insights. Outside insight is equally essential for career planning. Not only does a kid need to establish an intimate acquaintance with herself, but she should as well become a keen observer and interpreter of the outside world. She has to extract the right conclusions from what's going on all around her, interpreting accurately the many ideas, issues, motives, and questions confronting her. Three growth processes foster keen interpretation: comprehension, pattern recognition, and evaluative thinking.

COMPREHENSION

Here's a true confession from a dazed twenty-four-year-old: "You know, I'm pretty sure I was able to wing my way through school just by memorizing and imitating. I pretended I understood. I even fooled myself into believing I was getting everything. But really, I never bothered to understand what I was doing or what they were trying to teach me. Luckily, I had no trouble remembering the details—at least when it came to exams. Now, here at IBM, they assume that I totally understand what I'm doing and saying, and there are very smart people watching me and listening. They can see right through me, and boy, do they ask tough questions. I have to really know what I'm talking about. That's harder, a whole lot tougher than spitting out a bunch of facts on some European history exam in college. I used to think I was so smart, but now, frankly, I'm finding out that I'm not very good at understanding things in depth. It's as if I'm being forced to use some muscles in my brain that I never had to use before!"

More than Just Remembering

Racking up passing or even honor grades in school is no guarantee that you know how to understand. It is common for students to obtain diplomas and degrees largely through the deft use of memory and the rote learning of procedures.

There are many different channels of understanding, and any individual is likely to understand best through one or several of them. Some people process visual information well (such as a complex wiring diagram), while others are better at unraveling meaning from language (understanding the symbolism in a poem or following verbal directions). There are also differences in how rapidly a person can understand something and the extent to which he can comprehend information when it is delivered in large amounts (for example, in a lecture or an extended explanation). Understanding can also be very subject-specific; a kid might have no trouble understanding how a jet engine works but have serious problems comprehending algebra. Any of these potential strengths or deterrents to understanding can play a pivotal role in determining the success of the startup years.

On the job, understanding includes comprehending work demands or expectations, justifications, and concepts. In chapter 10 we'll tackle a related facet of comprehension, figuring out people.

Decrypting Expectations

In chapter 4, I described some mistakes made by individuals early in their careers because they failed to understand what was expected of them. A new employee has to think not only about his written job description but about all the unstated, encrypted expectations. If the person can decode these expectations, he'll be more likely to hit the target and satisfy spoken and unspoken job demands. Learning how to understand what's really expected of you is a growth process that should begin early in life.

Some unstated expectations are generic; they could pertain to any job. And some are job-specific. Here are some examples of generic hidden expectations.

SOME GENERIC HIDDEN EXPECTATIONS

You will act upbeat on the job.

You will work extra hours when you need to.

You will make sure your work is done thoroughly and with care.

You will pitch in and work well with your colleagues.

You will show respect and admiration for your supervisor.

You will be eager to acquire new skills and knowledge.

You will help create harmony among those you work with.

You will ask good questions.

You will offer suggestions and solutions.

The job-specific hidden expectations are easily overlooked. Dr. Jack Gable was an outstanding intern and resident, and during his specialized training in infectious disease, he did a lot of clinical work consulting on patients hospitalized with various infections. He also participated in research and taught medical students. When he finished his fellowship in infectious disease, Jack remained at the hospital where he had been trained and was sought after as a consultant when patients had fevers of unknown origin and other illnesses that stumped most doctors.

After about three years, the chairman of the department informed Jack, who thought that he had carved out an essential niche at this high-powered teaching hospital, that he would have to depart. Jack felt as if he'd been electrocuted. The chairman acknowledged that Jack was a first-rate clinician but pointed out that he had done no research nor applied for any grants and could not be employed as "just a clinician." Jack had never figured that out for himself. He had floated along without analyzing what it takes to survive in the long run in his beloved academic milieu. The department, in fact, needed Jack's salary to fund someone who could be a genuine "triple threat," a young professor who would undertake research, plus teach, plus do clinical work. In fact, they had such a rising star in mind. Jack had never understood the job-specific expectation that he become a triple threat. He found himself stranded, out of work, and he sank into depression for months. An excellent high school student, a cum laude graduate of a high-powered college, a top graduate of his medical school class, his parents' pride and joy, Jack at age twenty-nine now felt worthless. Furthermore, he was the dad of a two-year-old, his wife, Susan, was pregnant, and he had medical school loans to pay. Eventually he got a job in a health maintenance organization as a general pediatrician. He could pay his bills, but he deeply missed the gratification and intellectual stimulation he had savored as a consultant on complex cases. He felt woefully unfulfilled.

Natalie was an attractive, unmarried twenty-four-year-old woman when she was laid off from her job as an assistant sales manager at an upscale shoe distributorship. She had obtained the job through family connections and was nothing less than ecstatic about her career. After two and a half years, she believed everybody at work adored her. True, she did have a winning personality, including an indelible smile and an ability to make other people feel good. While she was a totally reliable nine-to-five worker, Natalie spent long hours on the phone socializing with customers (and others) but failed to harvest new accounts. When the company suddenly had a disappointing season, she was abruptly laid off; her lack of a track record in obtaining new outlets made her dispensable. The company was interested in her productivity, not her social skills! Somehow Natalie thought she could thrive on personality alone. She had misread expectations; she hadn't studied what it would take to succeed.

The culture in which young people are growing today deprives them of opportunities to understand expectations. Mothers and fathers who are fearful of their kids (page 45) may offer only minimal and completely obvious expectations (do well in school and stay out of trouble). When kids have few responsibilities, there's not much need for them to know how to do their jobs well. And when entertainment or gratification is almost always available on demand, you don't need to fulfill expectations to get what you want. Children who have no desire or opportunities to study grown-ups (page 30) may eventually have trouble deciphering the priorities of a boss or a customer.

Who teaches students how to unravel underlying expectations? Such instruction seldom, if ever, takes place. How, then, are they supposed to understand expectations that are not stated explicitly? Some may be able to do so intuitively, but most will need coaching. All kids should undergo that growth process before they turn twenty. Students should be encouraged and helped to analyze the demands placed on them in middle and high school. Periodically they should be asked to submit what I call "expectations analyses." Here's an example of a paragraph written by a ninth grader.

MY ANALYSIS OF MY HISTORY CLASS
by Susan Heartwood

Mr. George is a really strict teacher. But I think he's fair. He expects you to study hard and gives you a lot of quizzes. On his tests he's not so interested in how many facts you can remember from the textbook, but he wants to know your opinion about everything. And you better be able to defend what you say or write because Mr. George likes to argue with kids, not to give them a hard time, but just to make sure they've done their thinking. The kids who just memorize facts don't impress this teacher. You get a good grade from Mr. George if you have interesting ideas that you can defend. I think that's why I got an A in his class. And I think that's why I now love history. I used to believe it was all memorization.

Both kids and adults need to be taught to pause long enough to analyze and tabulate hidden expectations—both the generic and the job-specific keys to success. Here are some steps they can take.

1. Make a list of the most obvious on-the-job or classroom demands.
2. For each demand, list several ways to ensure the job is done well (for example, have someone else look over the work, put in a few extra hours, do it in steps rather than trying to get it done impulsively or all at once).
3. Then put yourself in the position of the boss or teacher and make a list of what would please you, what your unstated demands would be if you were that person (for example, show enthusiasm for the task, ask for suggestions, do a little more than was asked of you).
4. Then talk to some people you respect who have worked or are working with your immediate superior (boss, teacher) or in that setting to get their insights on important priorities and values (for instance, "She really likes it if you provide statistics in your report" or "She really likes you to come up with far-out ideas or suggestions").
5. Speak with someone who has succeeded in such a position and find out what she thinks she did that made a difference (for instance, "I went by to see him on a regular basis. I realized he really likes to have some kind of one-to-one relationship with you, but you have to take the initiative").
6. Translate steps 3, 4, and 5 into a plan of action that can undergo periodic review and revision based on your own ongoing analyses of what's needed.

Starting in middle school, students should be encouraged to interview kids who took a particular course in the previous year. Honor students should explain how they went about understanding and articulating the class's demands. Early in the school year, kids should hand in their proposed success plans. If they get some practice in ferreting out expectations, they may be more prepared to determine what it is they need to be doing so they won't be ambushed like Dr. Gable or Natalie.

I've met many students who chronically misread expectations. They had the uncanny ability to study the wrong things for an exam, repeatedly misconstrued assignments, and lamented that whatever they do, they can't seem to please adults.

Carl, a likable sixteen-year-old, was a plugger, a conscientious guy who wanted nothing more than to succeed in school and reap praise from his parents and teachers. But his academic life was an endless tale of losing streaks because the ever-upbeat Carl never quite understood what he was supposed to do to satisfy imposed demands. He chronically misinterpreted instructions, would grind away to churn out history reports that expounded eloquently on the wrong topics, and studied for exams without estimating what was likely to be on the test. It never occurred to Carl to don a clean shirt and shave his stubble before he went for his summer job interview. Poor Carl always seemed to miss the point, to fail to assess accurately what others expected from him. He suffered from weak expectation comprehension.

I think all kids and probably most adults need plenty of practice discussing questions that begin: What would it take to . . . ? What would it take to get an A in English? What would it take to win Saturday's football game? What would it take to receive a significant salary increase this coming year? What would it take to impress my boss or my chemistry teacher or my girlfriend?

Ideally, a person should reflect on expectations as follows: "To get an A in English, I will have to submit all five book reports this semester. I'll have to start spending more time on them. I know my teacher likes me to compare my point of view with the author's when I do a report. That takes time, so I have to budget more time to do these reports. Mrs. Morrison also likes me to participate in class discussions, so each evening I'll have to think up some comments to make about what we're reading. I'll volunteer so she doesn't call on me for something I don't know. If I have time, I might also read an extra book: she really likes kids who work hard and show an interest." The same kind of expectation analysis can be used to get a promotion at work or sell a lucrative insurance policy to an indecisive customer.

Getting the Concepts

At school and on the job, it is possible to slog through the daily grind without necessarily processing any key concepts; such tenuous grasps of essential ideas may lead to mediocre performance and ultimately to failure. A student can answer questions about kinetic energy or chemical bonds or ecological balance despite having only the blurriest notion of what these concepts mean. He can repeat memorized definitions and echo explanations as the teacher communicated them without really knowing what he's talking about. He is a first-class imitator rather than a true learner. The same scenario can take place at work, especially when someone never learned how to conceptualize in school. During the startup years, weak conceptualization is a widespread mind debt.

Hank was recently let go from a job he enjoyed working at the registration desk at a local hotel that was part of an international chain. He liked the hours, the work made him feel important, the job wasn't too taxing, and he could get some reading done during quiet times. Besides, he liked travel a lot and thought he might make a career for himself in hotels. During a series of training sessions for new hotel employees, Hank was taught various hospitality industry concepts, such as flexibility, responsiveness, image projection, customer service, eye contact, and courtesy. He scored 100 percent on a quiz they gave. But on the job Hank revealed that he didn't really understand these concepts, and so he could not incorporate them into his daily work. He seldom made eye contact with guests when he signed them in. There were repeated complaints about how unhelpful he was when someone sought to change rooms. He showed no real understanding of customer service. He could mouth these concepts but not internalize them. The best test of how well someone understands a concept is whether he knows how to apply it consistently and in a variety of situations. Hank couldn't do that, and it cost him his job. His boss told one of Hank's coworkers, "That kid just doesn't get it." Incidentally, in school he had fared poorly in highly conceptual classes like religion, political science, and literature.

Bethany had a similar experience. She had always loved working with children and wanted a career in elementary education more than anything else. Having done fairly well in college and as a student teacher, she was hired to teach third grade in a private school. She approached that work with unfettered gusto and charm. The kids all adored Miss Dean. But their parents had some concerns, as did the head of the school. The kids seemed bored and were not learning well in math and science. It turned out that Bethany was very rigid, adhering obsessively to a curriculum guide. In fact she had some trouble with the concepts she was trying to convey to her students, such as place value, integer, and internal combustion. She had the students memorize definitions, but she could never explain and provide examples in her own words. Eventually the headmaster realized this limitation and got Bethany diagrams of the concepts. That helped a lot, and Bethany's teaching improved dramatically.

Careers are saturated with concepts, and to complicate matters, the concepts keep changing. New ones are added; old ones become modified over time. If conceptualizing doesn't come naturally to you and you've never been taught to conceptualize, you could flounder through school and work without understanding why.

I often ask high school students to tell me what a concept is. I rarely hear an acceptable answer. It's usually a vague utterance such as, "I think it's some kind of an idea." Even teachers may not have a clear sense of the concept of a concept, making it hard for them to help students conceptualize.

I have spent a fair amount of time studying concept formation, and here's how I think about it. It's much easier than it sounds at first: a concept is a collection of critical features that occur together to set default expectations, and can be characterized with a specific term. Now that's a mouthful, I agree. Take the concept of fruit, which possesses the following critical features:

It belongs to the vegetable (as opposed to the animal) kingdom.

It grows on trees.

You can eat it.

It often grows in orchards.

It comes from a blossom.

You can purchase it at a supermarket.

Many members of the animal kingdom eat it.

It contains seeds (pits).

In view of the above, if you tell me an object is fruit, my default expectation is that it possesses all of the above critical features. Sure enough, an apple fits the bill. However, a certain fruit may boast some but not all of the critical features of the fruit concept. For example, there are fruits that are poisonous; they still qualify to be called fruit, but they fail to satisfy every one of the critical features. And watermelon doesn't grow on a tree. That's why we say a collection of features sets *default* expectations; we start by assuming they apply to a specific example until we discover otherwise. So it is that we have ideal (so-called prototypical) examples of religious fundamentalists, women or men who possess all of the beliefs or critical features of fundamentalists, but there are also those who show only fundamentalist tendencies or leanings. The latter may lack a few of the critical features. If you tell me a particular species fits the concept of bird, I will assume for starters that its members have feathers and can fly. I'll run into some trouble with penguins, but they still deserve to be considered birds, if not perfect examples like cardinals, prototypes who have it all.

For a person to understand a concept, she has to have a grasp of its critical features. She then needs to think of possible examples of the concept and decide which ones are perfect prototypes and which only partially meet her default expectations.

Countless unready startup adults are in serious mind debt because they never learned to form concepts firmly. Kids ought to have plenty of practice analyzing and applying the concepts they come across (page 224). Later on in life, during the pivotal startup years, there is much to be said for establishing the conceptual basis for whatever you're doing. Winging it is a dangerous game when you're under the gun to prove to yourself and others that you really know what you're doing (and saying). That means forming solid concepts—not just memorizing facts and procedures.

Active Processing

At a conference for middle school mathematics teachers, I asked a group of them if they were able to identify the strongest characteristic of their most proficient students. Several of them indicated that their top performers were kids who, almost as soon as they learned something new, were able to come up with ways in which they could use it. They were not just obediently absorbing skills in algebra; they could see applications for the skills in their lives. This contrasts with a common complaint repeated in this age group, "Why do we have to learn this? We're never gonna use it."

It's one thing to know something and another thing to put it to good use, gathering a record of accomplishment along the way. Learning to apply what you know starts with understanding it in some depth. That depth of comprehension is most likely to occur when a brain is in its most active state. The mind of a brightly responsive student gives a hero's welcome to new information, allowing it to ring bells, to resonate across different regions of his mind. A teacher might comment on a dishonest character in a short story. That comment then activates a listening student's internal circuits: "Oh yeah, that kind of reminds me of that time my sister Emily got punished, and I once got in hot water for the same thing, and my dad and I were talking about how politicians who lie keep getting caught and embarrassed for it, and I guess it means you shouldn't lie about your homework either." Such a chain of associations, rich connections to previous experiences, and future implications constitutes active learning. The opposite phenomenon, namely inactive learning, is all too common. A teacher states something meaningful, and the idea simply rests at a mind's front entrance, stagnating there.

Some kids are chronically passive in their learning and thought processes, and the educational system may be partly to blame for teaching in a way that encourages and even rewards spongelike learning. As one frustrated startup adult put it, "When I was younger, I did what I was told to do—without really thinking very much. Now I'm having a hard time with reading assignments in business school. It used to be in college and high school, I read so I could answer factual questions on quizzes. The other day each of us had to put together an airtight sales contract and demonstrate that we understood all its implications and potential glitches. I had to really use what I was reading. It takes me forever to do something like that and makes me feel out of shape. I don't think I ever really was forced to apply what I was reading—you know, like using the stuff to solve problems or unravel confusing issues."

As part of the active learning process, schools need to help, even require, kids to think in terms of the relevance and long-term applications of the facts and skills they are taking in. "I'm really glad I'm learning all about classical music. For the rest of my life, I can go to concerts and understand and enjoy what the orchestra is playing." "Finding out more about government will let me get more out of what's in the newspaper, and it will also help me decide how to vote in elections." "Learning all this human anatomy is really fun. I think I've always been a little curious to find out what all the different bumps on my bones and joints are called. Now I know. That's cool."

Students should try out immediate applications while thinking through possible long-term uses for what they learn. And teachers should do the same. They should constantly address the question, "Why am I teaching this? How will my students be able to apply this material in the short and long run? And how can I provide them with some immediate real-life practice in making use of what they are learning?" When faculty members are unable to answer such questions, they should seriously consider revisions to their curriculum. If a teacher is requiring his seventh grade class to memorize a list of African rivers, he might inadvertently be fostering inactive learning by encouraging the inert sopping up of information with no perceivable relevance.

Parents and teachers need to help kids engage in active processing. Asking good questions can help students to ring bells in their minds as new information enters their consciousness. The list that follows provides some examples of the sorts of questions that can stimulate worthy cognitive activity. Kids need to understand that truly excellent minds do not feel bored in school; they find things interesting because they never stop asking questions and fitting things together.

SOME QUESTIONS TO IGNITE ACTIVE PROCESSING

1. How do these facts or ideas fit or change your point of view or interests?
2. Can you connect these facts or ideas to other things you've learned recently?
3. What are some examples of things you've come across in the past that are related to these ideas or facts?
4. What are some ways these ideas or facts can help you in the future?
5. How do these ideas or facts change your mind or cause you to think a little differently?
6. How would you explain these ideas or facts to someone younger or less experienced than you are?
7. How can these ideas or facts be used to gain the respect of others?

Active processing can pay off abundantly during the startup years. Here's an example: Let's suppose you are an ambitious twenty-four-year-old salesperson at a home electronics store. The latest home entertainment center arrives, and you are given specifications of the glitzy new product. You may remember the amplifier wattage and speaker ohms and the colors and monitor screen sizes—or you may elect to look these up when a customer inquires. An active processing salesperson learns the information and translates it into a well-thought-out sales pitch. He thinks about the kinds of customers whom he might coax toward this model. He relates the new product to different service contracts and payment plans that might be made available to potential buyers. He thinks about whether any of his former customers or friends and relatives might be enticed into splurging on this new item of conspicuous consumption. You can go into a store and distinguish almost immediately sales personnel who are active thinkers and those who are not. The ones who make multiple connections are the ones most likely to succeed and keep on succeeding. Of course, such achievement is a necessity in any domain of work. Kids who are habitually passive thinkers are apt to start out at a serious disadvantage despite their sometimes impressive quiz scores and report cards. Parents can help by encouraging college-bound students to pick schools that stress learning as a give-and-take process rather than a matter of passive note taking.

PATTERN RECOGNITION

History repeats itself throughout our lives. Challenges, situations, impasses, and opportunities have a way of coming back as predictably as the seasons. In school we are introduced to words that contain letter patterns that are repeated but with different syllables before or after them. In music there are themes and variations. At a museum, we can identify a painting as the work of Picasso, Pollock, or Chagall, even though we've never seen that specific canvas before; we recognize an underlying pattern that gives away the identity of the artist. Awareness of recurring patterns is essential when it comes to understanding the outside world and doing your best at what you're doing. If you don't see the patterns, too much of what you are encountering seems unprecedented; you can't readily apply previous experience to new situations.

Some studies have shed light on the relevance of pattern recognition by comparing novices to experts in a wide range of adult pursuits. "How does an expert differ from a beginner in his ways of understanding things?" One powerful finding is that an expert has the ability to see similarities despite superficial differences. An expert chess player can perceive a pattern developing on the board. Even if he has never confronted that exact pattern before, if he peels away some superficial, trivial differences, he recognizes an underlying pattern that he has encountered in numerous previous matches.

A student with impoverished math skills may conclude that she has never before seen a word problem anything like the present one simply because it's about a horse and a cow. If she could penetrate the superficial details, she would find an underlying pattern (say, comparing relative speeds of two moving objects) that she's dealt with many times before. A previous problem may have entailed the same processes but dealt with a ferret and a kitten. As a frustrated father once sighed balefully, "Jeremy treats every math problem as if he's never been there before. You'd think he'd never seen anything like it, even when the problem is almost the same as one we worked on successfully ten minutes ago."

How does pattern detection and recognition come into play in early adulthood? During the startup years, a person is sensitizing his mind to the recurring patterns that will require his effective interpretation and response for years to come. As a pediatric intern, you are supposed to become sensitized to a wide spectrum of clinical patterns. For example, a newborn baby who is lethargic and has a very high fever should cause you to consider meningitis. An automobile repair person may recognize a pattern that calls for a specific repair in a car that is overheating and discharging thick fumes of a particular color from its exhaust. Over time, people in a career recognize an ever growing number of patterns that indicate the causes of phenomena and link these solutions that have or have not worked in the past. This is a major contributor to what we call sound judgment.

Throughout their startup years, people should be on a diligent search for patterns. No matter your profession, you have to become an astute diagnostician. You become skilled at diagnosing by recognizing the patterns when they arise. I was listening to the PBS radio show *Car Talk* one afternoon when a woman called in to complain that dog food came out of her car heater whenever she turned it on. I could not believe what I was hearing. But the knowledgeable expert hosts, who call themselves Click and Clack, recognized the pattern immediately. They asked the woman if she stored dog food in her garage, which she did. She was informed that mice or rats in the garage were nesting under the hood of the car and storing their coveted kibbles there. The rodents had chewed their way into the ventilation system and some of their reserve cuisine gushed forth whenever the heater was turned on. That's masterful pattern recognition—complete with significant remedial implications!

Kids with a poor sense of pattern recognition may grow into adults who fail in their careers. I believe strongly that teachers should always encourage students to identify explicitly underlying patterns and their implications. Parents can help out with this mission. Here are some recognition-enhancing strategies.

STEPS TOWARD ENCOURAGING PATTERN RECOGNITION

- In all classes, teachers should ask students regularly, "What's the underlying pattern here and where have we seen this before?"
- In seeking patterns, students should discuss how a pattern they've seen in the past has come back with some new twists or differences this time.
- Children and teenagers should link problematic or challenging patterns to solutions that have either worked or failed in the presence of such patterns in the past. History and social studies classes can examine historical events that may resemble current situations or dilemmas. They can consider the response to those patterns in the past and how that experience might guide present-day decision making.
- Often literature and poetry can best be understood by identifying symbols or allusions or themes that recur in one form or another in each chapter or stanza. That's a form of pattern recognition students can pursue consciously and explicitly. Character development within a novel is often a matter of teasing out behavior patterns or traits that reveal themselves as recurring patterns.
- Music and the graphic arts afford excellent opportunities to study themes and variations. Students should be able to listen to a musical piece and identify its basic theme and the way the composer has manipulated it. They can examine paintings and talk about the patterns that suggest a canvas was created in the eighteenth century or the characteristic brushstrokes that identify a van Gogh.

Pattern Recognition and Rules

Pattern recognition plays a pivotal role in solving all sorts of problems. For example, success in mathematics is dependent upon linking pattern recognition to solutions. A student detects a pattern, perhaps in a word problem, and then transfers from long-term memory the method that worked in the past when he has run into that pattern. That very same two-step operation—pattern recognition and method transfer—has a profound impact on an enormous range of life's problems. If a socially and politically competent person comes into conflict with a colleague or a supervisor, he can automatically refer to and invoke an experience he has had during similar interpersonal collisions and then transfer the strategy that has worked best. If the molding machine a worker operates every day in the factory starts to malfunction, that employee may be able to detect a pattern in the way the apparatus is faltering that reminds her of an earlier such impasse, thereby enabling her to recall what fixed it the last time this happened. It all adds up to a vital resource called cumulative wisdom.

Patterns that keep on returning translate easily into rules. Rules take the form of "if . . . then." So if you are aware of meteorological phenomena, you might come up with a rule that states, "If it's August and it gets very dark and windy in the late afternoon, then there is probably going to be a thunderstorm." Rules often imply a necessary action (that is, a method transfer), such as, "I'd better take my raincoat." It has been shown that many successful students are especially good at understanding and applying rules. Additionally, they are competent at devising their own rules when they become aware of two or more phenomena, such as dark skies and thunderstorms, that tend to go together.

Sensitivity to patterns and rules allows a student or a startup adult to detect irregularity, such as exceptions to the rule, and respond accordingly. Here's a statement from a successful car salesman: "As a rule I look at how someone's dressed. I focus mainly on their shoes and what kind of watch they're wearing. If their shoes look like they came from the local outlet and their watch looks like something they sent away for, I steer them toward our stripped-down economy models because I know they're shopping for price. But when I see a pair of expensive Italian shoes or top-of-the-line running shoes, I nudge those guys toward the loaded SUVs or luxury sedans. Shoes are always a reliable cue. Of course, once in a while, someone enters the showroom dressed like a destitute tramp and turns out to have a backyard full of hidden oil reserves and wants to trade in his two-year-old Ferrari. I might be able to tell by the way he speaks or by a comment his wife makes. That's when I toss the rulebook and instead show him our most profitable, price-inflated limited edition vehicle. But that's the exception to the rule." As this salesman recognized, rules are great for helping you detect irregularities, those acceptable or desirable violations of rules.

When Not Enough Looks Familiar Enough

On the job and in school, you learn from experience, in part by getting to know all the partly concealed recurring patterns, some of which you automatically convert into rules. The rules simplify your life; we sometimes call them "rules of thumb," handy devices for guiding your actions and making decisions that have a high probability of working out well. But what happens when a person is unaware of such patterns? She fails to operate on precedent, to learn sufficiently from experience. That might mean she keeps repeating the actions that never got her anywhere. She runs on a treadmill.

Betsy offers a vivid version of this plight. She was oblivious to the recurring patterns in her job as a stock market analyst. Her company in Chicago had assigned this very junior woman with her new MBA to cover the telecommunications industry. After only eight months she was laid off, much to her surprise and with no warning whatsoever. Her supervisor made it clear that he thought she was in the wrong field. He pointed out that all of the reports she wrote sounded the same, that they reflected an inability to see the big picture, to recognize the changing patterns that were emerging in the industry and make investment recommendations based on the patterns. For example, she could not answer questions about what startup companies in her field have in common. She couldn't identify successful patterns of management or strategy. Betsy was out of work because she just didn't exhibit pattern recognition.

I recall Pierre, an eleventh grader who had a long skein of struggles in all classes that featured rule-based learning. His brain suffered a dramatic meltdown whenever it was infiltrated with grammatical rules, mathematical rules, and foreign language rules. Pierre said that he had always had fun in English classes, except when they studied grammar. He pointed out that he could speak perfectly grammatical English but the rules "made no sense at all to me." We had Pierre keep his own private rulebook, a log in which he entered rules and patterns that recurred in the subject areas that were frustrating him. All students ought to do this, at least periodically, and they need constant reminders about the quest for patterns and hidden rules. That emphasis will serve them well throughout a career.

EVALUATIVE THINKING

In school and in careers, there is a never-ending need to evaluate ideas, people, and products (or proposed products). On the job and in the classroom, someone's reactions are often based on such evaluations. For example, you act positively toward people who seem competent and honest: that's an evaluation you have performed on them. An individual signs up to be part of a project because she evaluates it as one with significant potential. Both the ability and the frame of mind to be a competent evaluator vary considerably within a population of students and startup adults. Sooner or later everyone needs to become a capable critic.

A distraught mother described her twenty-one-year-old daughter to me as "one hundred percent naïve, the ultimate sucker." I had known Jessica for nearly ten years, having helped her deal with some minor learning difficulties. Now Jessica had graduated from a small college in Ohio and was insisting on moving to New York to pursue a career as a Broadway dancer. Her parents were panicked because Jessica was inclined to follow anybody and do almost anything anyone asked her to do—just to please people and win their acceptance. She also had a penchant for believing everything she was told. She would fall for absurd TV infomercials and become victimized by ridiculous propositions from her friends at school. The latter led to problems with drugs and smoking. Her parents rightly worried that their daughter could "get sucked in" by any big-city schemer or get taken by drug dealers, con artists, and potential beaux. In short, they were distraught over Jessica's dearth of evaluation skills.

At the other extreme are people who are hardened cynics. I remember one nineteen-year-old who was looking for work. He seemed to rule out every opportunity he faced. Here are some typical responses, each referring to a different job opening: "I wouldn't work for those rats. All they care about is ripping off everyone who walks in the door." "I could make more money on welfare than they would ever pay me." "No way, restaurants treat their employees like shit." His parents recalled that this kid verbally dismembered his teachers, other kids, his parents, and their church. He always had something negative to assert and seldom saw the positive side of things. Like Jessica, he was low on evaluative skill, overly judgmental to the point of abject cynicism. He never slowed down long enough to assess open-mindedly the pluses and minuses of any opportunity. Now he was virtually paralyzed by his own cynicism. His habitual negativism had become a reflex response. Evaluative thinking falls between the extremes represented by these two young adults.

First and foremost, evaluation takes time. We all are aware of the hazards of snap judgments and impetuous decisions and actions. Fortunately, the brain's prefrontal lobes (page 109) are home to our production controls, the mind regulators that enable us to slow down and think through situations and possible actions. Evaluative thinking involves the following steps:

TEN STEPS TOWARD EVALUATIVE THINKING

1. *Entering a thoughtful mode:* Slowing down to think through and assess something rather than jumping to an immediate conclusion or snap judgment.
2. *Describing the target to be evaluated:* Objectively describing what you are scrutinizing—the actual facts about the person, idea, or project. This step calls for temporarily suspending judgment so as to prevent prejudging.
3. *Describing claims and outward appearances:* Determining the point of view or bias in what you are evaluating—for example, what someone wants you to believe about a product in a sales pitch or an idea in an editorial.
4. *Pinpointing questionable aspects:* Identifying the elements that call for investigation—for example, in a sales pitch, the pricing, the convenience, the practicality, the risks versus the potential benefits of a product.
5. *Researching:* Harvesting any available evidence or data that might influence the evaluation.
6. *Consulting others:* Factoring in their knowledgeable points of view, participating in discussions.
7. *Forming judgments on specific aspects:* Using personal values, outside inputs, and previous experience to form some preliminary opinions of the elements determined in step 4.
8. *Weighing the pros and cons:* Coming to a judgment and acting on it.
9. *Refining and communicating the evaluation:* Putting an assessment in one's own words.
10. *Monitoring:* Checking subsequently to see if an evaluation turned out to be right (with major implications for future assessments and reactions to people, ideas, and products).

Arlene, a twenty-two-year-old recent college graduate, has just gotten a job offer from a public relations firm, which she needs to evaluate. First of all, she has to overcome her usual impulsiveness and shift into a decelerated, thoughtful gear. Next she may ask herself, "What would I really be getting myself into if I took this job?" Then, on paper, she should rewrite the job description or offer in her own words as accurately and completely as she can. The act of transcribing it rather than passively reading it can clarify or bring salient issues to the surface. Next Arlene needs to consider statements the company is making to attract her. Are they believable? She then should list all aspects of the position that could become pluses or minuses. She might then learn more about the company by reading reports about the business. She should seek opinions about the opportunity by talking with some impartial "experts," such as her mother, her college roommate, previous employees at that firm, and her professor of marketing. Now well poised to seriously weigh the pros and cons of the job offer, Arlene should put her conclusions into her own words. Months and years later, Arlene may benefit by looking back at her evaluation of this job opportunity and gauging its accuracy.

PUTTING IT ALL TOGETHER

We have seen how the growth processes that foster accurate interpretation play powerful roles in school and later during the startup years. Blending the basic understanding of information with pattern recognition and evaluative thinking, an enthusiastic startup adult is able to launch and nurture a career with an excellent chance of "knowing the ropes." Accurate interpretations lead to the best decisions and actions, which engender a justified sense of effectiveness and the positive feedback that can inspire someone throughout his work life. It is imperative that our schools educate students to be such effective interpreters.

BECOMING AN ACCURATE INTERPRETER

Comprehending

Learning beyond memorization
Decrypting expectations
Forming concepts
Processing information actively and effectively

Recognizing Patterns

Perceiving recurring patterns
Matching patterns with what has worked
Appreciating and generating rules

Evaluating

Overcoming extremes of naïveté or cynicism
Assessing in a stepwise, deliberative way
Judging products, people, ideas, opportunities

9
INSTRUMENTATION
Equipping a Mind's Toolbox

My ideal job would be one in which I was working with my hands, doing something that is also mentally challenging, and yet have the chance to work and interact with people. I would like to be able to take apart not only things but also ideas, and put them back together in a better way.

C.T., age 24

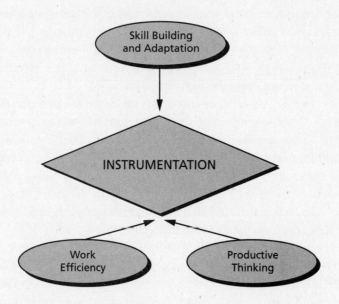

Instrumentation calls for assembling a portable kit of career tools. Every startup adult bursting forth from his teenage cocoon had better give some thought to the following vital questions: "What are the tools of my chosen trade (if I can identify one)? Do I know how and when to use them? How readily can I get my hands on the tools I don't have?" Many of them are not the kinds of tools you can plug in or transport in a steel box; they are part of your thinking. Without the right brain equipment, you too could become a fallen idol, a taker of the wrong roads, a perennial adolescent, or the owner of a mind in deep debt.

Last summer I deviously eavesdropped on a team of electricians installing a generator on my farm. I was surprised to discover that each man owned his own set of hand tools, and I was impressed and more than a tad jealous as I observed how each determined which size pliers, which wrench, which diameter drill bit was most suitable for each step in the installation. The implements looked like anatomical extensions of their hands. That led me to realize that thinking tools are at least as real and germane to my work life as screwdrivers and wire cutters are to an electrician's.

When I was in medical school, I and several classmates observed a renowned and somewhat arrogant surgeon as he performed a gall bladder operation. Before his flamboyant display, he offered an admonition I never forgot, saying simply, "If something you're doing is too difficult, it means you're not using the right instrument."

Educational administrators and policy makers must examine the demands of contemporary adult work to determine which instruments today's students are likely to require during their startup years and beyond. Although very different tools are required in specialized settings, such as a chemistry laboratory, a barbershop, a court of law, or the cab of an eighteen-wheeler, it is possible to identify some mental equipment needed across educational levels and occupations: skill tools, efficiency tools, and productive thinking tools.

From one generation to the next the repertoire of relevant career skills changes dramatically. All of us concerned with the futures of children need to examine closely the capacities likely to be needed by the next wave of startup adults. With continuing computerization and a steady decline in jobs for unskilled workers, many societies need to recognize not only the increasing need for sound basic academic skills but also the requirement for a range of technical and specific thinking abilities. Reporting on their research into the job market, Frank Levy and Richard Murnane (2004) state, "Those with strong skills do not have to worry about mass unemployment or underemployment. On the contrary: The great danger is the continuing decline in earnings opportunities for people who lack the skills to do work requiring *expert thinking* and *complex communication."* Many of the skills to be enumerated in this chapter, habits of mind such as brainstorming, evaluative thinking, creativity, and organization, fall within the realm of expert thinking. A startup adult needs to ask himself whether or not he is developing an area in which he is skilled at expert thinking. The complexities of communication are covered in chapter 10.

SKILL BUILDING AND ADAPTATION

Here's a statement that was made about a new employee who lacked the skills he needed to keep his job: "We hired Vernon to work in our fund-raising department, but he couldn't help organize our current campaign. Even though he had been an English major in college, he didn't know how to write a thank-you note or compose a letter to a prospective donor. He couldn't do the math required to calculate the size of a potential gift. We tried to help him, but he insisted he knew how to do everything. He just couldn't adapt his skills to our needs. It's too bad; he was such a nice guy to have around."

Nobody is skilled upon delivery from the womb. There is no such thing as a congenital skill. Skills are capabilities that are developed over time. Although there may be either inborn talents or congenital glitches that make the mastery of certain skills easy or difficult for an individual, all skills are the products or by-products of learning. Most are taught by teachers or parents; some are self-taught. The amassing of usable skills and the ability to mobilize the right ones to meet specific demands are the underpinnings of athletic trophies and medals, academic kudos, and ultimately career accomplishments.

We can divide skill building into four discrete operations: determining skill needs, building and applying skills, enhancing skills, and recalibrating skills.

Gauging Skill Needs

It is not at all unusual for adolescents and young adults to harbor certain career aspirations without the slightest idea what skills they will need to make them a reality. Kids need to be aware of the hard fact that many of the skills they need for school may be different from the ones they will need during a career (page 9). As I pointed out in chapter 6, it is common to be an undistinguished student in law or business school or basic training who nevertheless turns out to be an outstanding attorney or corporate executive or soldier. Likewise, some top students in professional schools become dreadful disappointments on the job.

A patient of mine desperately wanted to attend medical school. He applied and reapplied over a four-year period, finally getting accepted. I told him that, based on his prior academic record, medical school was going to be an ego-puncturing ordeal for him, but I assured him that once his formal training was behind him, he would excel in his chosen specialty. I was right: He barely made it through medical school; at age thirty-five he heads a well-respected internal medicine department. It's important for high school and college students to recognize that it's not necessary to thrive during training in order to be successful and gratified in a career.

In contemplating a career, a student should be helped to compile an inventory of the skills that will be needed for training and the ones that will come into play during the actual career. While few startup adults know in advance how their life's work will ultimately be framed, it is helpful to think through the options and derive some notion of the skills that will have to be incorporated at the training stage and the ones that will keep coming into play once the career gets going. A student who wants to be an economics professor needs to hone his quantitative skills to perform financial analyses. He should know that once he becomes a faculty member, he will have to develop a new skill, one that was not a priority during training but now is important, namely, an ability to write winning grant proposals.

Building and Applying Skills

Over time any successful individual makes use of a steadily expanding repertoire of skills. Academic skills, motor skills, life skills, and technical (specialized) skills are four common skill categories. They are described in table 9.1.

Academic skills consist of the venerable three Rs along with assorted requirements like note taking, outlining, and interpreting bar graphs. People find themselves in mind debt—perhaps even bankrupt—when they show up for their startup years with underdeveloped academic skills (chapter 5). Persistent reading problems that haunt an adolescent can strangle his career aspirations. I have received calls from countless law and medical students who are in danger of failing because they read too slowly or have horrible difficulty grasping or remembering material

TABLE 9.1
SKILL CATEGORIES

Skill Category	Description	Examples
Academic	Formal skills learned in school	The three Rs, note taking, library use
Motor	Trained muscular capabilities	Swimming, dancing, keyboarding
Life	Practical necessities for everyday life	Balancing a checkbook, shopping for food
Technical	Abilities needed for very specific tasks	Programming software, doing carpentry

they have gone over in a book or article. Many work-life-unready adults struggled with reading fluency when they were in school and are left with incomplete understanding, a slow and labored pace of reading, and problems with retention. To prevent this phenomenon, students can practice reading in steps:

1. Read the material over to get the overview, the "big picture."
2. Read it again for detail (underlining main ideas and key points and writing brief comments in the margins).
3. Do a quick scan of what you underlined.
4. Summarize what you read—either orally or in writing.
5. Apply it to accomplish a task.
6. Review the summary to make sure it fits with what was done.

Adults with weak reading skills may find it hard to decode individual words effortlessly and with accuracy, understand the ideas, and remember what they need to retain all at once. Reading in steps like this can help them get more out of what they read.

The other skills enumerated in table 9.1 also demand conscious cultivation and practice. Students might need to become adept at locating information on the Internet, being prepared for an important event (for example, knowing how to study for a test), taking notes, arguing for a point of view, and preparing budgets.

It is instinctive for kids (and adults) to crave one or another form of motor mastery, so ideally they all should strive for competence at a sport or with a musical instrument, in an artistic medium, or in some

other form of muscular achievement. Motor effectiveness does wonders for self-image. Additionally, an element of rigorous motor learning
is a necessity for some careers, from orthopedic surgery to flying a jet
to painting portraits.

Many kids with underdeveloped life skills have been deprived of
practical, real-world experience. Parents may worry endlessly about
how their child will ever be able to function independently by his mid-
twenties, but they may not do much about it. A mother or father may
wonder nervously, "How he will ever balance a checkbook, pay his bills,
take care of his laundry, and eat healthy foods?" But sometimes they fail
to pose these questions until their son or daughter is twenty-five and
living in life-skill squalor—a bit late in the game. Parents can help stave
off this plight by providing a home curriculum in life-skill education.
The life skills come in the categories summarized in table 9.2.

Kids should be encouraged or required to help with family budget-
ing, vacation planning, health-conscious shopping for food, and, of
course, menial chores.

Finally, there are technical skills, the expert thinking tied to a particular career. Every child should know what it feels like to have acquired
one or more technical competencies, such as playing the drums, drawing in three dimensions, using a particular kind of computer software,
or interpreting a blueprint.

TABLE 9.2
LIFE SKILLS

Category	Examples
Financial	Budgeting, balancing checkbook, not overspending
Medical	Regulating sleep, exercising, taking medication when needed, hygiene
Nutritional	Purchasing, preparing, and consuming a balanced, healthful diet
Personal needs	Obtaining the right kinds of clothing, shelter, transportation, managing money
Resource use	Knowing whom to call for what—personal problems, medical needs, car problems
Personal protection	Resisting exploitation by others, scams, misleading promises/advertising

Almost all startup adults, when seeking employment, are going to be assessed to determine their technical competence. Too often they are extraordinarily naïve regarding technical requirements. I remember interviewing a sixteen-year-old boy about his life plans. He told me that for years he had wanted to become a marine biologist, that he loved the ocean and "everything living inside it." Scuba diving was his favorite pastime, and he had been heavily influenced by Jacques Cousteau documentaries. During our discussion, I mentioned that all sorts of applied mathematics are used nowadays in marine biology. The boy was incredulous and stated, "I hate math. I've always done real bad in it. Like, I'm just about failing geometry this year." A lack of awareness of needed forms of expert thinking is a commonly seen facet of startup naïveté. This boy needed to do some thinking about the ways in which he could connect with the subject matter of marine biology without having to be a highly competent mathematician. Or he might decide to hunker down and pursue those elusive quantitative skills.

Enhancing Skills

The vice president of a local accounting firm wrote of an employee, "Sophie seems to know how to do everything, but her efforts lack luster and work takes her forever to complete. That takes all the joy out of everything she does. She concentrates on preparing taxes and does so diligently. But at tax time she can't keep up. It seems as if nothing is automatic for her; Sophie has to stop and think hard about every little thing. That makes her totally inefficient."

Throughout their school years, kids are admonished to become skilled—at reading, writing, and math, or when executing scales on the clarinet or playing a one-on-one defense in basketball. Over time, important abilities that are called upon repeatedly must improve in two major ways: they are expected to grow both more precise and more automatic. Precision enables someone to produce results that are on target, so jobs are properly executed. Less obvious, though, is the role of what is called automaticity. When skills become automatized, they can be used effortlessly and instantaneously, allowing a person to think about or express complex ideas while at the same time applying a necessary skill. A student can write on the subject of human rights without having to ponder the proper spelling of *rights* or the rules of capitalization and punctuation. The latter are on automatic pilot. Regrettably, there are too many students and plenty of startup adults whose skills are not automatic. Consequently, they work painfully slowly and ineffectively, and what they produce tends to be far less sophisticated than their thought processes.

Recalibrating Skills

Skills should never remain static or stagnant. It's one thing to have a diversified portfolio of abilities, but it's another thing to have the right ones and to be able to shape and reshape them to meet changing expectations. You may be a good reader, but can you decipher a new engine repair manual? You may be a good learner, but can you muster the flexibility to start using some radically new technology? You may be a terrific writer, but can you first create convincing advertising copy that appeals to contemporary teenagers and then switch to a piece aimed at folks in their fifties?

The ability to adapt to change promotes career success. A big part of this ability is the capacity to adapt your skills to meet new needs. Throughout a career, demands change, markets change, conditions change, even job descriptions change. An individual may need to adjust his sales skills to promote a new line of products, or he may have to revise his progress reports to satisfy the idiosyncratic expectations of a new manager. As children and adolescents conquer skills, they should be taught to modify their abilities to address a broadening range of demands. For example, different approaches are needed for reading fiction, editorials, technical manuals, contracts, tax laws, movie scripts, and poetry. Preparing kids to be flexible in applying skills will pay dividends during their startup years and beyond. They should practice writing in varied forms (letters, screenplays, essays, op-ed pieces) and for different audiences (little children, new immigrants, prospective customers) and discuss the variations called for in each of these circumstances.

WORK EFFICIENCY

There are immense individual differences among brains in their ability to conduct efficient mind work; some people seem to possess well lubricated working gears; for others, mental work takes too much effort. Those who enter their startup years saddled with inefficiency are true mind debtors who are likely to pay a high price to get out of debt—if

they ever do. Three growth processes assume key roles in building efficiency: mental energy control, organization, and strategic thinking.

Mental Energy Control

A tutor working with a ninth grader noted, "Buck almost never finishes
anything he starts. He simply runs out of steam when he studies for a
test, writes a report, practices the trumpet, or plods his way through a
worksheet in math. You can see the quality of his work head downhill
and eventually deteriorate as he goes along. Then he just plain peters
out; he runs out of gas."

In my books *The Myth of Laziness* and *A Mind at a Time,* I stressed
the critical importance of the fourteen attention controls that regulate
thinking, behavior, and productivity. With the approach of the startup
years, these controls have to operate as effectively as the knobs in the
cockpit of a Boeing 777. One set of controls is responsible for regulating mental energy, the power supply mobilized when a person needs to
concentrate. Some jobs take a substantial amount of time and are not
especially or immediately pleasurable. Parts of the human brainstem
(the reticular activating system and the locus coeruleus), in collaboration with other parts of the brain, are assigned the chore of energizing a
mind, enabling an individual to have sufficient stamina so that he can
stave off mental fatigue. When someone says, "Joe has such good ideas
and intentions, but he never really delivers the goods," we have to wonder if he has a mental energy shortfall. The four basic mental energy
controls are summarized in table 9.3.

TABLE 9.3
MENTAL ENERGY CONTROLS

Control	Description
Alertness control	Ability to mobilize sufficient mental energy to concentrate on incoming information
Mental effort control	Ability to generate and allocate mental energy for work output
Sleep-arousal control	Ability to turn down energy for sound sleep and then turn it up for work and concentration
Consistency control	Ability to put forth mental energy in a predictable, reliable (not erratic) flow

Individuals vary remarkably in their ability to regulate the flow of energy required for effective mind work. Some seem to possess supercharged minds that can blast through a work assignment, while others find most mind work unbearably arduous. Some find they can control their fuel supply only at certain times of the day (or night). Others seem to phase in and out of control capriciously; their bosses and customers call them unreliable. In some cases an individual has a long history of trouble in opening the fuel valve, initiating work, or settling down to process incoming data. These kids and adults often require a jump-start, such as someone who can write the first line of the report for them.

Others with mental energy that trickles instead of flowing run out of gas as they plod through a task. They may be show a chronic lack of persistence and have trouble finishing what they undertake.

A typical description of such an individual might go like this: "I don't understand Betsy. When she's on, she performs better than anyone else around here. She's nothing short of brilliant. But you never know if she'll even show up, and sometimes when she does get here, her work is just plain shoddy and meager. You can't depend on her." Usually you can trace such patterns of inconsistency back to student days. More than one teacher may have commented, "I know she can do the work. I've seen her work diligently and with great thoroughness when she's made up her mind to get the job done. But it seems that a lot of the time she's just plain lazy and unmotivated to do a good job." Many adolescents with such performance inconsistency often come to the conclusion that when they grow up they will need to be self-employed because no boss would ever tolerate their likely absenteeism and fickle work output.

Mental effort is most severely tested during activities that are necessary but not especially pleasurable. I have often heard mothers report, "My son can fritter away hours on end glued to his computer games, oblivious to the world around him, completely riveted to that tiny screen. But give him his worksheet in social studies or his math homework, and in less than ten minutes he is wiped out. And you can see his work decay right in front of your eyes."

The most praiseworthy fruits of a mind's labor require time to develop. Yet some individuals with weak mental energy controls constantly crave immediate results. Those who combine low or erratic mental energy with a profound hunger for immediate gratification run

the risk of becoming perpetual dabblers. They may never pursue anything substantial in depth. A career invariably requires investing effort
in ways that have a delayed payoff. Young adults for whom postponed
satisfaction is unbearable are very much at risk during the patience-
demanding startup years.

Accomplishment typically passes through three stages: initial attraction, extended toil, and fulfillment. Stage 1 might emerge sounding
something like this: Ralph thinks, "Wouldn't it be cool to play the trumpet." So he rents a glistening brass trumpet and starts taking lessons.

Stage 2 entails rigorously and religiously practicing scales on the
trumpet, ultimately surviving several years of disciplined practice,
trumpet boot camp. Then comes the long-awaited stage 3, when you
have a blast, playing trumpet in a cool jazz ensemble. But there are
countless individuals who can't ever seem to make it through stage 2 in
anything. Their life stories are strewn with episodes of initial excitement with little or no follow-through. Bear in mind that children today
are growing up in a culture that seeks to minimize any such postpone-
ments of pleasure. The Internet offers instant access to information.
Popular music contains very brief melodic lines and unelaborated language. Many of the games children play generate speedy results. Is the
delay of gratification going out of style? Is persistence passé?

I think parents and schools need to pressure kids to impose discipline on their interests so that kids don't abandon their quests when
faced with stage 2 drudgery. Table 9.4 provides some guidelines for accomplishing this.

Mental energy control is vital for building sufficient working capacity.
I have come to believe that schools are mainly responsible for teaching
kids how to learn and that parents should take on the assignment of
teaching them how to work. You cannot build a working capacity entirely in school. Home life has to include the role models, the daily routines, the setting, and the stringent expectations, in short, the soil in
which to cultivate minds that work. In our culture it is often the case that
mothers and fathers are recreation coordinators and entertainers of
their offspring. But a parent must assume the part-time role of a rigorous taskmaster, a benevolent dictator when it comes to expectations for
schoolwork as well as other responsibilities. And those demands have to
begin at an early age—by six or seven. It is treacherous to try to institute
new work policies for the first time in eighth grade! Below are some
things parents can do to build mental working capacities in their kids.

TABLE 9.4
HELPING KIDS SURVIVE EXTENDED TOIL EN ROUTE
TO ACCOMPLISHMENT

Measure to Take	Example
Reduce the intensity or frequency of practice/ drill without quitting entirely.	Temporarily cutting back on the number of lessons and practice sessions (not everyone needs to become a concert pianist).
Intersperse some stage 3 pleasure during stage 2.	Framing and displaying a child's art during stage 2.
Remind kids or show them how much fun they will have in stage 3—putting light at the end of the tunnel.	Letting a child know how "cool" it will be to be able to speak good Spanish when visiting Mexico.
Make a game out of stage 2.	Keeping score of proficiency with math facts, giving rewards for successes demonstrated during practice.
Establish a moral mandate that stresses persistence and perseverance.	Telling her that quitting dance class may be a bad precedent.

ENHANCING WORKING CAPACITY AT HOME

Establish consistent times for mind work whether or not your
   child has homework (call it "mental workout time").
Help your child get started with work.
Assign some household chores consistently.
Serve as a consultant, answer questions, but don't do work
   for your child.
Help organize your child's desk—labeled boxes, drawers,
   folders, etc.
Assist your child in organizing/planning work before starting it.
Set up a distraction-free homework area.
Assist with time allocation, prioritization, and scheduling.
Reward/praise your child for productivity rather than for grades
   on her report card.
Teach your child how to break big tasks into stages, manageable
   chunks of work.

Try not to let your child quit a job when the going
  gets rough or dull.
Be a role model; do mind work yourself while the child is
  engaged in mind work.

Some individuals can best mobilize and sustain the flow of mental energy when they are simultaneously expending strong currents of physical energy. I've met numerous children and adolescents who proclaim
that they would never want to "be stuck with a desk job." These motor-
driven types seek direct physical experience as opposed to pure mental
work, which is the essence of most schoolwork. Their minds may be an-
nouncing that their careers will have to feature significant motor in-
volvement, such as in outdoor or hands-on work. Others gain a boost
by listening to music while they work—it's worth a trial.

The psychologist and educator Mihaly Csikszentmihalyi writes about
a process he calls "flow" that is an important contributor to work output (Csikszentmihalyi and Schneider 2000). Flow occurs when an individual engages in activities in which the goals are clear, there's
immediate feedback along the way, and "although the task is difficult,
he can succeed at it." He cites a little boy tightening the chain on his bicycle. The boy knows what he needs to do, gets ongoing feedback on
whether the chain is getting tight enough, and feels challenged by a
task that is at once difficult and manageable. In all likelihood, kids can
gain from exposure to a range of different types of flow triumphs. In another section of their book *Becoming Adult,* Csikszentmihalyi and Bar-
bara Schneider stress the need for adolescents to put forth "intense
concentration in any activity that requires skill and discipline, regardless of its content."

Certainly, flow and intense concentration build working capacity and
propel productive output. Schools and parents should ensure a steady
supply of flow and concentration-building activities, which will lead to
productivity during the startup years. Eventually, a history of succeeding in tasks that feature abundant flow while demanding intense concentration will lead to gratification on the job.

A nineteen-year-old college freshman, Ethan, once confessed with a
smirk that he was determined to land in a career in which he'd never
have to work very hard. As he put it, "I've never been a worker and I
doubt if I ever will be. Yeah, I want success and all that, but I want to find

it the easy way; I assure you I don't want to kill myself at work every day." Reuben dropped out in the second semester of his sophomore year. I wonder whatever happened to him and to others like him, whether or not he was able to coast down a slope toward a gratifying life. I doubt it; the odds are against him.

Getting Up to Speed

Numerous startup adults falter because they do things too slowly. They fall behind because it takes them too long to complete individual tasks. In order to help someone who is not up to speed, you have to determine the reasons for that person's slowness. There are many possible explanations, including distractibility, a lack of awareness of the passage of time, delayed automaticity (page 151), slow retrieval of information and skills from long-term memory, a tendency to overfocus and devote too much time to minor details, trouble multitasking, difficulty translating ideas into clear language, and extreme perfectionism. Problems with organization (covered later in this chapter) may also dramatically reduce a person's work rate.

Just being aware of what's slowing you down is beneficial. The explanation for slow output has specific implications for getting up to speed. For example, someone with memory problems should surround himself with ready reference materials. To avoid getting bogged down, a person who overfocuses on trivial details or someone who loses track of time should use a stopwatch to give herself time limits for specific stages of tasks. Alternatively, an individual with a long history of slow input and/or output may want to seek a job where time is not of the essence, where deadlines are flexible and the pace is not frenetic.

Work Motivation

In chapter 7 we saw the ways in which motivation affects how a kid sets his sights on the future. But motivation is also a generous contributor to working capacity, and it demands ongoing cultivation. Kids need to see tangible evidence that their efforts are paying off. They need plenty of encouragement and recognition along the way.

During the school years, homework is the acid test for academic motivation. As I have mentioned, kids must develop their working capacities and habits largely at home rather than in school. But parents should handle their offspring with care. Homework battles often stem from a student's embarrassment about a messy handwriting, troubles with spelling, disorganization, careless mistakes in math, and a habit of rushing through reading assignments. Parents have to resist being overly critical, and they should comment on the positive aspects of what their kid is doing.

When you feel there's no way you can please the adult world, your stores of motivation become depleted. A frequent complication sets in when a student neglects all life's other priorities to devote herself exclusively to trying to please and gain acceptance by other kids. Then essential growth processes may never come to fruition; the outcome will be a mind in debt. In the absence of motivation, essential learning processes undergo what in medicine is called disuse atrophy.

Organization

A junior account executive during her first year working for a Madison Avenue advertising firm admitted, "I know my life would go a lot better if I could only get my act together. I'm a disaster at meeting deadlines, and I walk around feeling as if I'm buried, overwhelmed, always behind at work. Other folks seem to be keeping up, but I always fall behind, sometimes without even realizing it's happening—until it's too late. I think I'm in a total time warp."

Organization is the best policy for developing efficiency. Disorganized people are renowned for doing things the hard way. Kids need to grow in their proficiency in their organizational practices. In preparation for the inevitable workloads of a job, four forms of organization must be cultivated: time management, materials management, prioritization, and task integration. If we can equip students with these tools, they will have a leg up when it comes to productivity during their startup years.

Time Management

Some children and adults seem relatively oblivious to the passage of time. They have no idea how long it will take them to accomplish something and are likely to experience trouble meeting deadlines as well as difficulty sensing when they are running behind. Many people with time management confusion seldom tackle tasks in a stepwise progression; they may try to do everything at once. Melissa was a fifteen-year-old who ran late for everything. Her family was forever waiting for her to finish dressing so they could leave for the restaurant or get off the phone before supper got cold. As her father related, "Melissa has no idea how to go about doing anything in stages. When she studies for a test, I'm the one who has to help her come up with a plan for what to go over when. Otherwise she's at a standstill; she can't even begin to get started with her studying." The passage of time, like a soft breeze at her back, seemed never to faze her. She had no idea how long she'd been on the phone and couldn't believe it when she was told it took her more than an hour to wash up and get dressed. The instructions that follow may help school-age and adult Melissas adopt some stepwise approaches.

APPLYING STEPWISDOM TO ORGANIZATION

1. Clearly define the assignment or project.
2. Establish a final deadline.
3. Estimate time needed for completion (*hours, days, or weeks*).
4. List tasks needed for completion (*working backward from deadline to start*).
5. Arrange tasks in the best order.
6. Estimate time needed for each step (*minutes, hours, days, or weeks*).
7. Insert appropriate breaks (*intervals when the work gets set aside*).
8. List expected time or date of completion of each step.
9. Monitor progress (*checking off completed steps and time actually taken*).
10. After each step, determine if activity is on schedule.
11. Review the process after submission to evaluate plan efficiency.

Stepwisdom is as applicable in adult life as it is throughout the school years. But starting in elementary school, teachers should emphasize the taming of time in this way. Kids should engage in frequent long-term projects, for which they should submit work plans that more or less follow the time flow model. They should submit work in progress and gauge whether a stage took more or less time than anticipated.

Each Sunday evening, parents should preview with a child her schedule for the coming week and then compile a checklist of what will need to get done when and how much time will have to be set aside for each piece of work. Then each night before going to bed, the child can check off what has been accomplished that day. She can help compile itineraries for vacations and devise schedules for her work and play activities. For some children, time management is instinctive. Others have to be taught how time works and how to work it.

Temporal thinking is critical in every field of adult work, and its absence is a common reason for career crashes during the startup years. A commercial pilot has to show up at the airport in time for his scheduled flight. A cross-country truck driver has to estimate when she'll arrive in Moline, Illinois, to pick up the cargo she is taking to Seattle. A surgeon has to schedule time in the operating room; to do so, he needs to be able to estimate how long it will take him to remove that spleen. A building contractor has to know exactly when to schedule the arrival of the trusses. A magazine journalist must know how to meet the deadline for the story she's writing for the August issue of *Good Housekeeping*. Time planning requirements go on and on. Are we priming kids to meet the unforgiving temporal challenges they will meet in their startup years? Probably not.

Materials Management

Most jobs call for some equipment. As a student you have to be the responsible guardian of your notebook, your textbooks, your assignment pad, your keys, your backpack, your gloves, and your gym shoes—among other assorted items. Some kids and lots of adults too are overwhelmed when it comes to shepherding the massive collection of material objects that help get things done. Individuals whose earnest efforts are perpetually sabotaged by their material disorganization keep losing possessions and misplacing crucial slips of paper; they have trouble maintaining order (on a desk or in a locker or a closet) and seldom can find what they need when they need it. I personally spend much of each day in the aggravating quest for misplaced objects. People with my problem forge no memory linkages between an object and the site where it was left or last observed. Kids with material organizational woes have chaotic backpacks with binders that hemorrhage their three-hole paper, pencils that spontaneously flee from their pockets, and homework papers that vaporize en route to school. Imagine a bartender who isn't sure where he put the club soda, a cab driver who misplaced her license, a frequent traveler who can never remember where she left her car in the airport parking lot, or a prison guard who's lost his keys. Such people expend a lot of time and anguish at the expense of efficiency and quality of work.

We have to help kids develop effective tactics for materials management. This is mostly the job of parents, who can ensure that a kid's desk has color-coded folders, labeled boxes, specific places for everything. And every couple of nights some time should be devoted to renovating notebooks and restoring order to desktops, drawers, and other storage facilities that may have deteriorated. Parents need to take the lead on this, even when there's resistance on the part of the kid. Most children and adolescents with material disorganization are not at all concerned about it; in fact, they're likely to be completely oblivious to their self-inflicted chaos. We must help them cultivate a taste for order by creating that order for them when they can't seem to do it themselves. This assistance should be offered without threats or statements such as "You know, I'm not going to be here all your life." The key is consistency. You have to remember to put objects in the same places. And at key transition points during the day, for example, when leaving for work or school, a person should pause and ask himself, "Let's see, do I have everything I need today?"

Prioritization

This is the gist of what one college junior confessed: "I think I could write a manual on how to waste time without even trying. I can spend hours doing things that are totally unimportant, and they're not even really fun. Then I never have time to do the things I really need to do." A large cohort of children and adults lack the brain circuits needed to set and follow up on priorities. They are disorganized because they don't or can't determine relative degrees of importance of the items on their daily agendas. So they invest their minds and other resources in ventures that lead them nowhere and have no payoff, while neglecting the activities that really could count for something.

I once worked with a promising young assistant professor, a man who would never miss a campus lecture covering any subject or topic (even one he wasn't really interested in or one he already knew a lot about). He was like a religious zealot attending every conference and every questionably relevant meeting. Meanwhile, he could never get around to correcting exam papers, answering important letters, submitting grades, or assembling grant proposals. Various manuscripts he was invited to write lay incomplete in a bottom desk drawer. He was a razor-sharp analytic thinker and a hard worker (sometimes on questionably gainful tasks), unfailingly scholarly in his area of expertise. Yet this consummate genius was refused tenure because his academic output was so meager. He lacked the instrumentation needed for prioritization, spending much of his life engaging in low-yield activities. This is the explanation for countless tales of career underachievement. People fail when they are unable to establish and act upon priorities.

Schools and parents too often neglect the job of teaching students prioritization skills. Kids need to be taught how to rank their activities in terms of their likely payoff. They need to be able to differentiate between high-priority tasks that yield significant benefits (often in the long run and not immediately), lower-priority enterprises that are fun but not all that beneficial, and zero-priority (easily omitted) engagements that are neither fun nor productive. I have suggested to parents and teachers that they use a priority scoring system for kids and that adults can employ it as well. Once or twice a month various possible activities are rated in terms of their relative priority, as depicted in table 9.5. Using this kind of simple grid can help heighten awareness of prioritization while enabling a child or a grown-up to determine how much time and mental effort to devote to specific tasks or pursuits. By the way, there's nothing wrong with indulging in low-priority, frivolous ac-

TABLE 9.5
PRIORITIZATION GRID

Task or Activity	PRIORITY LEVEL				Proposed Time Allocation
	Very High	High	Moderate	Low	

tivities that are just for fun and result in immediate if transitory gratification. It's a matter of consciously balancing high with low priorities.

Task Integration

When a task has numerous components, like the moving parts of a fine Swiss timepiece, they have to be coordinated, calibrated, and synchronized. It can be nothing short of scalding torture for certain students to launch and steer themselves through the tasks and subtasks of a science, art, or social studies project. It is exceedingly frustrating for them to think up a topic, decide what resources they will need, locate those materials, extract what they need from them, start fitting it all together, come up with their point of view or interpretations, decide how best to present their ideas and the facts they have gathered, and so on. And what if you are involved in several projects simultaneously? That's an overwhelming mass of puzzle pieces to someone who has trouble integrating parts. And such challenges are common during a lifetime.

Some individuals are adept at jobs with only a single component (such as completing a reading assignment, filling out a geography worksheet, or changing a tractor tire), but they can't cope with the demands of complex projects and multitasking. Here's a vivid example of an up-and-coming floundering nonintegrator: Charles was a seventeen-year-old overtly ambitious kid who was an avid reader, a talented poet, a good athlete, and a universally popular guy. He scored sky-high on his SATs and was a robust college applicant. But poor Charles had an awful time getting together his college applications. He felt as if he were drowning and kept procrastinating. He just couldn't seem to integrate the subtasks of filling out the forms, writing essays, getting letters of recommendation, discussing college choices with his guidance counselor, making a list of his interests, and arranging for interviews. Even with his parents' benevolent offers of rescue, he felt overwhelmed at the prospect of the process. There were too many fragments, and he sensed he couldn't cement them.

Integrating multiple task components forms a large part of what I like to call a project mentality, a frame of mind that should become firmly established in the education of all children. Across the curriculum, we can prepare students to integrate subtasks in a lucid and explicit manner. Before undertaking a project or studying for an important examination, students should be required to identify the subtasks. They can arrange these components in a circular fashion (see

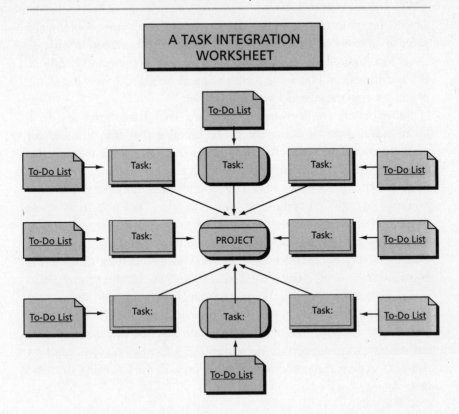

A TASK INTEGRATION WORKSHEET

the worksheet above) and make a small to-do list for each subtask. There is no need to complete all the items in a set order; they can keep returning to certain subtasks to revise or polish them or they can add new ones. In this way students develop the mental agility to organize all the moving parts. The worksheet can help children and adults contend with the multiple tasks within a complicated project. Multiple projects may require several such grids. As a teenager, you can use this approach to plan your graduation party, to write a biology term paper on termites, and to apply for summer jobs. In adult life, a project mentality can help you write an outstanding book, design and implement a new science curriculum, and launch a manned satellite.

Strategic Thinking

Here was one mother's notation about her child, age thirteen, as a strategist: "My daughter does everything the hardest way possible. She uses no strategies whatsoever, and when the going gets rough, Lizzie simply throws in the towel. When she can't solve a math problem, she gives up entirely or just goes to pieces. When she has a run-in with another kid, Lizzie crumbles and has no idea how to cope and handle it. It's as if she doesn't have the tools she needs to smooth over life's little obstacles, the ones we all have to surmount."

Some people are born methodologists. They have clever and well-thought-out ways of doing things, techniques that they consciously apply to complete tasks efficiently. Their strategies work like booster rockets for their work output and enhance the overall quality of their output. Other folks never stop to ask themselves the pivotal question, "Let me see now, what's the best way to do this?" They just do it—most often the hard way. I call them nonmethodologists.

As they progress through school, students need to keep being asked, "What strategies do you think you want to use for this?" While planning their work (which too few do), they should be prompted to articulate the strategies they expect to employ. For example, before taking a final examination in chemistry, every student should submit his or her strategic plan for studying, which would describe what strategies he will employ to make certain he retains the information to succeed on the test. An eleventh grader might come up with the following strategic list:

1. I'll try to figure what's really key, what's most likely to be on the test.
2. I'll make a list of those things.
3. I'll read over that list a couple of times.
4. I'll try to answer the sample questions at the end of the chapter.
5. I'll try to think up some questions of my own and guess what might be asked on the test.
6. I'll go over my homework and redo some of the chemical equations.
7. I'll call Fran; she's good at chemistry, and we can quiz each other over the phone.
8. I'll study hard right before I go to sleep and do a quick review during breakfast.

Those are commendable study strategies. Regardless of how that student fares on the examination, he is becoming a master methodologist, a strategic planner and thinker. This is so vital that schools should start to grade kids as much on their strategies as they do on their test results.

Teachers should evaluate and reward students for the way they went about doing something as much as for the right answer or a stellar essay. (This is often done in high school mathematics, but rarely in other subjects.) The kids might submit documentation called "my strategy plan" for an assignment or test. Before some of their examinations, students should submit and be graded on their study plans—just as pilots have to submit their flight plans.

Plenty of students, when asked how they study for a test, respond simply by saying, "I just, like, kinda go over the stuff." That's hardly strategic. How will they demonstrate strategic planning capabilities during their startup years, a period during which strategic thinking is crucial?

We should sensitive students to the vast range of challenges and settings where the right strategies can come to their rescue. Table 9.6 lists some common subtypes of strategies.

Kids should look over the strategy subtypes, then cite examples of each and either write or talk about strategies they might apply in their examples. Getting into the habit of strategic thinking helps prime a child to emerge as a productive young adult, and it does wonders for self-confidence, resistance to stress, and overall resiliency.

TABLE 9.6
STRATEGY SUBTYPES

Strategy Subtype	Possible Application
Self-marketing	Figuring out how to come across during a job interview
Interpersonal	Deciding how to go about becoming friends with someone you admire
Conflict resolution	Settling a dispute amicably with a dissatisfied customer
Sales	Working out ways of promoting your ideas or products
Political	"Campaigning" to get promoted or chosen for a new position
Coping	Coming up with ways to handle stress or personal setbacks in life
Task-oriented	Devising the best and most efficient ways of meeting academic or workplace demands

PRODUCTIVE THINKING

Productive thinking is brain work culminating in a useful or meaningful outcome. That endpoint might be a visible product, an innovative concept, or a solution to a thorny dilemma. We can divide productive thinking into three somewhat overlapping processes, namely, competent decision making, creative thought, and brainstorming.

Competent Decision Making

No one would dispute the fact that we would like to equip our kids to become excellent decision makers. But numerous kids and adults make too many decisions impulsively. They don't inspect a challenge, identify it as such, and then slow down their thinking to consider how best to tackle it. Saying to yourself, "Oops, that's an important decision that I really need to think about" is half the battle.

Some nondeliberators fall back on aggression—sometimes verbal, sometimes physical, and sometimes just pure spite or passive aggression. When confronting a tough decision, they either glibly feel sure they know its solution or become paralyzed. There may be no middle ground, no helpful internal voice saying, "This is hard; I'd better try to figure out the best way to decide this." For startup adults, heavy-handed impulses can be like land mines pulverizing the foundations of their careers.

A competent decision maker knows how and when to slow down and reflect. He proceeds through a sequence of steps to arrive at a desirable solution. Some of these steps may fall into place automatically; the decision maker's inner voice may vocalize other steps. Children should be prompted to use some internal narration to help navigate their decision making.

Competent decision making inevitably is a multistep process. It involves highly flexible thinking during which multiple alternative decisions are generated and considered. It is also a procedure in which a person refers to problems faced earlier, so that experience and precedent can be brought to bear on a current decision (relying on pattern recognition, page 133). While children are growing up, their decision-making tactics should be talked about and made explicit. Also, kids need to perceive decision making as a problem-solving process with a broad range of applications, such as settling a dispute with your girlfriend, picking a topic for a report, determining which policies the

United Nations should enact in the Middle East, and figuring out the best way to tackle a tricky word problem in math. In early adulthood, competent decision making can meet such diverse needs as deciding whether to act sophisticated or naïve and youthful during a job interview, choosing between finding a job and heading back to school, selecting clothes that convey the best image, and determining what style would work for a new necktie you are about to design. Learning to undertake the decelerated steps outlined below will help a child or adult become a competent decision maker.

COMPETENT DECISION MAKING

1. *Identifying a decision as a decision (that is, knowing one when you see one):* The first step when you come across a challenge is to realize that it will take some time and effort to think it through. Example (from an ambitious startup software engineer): "Should I go ahead and accept the job offer from the startup company my buddy Virgil is launching?"
2. *Stating in detail the decision to be made:* You try to describe the question and its ramifications (often using the formula "if . . . then"). Example: "The opportunity sounds exciting. Virgil is real smart and the company should do well. If the company does well, then I'll be on a roll. But it's risky, and they don't have enough money yet. I'll get less pay for now, but the potential for future advancement and more money is there if I'm patient. On the other hand, I like where I work now, and my boss thinks I'm terrific. But there are lots of other good people working here, and I'll have to wait a long time to get a decent promotion."
3. *Previewing the desired outcome(s):* You look ahead and describe how you would like things to work out or what they will look like once the decision is made. Example: "Whatever happens, I want to end up making plenty of money and feeling I'm advancing pretty fast in my career. I also want the freedom to create some of my own products for the company."
4. *Enumerating your options:* You list alternative final decisions. Example: "I could go ahead and take the job, or else say no to Virgil, or tell my present boss about the offer and see if he'd pay me more to stay or promote me soon. I could just stay put, be patient, and not

risk alienating the boss, or I could tell Virgil I want to sit tight and see what happens with the new venture before I commit myself to it."

5. *Referring to previous experience:* You recount similar decisions in your past work life and how they were resolved—successfully or not. Example: "The last time I got an offer from a new firm, I decided not to take it, and they later went belly-up. So I'd better be cautious."

6. *Getting help:* You consult other people, do the needed research, or gather information to aid in the decision-making process. Example: "I'm going to discuss this with my wife; she's logical and she has a stake in this."

7. *Weighing and deciding:* You rate the relative merits, demerits, or likely consequences of each option: "I have to weigh heavily my need for money right now to cover my living expenses and debts. I also don't want to get into a rut and stagnate where I am; that counts for a lot. And I don't want to feel three years from now that I made a dumb decision; that would kill me. I think I'll keep my options open by telling Virgil I need a few months more to think over his offer."

8. *Monitoring:* You evaluate the extent to which the ultimate decision is working or has worked. Example: "Virgil's company never got going. I'm so relieved that I didn't just impulsively go for Virgil's offer."

Some people might prefer to substitute the term *problem solving* for what I have been calling *decision making.* I favor the latter term because we need to connote to kids and startup adults that something does not need to be a problem to lend itself to systematic deliberation. Problem solving should be thought of as one form of careful decision making. There are other applications of decision making, such as resolving dilemmas, choosing between multiple desirable alternatives, and exercising good taste, that do not constitute responses to problems. You don't have to have a problem to think in an organized fashion.

The steps itemize the sequence of thought processes that can be applied across the spectrum of life's important decisions. Foreign policy decisions, clinical decision making in medicine, and critical career decisions as a startup adult all lend themselves to such a stepwise approach. It can be used as well for such ubiquitous moral dilemmas as: Should I call in sick so I can go to the beach? Should I tell the geometry teacher that Susan cheated on yesterday's exam? Should I lift this information from the Internet? Should I indulge in insider trading using what I just found out about my company? Competent decision making is far better than glossing over an issue or lurching into an impulsive approach. There's much to be said for teaching kids how to recognize a decision-making challenge when they come across one. Too many startup adults with work-life unreadiness have too little experience treating important decisions systematically.

Creative Thought

Every startup adult should want to make a contribution. And some of what can be contributed comes from having original ideas or unique personal approaches. Such creative thought takes off like a missile when a mind feels free to explore. While original thinking is at its heart, the creative process contains other features as well. Table 9.7 lists some of these key components.

During the startup years it can be tremendously beneficial to identify and market one's area(s) of applied creativity, since that is where a per-

TABLE 9.7
SOME KEY COMPONENTS OF CREATIVE THOUGHT

Component	Description
Fluid/divergent thinking	Allowing a mind to free-associate, operate in an open exploratory way, spawn possibly unorthodox thoughts
"Erasing the board" in your mind	Trying to suspend most or all preconceived notions; going back to a naïve state of mind
Risk taking	Being willing to go "out on a limb" and come up with ideas that might be criticized
Autonomy/independence of thought	Being willing to operate on the social fringe, perhaps questioning the status quo, conventional norms or values
Medium discovery and use	Finding a means of delivering creative effort, such as an art form or a mode of communication
Discipline and technique	Mastering the above form or mode to meld technical proficiency with creative effort

son is likely to make his or her richest contribution to a company or organization. Creativity is as well a potential reservoir of personal passion. Such intense attraction can be a reliable compass when it comes to engaging in what excites you the most.

Brainstorming

Both creative thought and decision making thrive during brainstorms, which are more frequent when you are willing to devote time to open-ended thinking, starting with few if any preconceived answers, letting ideas erupt spontaneously, and then determining which thoughts to discard and which to refine. This kind of freewheeling, trial-and-error thinking can be portrayed as, "Let me see what I can come up with, and then how I can make it better." For example, when I have to produce a title for a new book or article I am writing, I am apt to sit down with a cup of coffee, a sharp pencil, and a fresh lined yellow pad. I will then jot down all of the options that leap from my brain—the awful ones as well as those that have some potential. I try to come up with ideas "out of the blue." Then once a reasonable candidate surfaces, I try creating an assortment of variations on that idea. I critically examine each variation and decide whether it's time to hatch more entirely fresh thoughts. At a certain point I decide I'm getting stale, so it's best to put away the list and return to it at a later time.

The chemist Linus Pauling once said, "The only way to have a good idea is to have a lot of ideas." What an awesome idea! Parents and teachers should frequently ask kids to come up with and express their own ideas. At the dinner table, ask, "Brent, what new ideas did you come up with today?" Brainstorming should be as open-minded, as unfettered as possible. All ideas should be viewed as candidates for further use and future development.

Sometimes it is best to divide brainstorming into sessions. Each new round allows for a fresh view of previous options and the chance to synthesize entirely new ones.

STEPS IN THE PROCESS OF BRAINSTORMING

---

1. Identify a need.
2. Produce as many possible ways of meeting that need as can be thought of—thinking out loud.
3. Write down every idea as it comes to mind.

4. Visually inspect and verbally elaborate on each new idea.
5. Think up variations on that idea that might improve it.
6. Think up variations on the variations that might improve them.
7. Periodically reexamine, add to, and refine the list of ideas and variations.
8. Take breaks, making use of multiple brainstorming rounds.
9. Review the list and highlight the leading candidates, the best ideas.
10. Talk through the pros and cons of each of the best ideas.
11. Select the idea that best satisfies the need stated in step 1.
12. Schedule a final session to review and verify the choice, possibly soliciting outside opinions.

The following blank form is excerpted from a brainstorming worksheet.

Idea no.	Idea	Variations
1		
2		

Brainstorming, consciously or not, can become a key step in both creative thinking and decision making. A creative poet may need to brainstorm possibilities to come up with a fitting word within a stanza.

Someone trying to improve upon some software may need to brainstorm the many options to create the best program.

Some of the most productive brainstorming occurs when two or more people collaborate, refine the list, and arrive at a consensus. Students of all ages need both kinds of experiences—solo and joint performances of brainstorming. In school, kids should periodically fill out a brainstorming worksheet and submit it as a way to demonstrate the richness and flexibility of their thinking. This exercise can help kids get out of the habit of generating ideas by settling for the first thing that comes out of their minds.

Closure

Productive thinking is all about getting things done; it must have a discernible outcome—either a product or some form of closure, such as arriving at a deal or resolving a conflict. The capacity for productive thinking is a critical growth process contributing to work-life readiness.

Kids may need help becoming productive thinkers. My boss at Children's Hospital Boston, Dr. Mary Ellen Avery, was a brilliant source of sage guidance to me early in my career. I remember her description of what she called "the promises, promises syndrome." Dr. Avery noted that people who came to see her with this syndrome described all sorts of grandiose plans and ideas they were incubating, but she would never see the fruition or implementation of a single one of them. This is one reason why students' productive thinking should be part of a project mentality. Through projects they can be helped to take an idea from its early conceptual stages through its birth to results.

INSTRUMENTATION AND BRAIN CHANGE

Is there an optimal period during which the compiling of a basic tool kit needs to occur? Although instrumentation goes on throughout a child's education and on into adulthood, there are strong indications that the period from age eleven to twenty is an especially optimal time for tooling up. Dramatic changes are taking place in the human brain throughout these years, and these modifications in function and structure represent prime growth opportunities for instrumentation. Three forms of change are especially germane: the spread of white matter on the surface of the brain, the pruning of underutilized nerve cells and connections, and the development of the prefrontal region. Let's examine these recently discovered phenomena.

Using sophisticated brain imaging techniques, neuroscientists recently have demonstrated that between the ages of eleven and twenty the brain's surface evolves from being predominantly gray matter to becoming mainly white matter. During this time many nerve cell extensions become covered with a white waxy substance called myelin that is rather like the insulation surrounding an electric wire. It turns out that the cells most often utilized are the ones that are rewarded with myelinization, which tends to make them more or less permanent brain gear. Imagine a rural town in which some dirt roads are chosen to be paved; obviously, the ones with the most traffic get picked. The same is true in the brain: namely, the paths that get put to use most become enhanced through myelinization. In the meantime, the process of pruning is also occurring, as cells that seldom operate get trimmed, eliminated so as to enhance the efficiency of the working pathways. The significance of these two processes is enormous. It means that between the ages of eleven and twenty, we need to make sure that kids are developing and using with frequency the best habits of mind, the techniques, the mental tools they will need throughout their lifetimes. If they are underutilizing essential tools, those will be pruned away, eliminated. If they are spending their time wasting time, the wrong patterns may get established. Parents and schools need to determine which brain roads they would like to have paved and then proceed to pave them through their active and frequent use!

The development of the prefrontal lobes of the brain is another significant process unfolding during the years from eleven to twenty—and beyond. This region enables kids to slow down their thinking, look ahead to anticipate the outcomes of their actions, consider their alternatives before making decisions, keep an eye on how they are doing, and make use of prior experience to guide their judgment, decision making, and behavior. In other words, the prefrontal lobes, as they mature, protect people from any tendencies to act on impulse rather than careful reflection. While this capacity is growing, the time is ripe to install those tools of decision making, strategy use, and other mind-based devices that I have mentioned in this chapter.

Clearly, these neuroscientific findings should reinforce our determination to make sure that adolescents are being taught to use the tools needed for a productive work life. Failing to do so in a systematic way will worsen any epidemic of work-life unreadiness.

Below is a review of the important components of instrumentation.

ACQUIRING INSTRUMENTATION

Building and Adapting Skills

Perfect general and job-specific abilities by
- mastering important skills
- enhancing and automatizing select skills
- recalibrating skills to meet evolving needs

Developing Work Efficiency

Mobilize and direct high output by
- activating and focusing mental energy
- harnessing and sustaining mental effort
- organizing time, materials, priorities, and complex tasks
- attaining a project mentality
- developing and using strategic approaches

Thinking Productively

Move toward intelligent output by
- making decisions competently
- brainstorming
- thinking creatively

10
INTERACTION
Crafting Interpersonal Skill

I had no idea about those office politics issues when I left college. I was a little naïve and thought it couldn't happen to me. But the world just isn't like that.

B.W., age 25

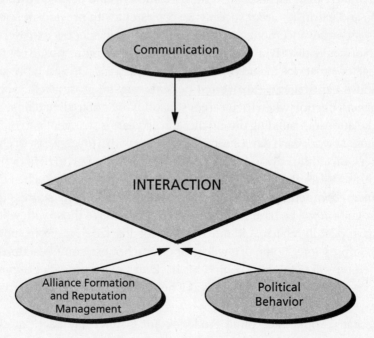

"

I'll tell you, my boy sure don't have much book sense—with the trouble he's got with readin' and spellin' and all. But tell you what: he's the best darn people person you'll ever get with. Everyone likes Frederick, and they all follow him." That was a loving statement from a cattle and hay farmer near my farm in North Carolina. His son was a delightful boy, aspiring (but perspiring) to be promoted to tenth grade. And his dad was right on target in highlighting Frederick's charm and charisma. In the long run, knowing how to relate well and endear yourself to others plays a more substantial role in career success than precision in spelling or punctuation or geography.

Frederick was the consummate extrovert—outgoing, able to give and take gratification from his interactions. In their studies of personality factors affecting career success in adults, Scott Seibert and Maria Kraimer (2001) concluded, "Extraversion was related most consistently to career success, exhibiting positive relationships with salary, promotions, and career satisfaction. Positive relations found between extraversion and extrinsic career success are consistent with previous research on career advancement. . . . In terms of intrinsic success extroverted persons may display a general tendency to react more positively to a range of situations including their career situations. Or, as a more substantive explanation, extroverted persons may be more likely to take corrective action when their career situations are not to their liking."

Relationship building during the startup years is stringent and unforgiving. At work each day a startup adult deals with a diverse cast of characters, including coworkers and individuals in a position to help or hurt him, as well as members of highly judgmental "audiences," such as customers, competitors, clients, and job interviewers. Early success and recognition will be based on the candid judgments of those with whom a startup adult relates. And much of that feedback derives from subjective impressions. Some of it will be open and honest; some reactions to a person will take place behind his back and may contradict outward appearances. Someone who acts as if he admires you may secretly damage you.

Some people like young Frederick are instinctively adept at constructing relationships. Others are career-crippled, particularly when they find themselves immersed in jobs that feature heavy-duty interpersonal actions and transactions. A highly interactive workplace or steady contact with clients or customers may be the wrong road taken for a person with misguided social insights and behaviors.

In my book *A Mind at a Time,* I described a neurodevelopmental system called social cognition, a set of verbal and nonverbal processes that enables people to succeed in their interactions. Social cognition plays a key role in the quest for happiness throughout the school years and, if anything, its importance intensifies as careers are set in motion. Adults, like kids, crave and thrive on friendships. But a social life embedded within a career life differs from the interpersonal scenarios that play out in and around school. In their social transactions, adults must know how to appeal to different groups and to build durable relationships. This demands more than a jolly patina of ebullient personality and glistening charm.

Startup adults are under pressure to inspire long-term trust and to communicate in a way that strengthens on-the-job relationships. So an employee might tell a colleague, "I realize you're going to need my help operating this new software. Feel free to call me anytime you need assistance." Then, of course, that speaker needs to follow through on his reassuring statements. An adult also must be able to convince, collaborate, negotiate, and come across as supportive to customers, coworkers and bosses who may have totally different educational, cultural, ethnic, and family backgrounds. Your social communication style may have to be recalibrated to meet the needs of such diverse audiences. This broad outreach may contrast dramatically with the tight adolescent relationships forged in cliques, gangs, athletic teams, and clubs, where there may have been a tendency for young people of similar backgrounds or interests to find each other.

Unlike at parties, in the workplace a person has to be effective at communicating ideas in a manner that will impress and elicit the confidence of others. In other words, you have to do more than just come across as a cool guy or an affable woman; you need to communicate that you're competent and trustworthy, someone who knows his stuff, a person who can be relied on. A knowledgeable, dependable, caring-about-what-you're-doing demeanor that radiates an overall competence might not have made you popular at a college mixer. Yet, patients coming to your surgical clinic or customers at your accounting firm respond positively to that aura of expertise and reliability.

Some startup adults mistakenly assume that the ultracool actions and poses that they parlayed so masterfully in school and at parties and proms will transfer to on-the-job social acceptance and credibility. But the scenarios are vastly different. These individuals may be showing the symptoms of twenty-year-olds trapped in their adolescence (chapter 2). A teen can be disarming, ingratiating at a high school or college dance, and subsequently be way off base socially on the job. In some instances, the opposite phenomenon prevails; an individual may interact effectively at work while being a relative loner. Transmitting strong social signals and jelling with others at work depend heavily on the cultivation of three seminal growth processes: communication, alliance formation and reputation management, and political behavior. Let's examine these growth processes and how fostering them during the school years can help ensure work-life readiness.

COMMUNICATION

While preparing *Ready or Not, Here Life Comes,* I had a chance to speak to the experienced chief operating officer of a major company. I asked him if he could pinpoint the most prevalent weakness among his current crop of young executives and sales staff. His response: "Oh, that's easy. They have no idea how to communicate. They can't get their ideas across at a meeting and they are shamefully inept when it comes to speaking with customers. They alienate people without realizing it. They sound indifferent or sometimes even condescending without intending to. And they can't explain things clearly to potential buyers. I'm sure they lose us a ton of business. What I don't get is why these supposedly well-educated young folks were never taught how to talk—or, for that matter, write."

Are we experiencing a communication crisis? I think so. The ability to speak and write clearly brings high marks in school and then yields generous dividends at every stage of a career. Therefore, we need to equip kids with the verbal equipment needed to be appropriate and precise. In particular, they have to be able to operate the two most heavy-duty communication engines: thought translation and verbal transaction.

Thought Translation
An eleventh grade English teacher said of a student, "Sandra seems to have no shortage of terrific ideas, but she is way too quiet in class. Somehow she has trouble communicating her rich thoughts, getting them out, or maybe it just takes her too long to express herself. Sometimes it appears that she is extremely shy and inhibited in a classroom, yet she's noticeably verbal and spontaneous when she's with her friends." If Sandra doesn't overcome this limitation, her mind debt as a communicator could become a lifelong hindrance. Being a competent

conveyer of complex thoughts is a prerequisite across the gamut of professions. A wrong road will have been taken if an inarticulate person opts for teaching, sales, litigation law, or politics! Virtually all jobs call for some form of effective communication. Quite a few people in their twenties get stuck on the exit ramp that leads out of adolescence because of unrecognized communication shortcomings. Like Sandra, they cannot go beyond everyday banter with friends.

Throughout life we need to translate complicated thinking into decipherable statements; that way, we can share our impressive thoughts with colleagues and clients. In a sense, everyone sooner or later is called upon to become a salesperson. Lucid expression of thoughts enables a person to sell herself and promote her ideas. And too, persuasive language helps her recruit others to her way of thinking. Kids need lots of experience verbally promoting their ideas and points of view. Instead of fruitless renditions of "what I did last summer" or "why I liked reading that book," they should strive to be articulate about "how I think we can conserve our energy resources" or "why animals shouldn't be used for experimentation." Verbally defending something you believe in is a great way to build oral language, while adding rigor to your own thinking about an issue.

We are currently witnessing a dramatic downgrading of oral language among children and adolescents, a virtual verbal famine. Too many of them cannot construct sophisticated speech, despite their fluency with everyday chitchat and the almost raplike banter they enjoy with their intimate friends. They struggle and fumble with what is called literate language, the linguistic sophistication needed to formulate and transmit complex thinking and precise points of view. You can detect this language deficiency just by listening to adolescents when they attempt to discuss an abstract concept or an issue in the news; they may do so in a way that sounds as if they are talking with a friend on the phone.

In class discussions, one encounters numerous students with conspicuous verbal imprecision and dysfluency. They reveal noticeable hesitancy, a high volume of *uhs, ums, likes,* and *you know what I means.* You can practically hear the linguistic gears grinding and see the dark exhaust spewing from their minds' engines when they strive to communicate on a high plane; vocabulary and proper sentence construction are too much work. You feel the compulsion to send in a verbal rescue squad, to inject the proper words into each halting speaker's larynx.

Kids need frequent practice making oral presentations, summarizing lengthy information, verbally defending their views on issues, and elaborating upon ideas. They have to be capable of explaining what they know and how they are thinking. Sadly, kids are growing up in a culture that is decidedly antilanguage.

Much of what they savor outside of school comes to them brightly packaged in nonverbal or verbally minimalist formats. Instant Messaging, contemporary music lyrics, and Internet websites deliver linguistically desiccated and highly condensed communication. Prolonged submersion in computer games, skateboarding, and spectator sports does nothing to cultivate or stimulate linguistic productivity. Many startup adults can't seem to craft a convincing argument to promote or defend their ideas on the job. And their deficient oral language is frequently echoed in their barely literate written communication, creating a rippling crippling effect. Table 10.1 lists and explains some key roles of expressive language at work.

A soundly defeated candidate for the school board in her community mournfully confessed to me at a conference that she hated making oral presentations in front of an audience. As she put it, "I completely choke up. It's not just nerves or panic. I have an awful time finding the words for my ideas; too often what I end up saying is way off the mark. I mean,

TABLE 10.1
EXPRESSIVE LANGUAGE OPERATIONS AT WORK

Expressive Language Role	Explanation
Persuasion and salesmanship	Getting others to buy your ideas, your products, and yourself
Thought development	"Thinking out loud" as a way to generate and enhance your own ideas
Written expression	Documenting and developing your thinking
Interpersonal relationship building and maintenance	Nurturing friendships and collaborative relationships
Self-coaching	Guiding yourself through tough challenges
Advice giving	Reaching out to help others cope and succeed

it doesn't say what I'm trying to say. That makes me nervous, and my nervousness makes my speech worse. I had so much I could have offered to the school board, but I fall apart when it comes to public speaking."

Here's a pediatric version of the same confession, a statement from a thirteen-year-old patient of mine: "I sit there in class a lot of times scared out of my mind. I can hear my stomach gurgling like a washing machine and sometimes I feel like I have to go to the bathroom whenever Mrs. Fenton starts calling on us in class. When I say stuff in a class discussion, it sounds real dumb, and it always takes me a really really long time to figure out how to say ideas. By the time I figure it out, the class has started talking about something else. I like classes where the teacher lectures and you don't have to say that much."

Apprehension about public or even semiprivate speaking is an increasingly common phobia among kids and adults. And this should not be the case. Throughout their school years, all kids ought to have abundant practice delivering oral presentations and participating in class discussions. They should be given discussion questions in advance so that they can have time to polish their expressive language fluency and accuracy. There needs to be a major educational push for oral language sophistication, helping students realize that expressing ideas well actually improves on those ideas. A person can work through his thoughts by talking them through. Thus, speaking (and writing) are ways of thinking. (As some people might say, "How do I know what I think until I hear what I say?") Language is more than a means of communicating thoughts; it also serves to synthesize and refine them. Here are suggestions for building verbal thought and communication in kids.

BUILDING VERBAL THOUGHT AND COMMUNICATION

Educate students to understand the importance
    of building literate language abilities and the capacity
    to elaborate verbally on their ideas.
Teach the differences between social and literate language.
Encourage children to use full sentences and elaborate
    on ideas, especially on topics that interest them
    (for example, sports, animals, TV shows, clothing).
Require frequent oral presentations in school.

Assign significant amounts of expository writing across subject
   areas in the curriculum.
Encourage long-term writing projects—with frequent revisions.
Have children summarize experiences, TV shows, movies, books,
   events in the news.
Give kids practice teaching younger children.
Ask students to describe in their own words how they went about
   accomplishing something (such as solving a tough math problem,
   scoring a soccer goal, picking out a blouse, or settling a dispute
   with a friend).
Teach and have students frequently apply the skills of debate
   and argument.
Conduct regular practice sessions with children using persuasive
   speech (trying to sell their ideas or a product).

The measures listed above can and should be implemented throughout the course of a child's education at home and in school. A sustained
emphasis on verbal thinking and expression will reap plenty of benefits
in work-life readiness.

Verbal Salesmanship
The world of work involves a rich blend of translation with salesman-
ship. Often the dual processes need to be deployed simultaneously. A
salesman must convince a customer of the value of his product and,
at the same time, urge her to buy it. People use language to sell themselves on a day-to-day basis. An employee has to interact amiably with
coworkers. When verbal transactions serve to alienate rather than attract colleagues, career crises are practically inevitable.

A perceptive administrative assistant at a stock brokerage firm offered the following observation: "It seems as if William has a knack
for turning off or alienating nearly everyone whenever he opens his
mouth. He keeps saying inappropriate things or jokes around in a way
that seems totally out of place. I sometimes feel embarrassed for him.
He doesn't seem aware of how his statements are affecting others.
Every time he lands a well-heeled new client, he broadcasts his victory
to all the other brokers in a tone of voice that conveys sheer arrogance.
Of course, they're a bit jealous, but William really rubs it in—probably
without realizing he's doing so. Even the vice president he reports to
can't stand the guy."

William is in jeopardy because people talk their way into or out of working relationships. In doing so, they make use of some social language tools, referred to collectively as verbal pragmatic functions. Some elements of social communication are nonverbal (such as the nuances of body language, facial expressions, and hand gestures), but spoken messages make up the principal communication cable connecting people. Many children and adults who are authentic "people persons," who demonstrate impressive interpersonal performance, are likely to be social language virtuosos, supreme verbal pragmatists. Others need help to understand the intricacies of interpersonal communication, and we can't afford to take it for granted that they will somehow acquire this awareness on their own.

It is not unusual to come across a kid rejected by his peers and described by adults as "totally lacking in any social skills." Much like William, "every time Aaron speaks, he manages to alienate just about every listener within hearing range. That boy just can't keep his foot out of his mouth," according to his dad. Aaron, along with many others like him, talks in a manner that sounds abrasive or hostile or arrogant or in some other way verbally out of step. Such kids may present themselves as downright ornery without intending to. Or they may keep picking inappropriate things to say, somehow disregarding the values and tastes of people around them. It is uncouth to broadcast an off-color joke in front of your boss's wife, whom you've just met for the first time. But kids and grown-ups with verbal pragmatic dysfunction often fail to realize that what they say, to whom they say it, and the way they say it may repel people as effectively as a spray of Mace.

Some young adults who managed to make the grade socially as kids are now unable to calibrate their interpersonal communication for on-the-job transactions. They may strive to sound like cool cats when a more businesslike, professional tone of voice and choice of words would work better for them. They may come across as adolescents in their twenties. Sometimes they seem unable to modify their language code according to the audience and the setting. One startup adult "dude" was described as a person who "always addresses you as if you're chugging a beer with him at Tony's Tavern." His ultracasual, supercool lingo failed to win him the confidence of his sixty-two-year-old, stiffly formal, brutally judgmental boss.

What contributes to effective social talk? One big-ticket item is your ability to inject just the right feelings into your speech. If you want or need to transmit enthusiasm regarding an idea someone is proposing to you, the pitch and rhythm of your voice, your selection of upbeat words, and your vocal inflections should be interpreted by listeners as unquestionably committed. "That sounds awesome; hey, I'd love to be a part of that project. That would really fit well with my interests." This kind of response contrasts with that of a highly artistic, blasé teenager, who, when asked to help design scenery for the spring musical pageant, replied, "That'll be all right, I guess. I don't mind. I guess I can do it for you this time." His muted tone and less-than-lukewarm words came across as smug, concealing his deep pleasure and gratification at being asked to help. He sounded as if he was barely willing to do this as a favor. He just could not project positive feelings through language, so his colleagues came to think of him as a loner, someone who didn't value their collaboration or friendship. In truth, he craved relationships and wondered why he was so infrequently approached by anyone. He was socially misunderstood because of the way he talked.

Closely related is a verbal pragmatic function called affective matching, where if someone is sad, you deploy a tone of voice and choice of words that reveal your compassion. Some people—both kids and adults—have a way of broadcasting inappropriate feelings, perpetually mismatching the moods they convey with the moods of the people they are with; their speech sends out jarring feelings like a fingernail grating on a chalkboard. As your manager and fellow marketing specialists at the department store are intently planning a winter sales campaign, you should not try to play the role of local jester. Hold back on your off-color jokes and clever puns—at least for now.

Additional facets of social communication include selecting appropriate items to talk about (called topic selection) and dwelling on them for the right length of time, knowing how and when to use humor, coming up with words that praise, reassure, or reinforce others, and using a language code appropriate to the people you are with (called code switching). The latter means you don't talk the same way to your boss as when you gossip with your closest chum. It sounds obvious, but many kids and adults can't figure out these social verbal fine tunings.

Imagine the following: Craig, a college freshman, is asked to see his economics professor about his failing grade on the final examination. He enters the distinguished faculty member's austere office and utters this spontaneous discourse: "Jeez, you know I'm real sorry I blew your exam. Believe it or not, pal, I studied my ass off, but I guess I blew it. Must have studied the wrong damned stuff or maybe partied too much the night before—just kidding—but for sure, I'm not making up excuses, buddy." The student is oblivious to the inappropriate jocularity and disrespectful tone. He could be immersed in a bull session with one of his fraternity brothers. Craig's no code switcher, and he's in for some rough sailing during his career.

Code switching has a diagnostic side: perspective taking. A competent speaker is able in a sense to peer into the mind of the person she is addressing. She can figure out what her listener already knows and needs to know at the same time that her communication X-ray apparatus is picking up moods and attitudes, so she doesn't come across as too glib or witty or carefree when her colleague is dismayed or depressed. A child with poor perspective taking may mention to his teacher that he went to the carnival with Bill. It doesn't occur to the boy that Mrs. Franklin has no way of knowing who Bill is. A perceptive perspective taker would have said, "I went to the carnival with my *cousin* Bill." As a first-year medical student I was once condemned to attend a lecture given by a young biochemist. The brilliant scientist's pedagogy was tedious, monotonous, and esoteric. I, for one, felt as if I'd been gagged and bound in my seat. He kept using terminology and concepts we students had not yet encountered, and he was oblivious to our audible yawns and transparent struggles to maintain our heads in a vertical plane as he spoke. He was later astonished to learn that we ranked him the worst teacher in his department, one reason he failed to get promoted to associate professor.

Table 10.2 summarizes some key aspects of verbal pragmatics. In my experience, people with verbal pragmatic dysfunction are rarely sufficiently aware of their shortcoming. Affected people have to perceive how the way they talk is alienating others. At the very least, they need to have their problem demystified and to receive periodic feedback from those close to them. They should be reminded when their choices of words and topics, their tone of voice, or their language code is causing interpersonal problems. There is a great need for professionals who can coach and counsel individuals with verbal pragmatic dysfunctions; at present these needs often go unrecognized and neglected.

ALLIANCE FORMATION AND REPUTATION MANAGEMENT

Igniting a career takes a lot more than just talk. A startup adult needs to gain penetrating insights and employ proper social tactics to forge cooperative and constructive alliances. In other words, he needs to know

TABLE 10.2
VERBAL PRAGMATIC FUNCTIONS

Function	Explanation
Conveyance of accurate feelings	Using the right words and intonations so that you don't sound angry, hostile, or inappropriate
Affective matching	Talking in a way that fits with the mood of those around you
Perspective taking	Judging and monitoring the needs and reactions of a listener
Code switching	Speaking differently with different people, depending on their relationship with you
Topic selection and maintenance	Choosing what to talk about and for how long
Humor regulation	Knowing when, how, and whether to be funny
Communication monitoring	Watching how others react to what you say, so that you can make adjustments
Conversational skill	Showing a give-and-take approach to communication (instead of delivering a monologue)
Complimenting	Communicating to help people feel good about themselves and you

how to interact, how to become a team player, whether in an operating room, at a gathering of military officers, or on the sixty-sixth floor of corporate headquarters. What does it take for a startup adult to form the alliances needed for such teamwork? First of all, it helps if she projects an image that works, exhibiting a personality and a pattern of behaviors that convey acceptability and affability.

Etching a Personal Image

Reputation management is a survival skill in school and in the workplace. What others say about you has a major impact on your happiness and your effectiveness. The image you project is a major factor in developing a reputation. Creating a positive image at the start is important because it is hard to change a reputation once one is established.

Startup adults must pass beyond most of their residual obsessions with coolness (chapter 2) and learn to come across in a more serious way.

IMAGE ETCHING

For Adolescents

Ultrarelaxed demeanor
Bravado and confidence
Minor risk-taking/rebelliousness
Tastes loyal to current trends
Appearance appealing to peers
Acceptable body "choreography"
Membership in a clique or gang
Sense of humor/cynicism
Physical attractiveness

For Startup Adults

Acting the role you're playing
Conveying specialized expertise
Pursuit of fitting recreation
Attractive physical appearance
Listening/sharing ability
Empathy, amiability, and caring
Reliability/honesty/dependability
Sense of humor/self-deprecation
Collegiality/collaborativeness
Enthusiasm/commitment

Well-crafted image building and appropriately subtle self-salesmanship are basic instincts for those who are born self-promoters. But vulnerable individuals, both kids and startup adults, have a tendency to keep bungling the job.

Adolescent image etching may continue through college, but an obsessive interest in coolness tactics and traits often becomes counterproductive, a serious deterrent during the embryonic stages of a career. Can a kid alter his adolescent marketing strategies at entry into adulthood? Many seem able to do so, but some don't—or can't.

A startup adult must project conscientiousness, readiness to roll up his sleeves and make an earnest contribution. He has to put a lid on boasting, show some humility, and reveal a willingness to grow, learn, and respond to supervision. He needs to display some loyalty to those above him and can no longer afford to disparage the adult world; he's now in it for the duration. He has to exude competence in his specialty, talk impressively about what he knows a lot about, and dress for the part. So the startup adult must ask herself, "Do I want to come across as an academic, a fashion-conscious person, an artist type, a benevolent caregiver, a techie?" She must discard the outmoded adolescent images of a nerd, geek, preppy, jock, dork, or cool dude.

It's never easy to know how you're coming across to others. Whether it's a teenager interacting with classmates and teachers or an employee relating to fellow workers and a boss, knowing how they're doing is a challenge for them. A startup adult has to be especially sensitive to how he is being perceived on the job. He needs to get in the habit of slowing down and observing how others perceive his ways of acting and reacting. "Am I being too outspoken or agressive?" "Do I come across as bossy?" "Am I curt or rude when the place gets busy?" "Do I need to be more assertive?" A startup adult may encounter rough going if she's rubbing people the wrong way and is unaware of it.

Creating a Market for Oneself

Once a startup adult determines what his projected image should be, the next task is to locate or create a demand for what he has to offer, and to identify the people with whom to form alliances. In school these aggregations take the form of cliques, or else they comprise collections of students with common interests (jocks, band members, computer game enthusiasts, skateboarders, cheerleaders, and so on). Successful participation in an alliance is both uplifting and protective. Kids crave inclusion, and some will sacrifice almost anything to obtain it. In its worst-case scenario, submersion in a clique may cause a teenager to lose all interest in schoolwork and family life.

Alliance formation in college seems almost mandatory for undergraduates in fraternities and sororities, and all sorts of clubby congregations. Many college students feel most comfortable as part of a herd. After college some alliances may continue. Recently there has been interest in what are called urban tribes (Watters 2003), groups of mostly startup adults who hang out together after work and on weekends.

They become almost families, many members marrying late, if at all, and feeling strongly supported by their fellow tribal members. Such a feeling of belonging can provide a sense of security, especially for those startup adults who have trouble starting up, those who still can't decide who they are and where they need to be heading in their lives.

Alliances get forged in the workplace too. Three abilities and behavior patterns are key in fostering solid alliance building at work: control level, collaboration, and conflict handling.

Control Level

To what extent does an individual feel compelled to be in total control, to dominate others and try to run the show single-handedly? There are countless kids repudiated by their resentful classmates because they must have everything their way; naturally, this insistence incites the wrath of their peers. That very same drive to dominate may hinder alliance formation in young adults. Most often, the best course is not to seek to dominate the team, not to strive in an obvious, aggressive way to be in control all of the time. At the other extreme are blind followers, those who have ceded all of their autonomy and are willing to go along with whatever the group seems to mandate or legislate. These sheep-like creatures may ultimately lose the respect of their teammates. Somewhere between compulsive group domination and total compliance with the will of the gang there exists an appropriate level of social control. Groups work best when leadership roles rotate imperceptibly and unintentionally among members. Each individual can decide from moment to moment or day to day whether she is being too assertive or overly passive as an alliance member.

Collaboration

Role definition and sharing make up the high-octane fuel mix for alliances. Each member of an alliance should have a sense of what he is bringing to the table and what benefits he is gaining from other members. To compile a strong record of collaboration, an individual student or startup adult should be able to describe lucidly his actual or potential role in the group and that of others. He should willingly share the risks, the blame, or the credit for the alliance's accomplishments or lack thereof. A lot of kids learn this when they play on a well-coached athletic squad. Others may harbor a built-in instinct for sharing. But some kids incessantly hog the spotlight, blame others for dropping the ball, or try to do it all. They are perceived as prima donnas, avowed soloists, and as such they have no allies.

Collaboration skills developed during the startup years may plant the seeds for two critical attainments that can arrive later, namely networking and leadership. As a person collaborates constructively, she may find that her group of allies keeps expanding, often beyond her own limited work site. She gains in her influence and has the gratification of knowing that she is having a broad impact. Leadership opportunities often follow. And it all starts with well-orchestrated collaboration.

Appropriate Competitive Behaviors

Competing is a common and perplexing component of interaction. Many kids learn sportsmanlike competitive skills through athletics. Others may be competitive in their quests for good grades, leadership opportunities, or popularity. The trick is to carry out a competitive effort without being too obvious and too brutal in the process. A competitive drive that is too transparent may offend your closest allies, the very people who can help you succeed. It can also intensify the desire of others to defeat your purposes. Kids need opportunities to talk and think about the areas in which they are competing and what it is they are competing for. They need help differentiating between socially sound and socially unwise ways of competing. They need to recognize that excessive boasting, verbal or physical aggression, cheating, and intentional sabotaging of other people's work are not effective ways of competing.

Some children and startup adults suffer from an intense fear of competition. That may lead them to become conservative non–risk takers or it could cause them to pursue areas of endeavor in life that seem, at least on the surface, not to entail competition. Sometimes they are later surprised to find out how ubiquitous competition actually is; it's better to learn how to compete.

Conflict Handling

No relationship always goes smoothly. Every sustained interaction has its unsightly potholes. Therefore, a key instrument of interaction is the ability to deal with the impasses and disagreements that sooner or later pepper all enduring relationships. For kids and for grown-ups, the challenge lies in resolving conflicts without resorting to aggression—verbal or physical—or to insidious passive aggression.

Deft conflict handling and negotiating can heal many a career glitch and cement working relationships and friendships. Most of all, conflict resolution is facilitated by talking—first to yourself and then to those with whom you are in conflict. Verbal mediation is a first-rate relationship lubricant and often totally eliminates friction. Often very young children who explode behaviorally when they can't bounce back from a conflict are told to take time-out, to go somewhere and cool off before they come to the negotiating table. Adults also should know how to impose a time-out on themselves during conflict resolution. This is tantamount to declaring a cease-fire. Then they should acknowledge that the cleverest resolvers of social conflict are those who are virtuosos in the art of compromise. Such people know how to formulate treaties; they can determine what territory to concede and what to hold onto. The give-and-take of negotiation is a skill that we should teach kids through active role-playing and the study of real cases of conflict. Adolescents who are talented negotiators will have an asset they can use throughout their careers. Those who are perpetually stymied in the face of conflict will carry serious mind debts.

EFFECTIVE CONFLICT HANDLING

Faced with interpersonal conflict, a person should be willing to:
- slow down and consider options
- rule out aggression as an option
- be flexible in thinking (as opposed to "digging in one's heels")
- talk things through (internally and interpersonally)
- admit when you're wrong (the ultimate social ploy!)
- compromise/make concessions
- offer some apologies as needed

POLITICAL BEHAVIOR

Whether a student is tuned into it or not (and surprisingly few are), he is embroiled in politics throughout his years at school. There is a never-ending chain of unconscious or intentional power plays, efforts at influence peddling, and attempts to gain the favor of important people, folks with clout who could influence profoundly your short-term happiness and your long-term well-being. For one thing, kids need to reckon with student leaders who have the clout to turn the tide of peer public opinion for or against them, making life a joy or a wreck. Even ignoring these people can be treacherous. And if you happen to be one of those omnipotent tastemakers, you have to be savvy enough to know how to sustain your power.

Most kids are veterans of stormy political conflicts in the form of sibling rivalry, as they compete for the favor and resources of their all-powerful parents. I sometimes wonder whether those homegrown civil wars represent basic training for grown-up battlefields.

But that's not all there is to juvenile politics; many successful students are keenly aware that they need to "polish the apple" when it comes to cultivating their teachers and professors. Such campaigning never abates, and so into and throughout the startup years, young adults encounter politics as usual, in the form of early career political maneuvering. Sadly and sometimes tragically, many startup adults are politically naïve, dangerously ignorant of the political arena they are entering. The battle casualties are numerous among such unsuspecting victims. At the conclusion of my pediatric training, one of my mentors told me that I was an intellectual giant and an institutional midget. That statement made little sense to me at the time; it definitely has meaning today. To succeed, it is not sufficient to know a lot, work hard, and turn out quality products or services. You have to make yourself liked, and you have to show you like the people you want to have like you. That's politics.

Political skill is vital throughout a career. Alain de Botton, in his book *Status Anxiety,* stresses the role of political behavior in the quest for career advancement. Moving up in an organization takes more than just competency on the job. As de Botton points out, "the path to promotion or its opposite may have an apparently haphazard relationship to performance. The successful alpinists of organizational pyramids may not be employees who are best at their tasks, but those who have mastered a range of political skills in which ordinary life does not offer instruction." That makes it essential that startup adults become students of their own political behaviors.

Self-Studying

Table 10.3 lists some of the political self-studying questions that can help an individual paddle through the currents of early career survival. These questions often are dealt with semi- or unconsciously, but they ought to be posed explicitly to ensure that a person slows down and

TABLE 10.3
POLITICAL SELF-STUDYING DURING THE STARTUP YEARS

Questions	Possible Answers
Who are the power brokers I need to please/impress?	*My supervisor, the boss's assistant, the COO, the human resources person.*
What will it take to please/impress them?	*Show up early, leave late, do more than they expect from me, act loyal to them.*
How can I remain on their good side?	*More of the above!*
How can I make them think I respect/admire them?	*Ask them good questions, offer them praise.*
How do I act to support, reassure, and win over my coworkers?	*Compliment them, assist them, socialize with some of them.*
How do I develop a constituency of backers (allies)?	*Confide in a small group of them, show them respect, offer them praise.*
What are my competitive avantages that can boost my status?	*I'm good with the details. I'm a plugger and a strong problem solver.*
How can I use my competitive advantages without alienating others?	*I'll be careful not to boast or tell people how hard I'm working.*
How can I tell how I'm doing politically?	*I'll ask for feedback. I'll keep a close eye on facial expressions when I speak. I'll notice who tries to go to lunch with me.*

thinks them through thoroughly. The examples obviously have no absolutely right or wrong answers, but they are worth bringing up and reconsidering on a regular basis, for they form the core of astute political thinking. It is crucial to ask oneself, "Okay, now, what's my present political situation?"

How do kids and young adults acquire the habit of active political self-investigation? I'm afraid for the most part it's hit or miss! To make things less haphazard, I would like to see kids taught about career politics while they are still in school. Table 10.4 poses the same basic political questions to a high schooler.

Kids can benefit from performing frequent political analyses on themselves in writing. Every student should be required as well to plan

TABLE 10.4
POLITICAL SELF-STUDYING: THE STUDENT VERSION

Questions	Possible Answers
Who are the power brokers I need to please/impress?	*My teachers, a student leader, two other popular students.*
What will it take to please/impress them?	*I'll ask my teachers good questions, see them after school, show interest; I'll join, help, and support the student leaders.*
How can I remain on their good side?	*Keep trying to be helpful and supportive.*
How can I make them think I respect/admire them?	*Ask their opinions, seek their help, keep letting them know I admire them.*
How do I act to support, reassure, and win over my fellow students?	*Make friends with them, join them at lunch, invite them to do things with me.*
How do I develop a constituency of backers (allies)?	*Join a team or club, form a committee, try to be seen as a leader.*
What is my competitive edge that can boost my status?	*My personality, good looks, athletic ability, computer skill.*
How can I use my competitive edge without offending others?	*Help them, avoid boasting, say some things that put myself down.*
How can I tell how I'm doing politically?	*See if I'm getting phone calls, good teacher comments, party invitations from peers.*

some hypothetical campaign to attract customers, to get a raise or promotion, to win an award, or to gain supporters for a cause. If they do so, political self-questioning can evolve into a habit, a practice kids will perfect through their startup years, and one that will reap abundant dividends.

Diplomacy

Once an individual acquires a realistic view of his status and needs, he can develop ways to maintain or increase his effectiveness in the political arena. To do so, he needs to hone his diplomatic skills and make use of some well-thought-out strategies. He needs to know which working relationships could stand some strengthening and which are of less consequence or are in better shape. He can then take aim by being careful to convey loyalty, respect, and competence in his communication with important people. He can also determine how he can best support the causes represented by such individuals. The causes may include a profit motive, an altruistic mission, or a quest for fame or power. That's diplomacy, an essential requirement for work-life readiness.

WORKING ON WORKING RELATIONSHIPS

The French existentialist philosopher Jean-Paul Sartre once wrote, *"L'enfer, c'est les autres"* ("Hell is others"). All too easily we can become tyrannically controlled and lose our freedom and our identity at the hands of others. Startup adults need to be alerted to the ways in which they can be wounded seriously as a result of their interactions. They must also realize that they can prevent such harm by becoming communicators, alliance and reputation builders, and wise politicians.

Relationship building is ongoing, and we all keep learning more about the process through direct experience. As we interpret such experience, we modify and diversify our styles of interaction to meet changing needs. The underlying themes of communication, alliance and reputation building, and political practice persist, but there is always room for growth. And that growth is most likely to occur when it is consciously cultivated and monitored.

DEVELOPING SKILLS OF INTERACTION

Communication

Conveying thoughts
Transacting with language
Using good verbal pragmatics

Alliance Formation and Reputation Management

Etching a personal image
Creating a market
Regulating control
Collaborating

Appropriate competitive behaviors
Handling conflict

Political Behavior

Studying one's own political needs and actions
Using effective diplomacy

Part Three

MIND GROWERS

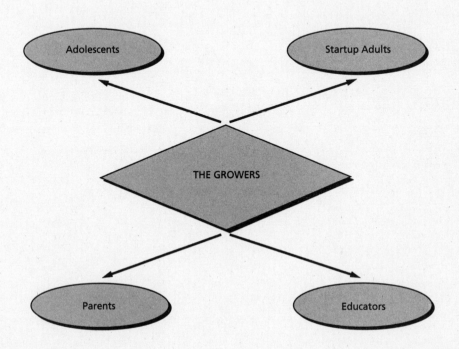

Preventing and remediating work-life unreadiness has to be a cooperative effort among parents, the educational system, teenagers, and
startup adults themselves. In part three we will explore what roles parents, educators, adolescents, and current startup adults should play. It
examines the ways in which the growth processes covered in part two
can be nurtured through a combined and concerted effort. These chapters are intended as a summons to action, a stimulus for changing some
of the ways in which we raise and educate kids, and a rethinking of the
manner in which teenagers and startup adults regard their present and
future lives.

11
PARENTS

Achieving the Right Mixes

My lack of ambition severely limited me if you look at a career as how far you could go. My dad has always been disappointed in me because I took this set of skills that I have and abilities and kind of curtailed them to fit my happiness. He grew up in the generation where you go as far as you possibly can to provide for your family.

D.M., age 28

ere's an excerpt of a telephone call from Adele Stone, the mother of Clifford, a patient of mine with some mildly persistent attention and language dysfunctions:

Mrs. Stone: Dr. Levine, I can't stop wondering if I know what I'm doing when it comes to raising Clifford.

Dr. Levine: What do you mean?

Mrs. Stone: I mean he's doing so much better in school these days, and he seems a lot happier. His self-esteem has improved, and he is concentrating better at home and in school. But you know, he's still very demanding. He wants attention all the time, and Clifford longs for truckloads of entertainment or new toys or special events. He's very manipulative until he gets his way or outlasts us.

Dr. Levine: Well, you know that's not so abnormal at his age.

Mrs. Stone: Yes, but we give him so much of our time and energy and even our thinking: he forces us to think about him all the time. We keep saying we want him to be happy; we're so afraid to displease the kid.

Dr. Levine: I guess it's a matter of degree. You shouldn't be catering to his every whim, and you need to set some consistent limits.

Mrs. Stone: We try to do that, but he still gets so much from us and from others. Most of the time, he's on some kind of nonstop, totally self-centered high, just having a ball. He's so cute and ingratiating that even his teachers seem bent on entertaining him (and the other students too). There's part of me that's happy to see him so happy most of the time and part of me that feels he would be much better off if he were more deprived or frustrated. I know that sounds awful, but I'm really worried that his childhood will be an impossible act to follow! When you've gotten so much as a kid, what is there to look forward to as a grown-up? How does having twenty pleasure-packed years get you ready to take on the next fifty in the real world?

Dr. Levine: I have to agree with you, Mrs. Stone. The challenge will be to find for Clifford the right mixes of fun and of lessons to be learned. . . .

Numerous ingredients go into the mix as a child is raised. The ingredients tend to come in pairs that have to be balanced to create just the right mixes. Some of the most influential and challenging mixes are summarized below.

THE RIGHT MIXES

Ingredient			Balancing Ingredient
praise	←	→	criticism
discipline	←	→	freedom
parental intervention	←	→	self-help
free play	←	→	programming
leisure	←	→	work
cultural assimilation	←	→	cultural insulation
individual pursuits	←	→	group activities
interaction with adults	←	→	interaction with peers
family life	←	→	life beyond the family
general abilities	←	→	specialized affinities/skills
body	←	→	mind
the present	←	→	the future

PRAISE AND CRITICISM

Kids thrive on the right mix of positive and negative reinforcement. Most of all, they need to feel that they perform well for an appreciative yet constructively critical audience. And there's no more influential and motivating audience than their parents. I meet many kids who in their hearts believe they disappoint their mothers and fathers. They may grow into the startup adults with heavy mind debts described in chapter 2. Kids know their parents love them, but they need to feel that their parents respect them. They should overhear their moms and dads boasting about them to friends or relatives on a regular basis. That provides momentum, the incentive and optimism about the future they'll need to keep going along their trajectory to the startup years.

Praise does not preclude constructive criticism. But negative feedback must be worded tactfully. It should refer more to the future than the past. "Joe, from now on I think you should start your homework right after supper and then take time off before you go to sleep." Critical comments should be phrased as serious recommendations rather than condemnations or indicators of disrespect for the child. Statements like "You're never going to amount to anything" run the risk of becoming self-fulfilling prophecies.

DISCIPLINE AND FREEDOM

In chapter 3, I pointed to a growing tide of parents who are fearful of their kids, especially teenagers, who in so many cases have usurped the power in a family. Domestic anarchy is in no one's best interests, so parents should strive to overcome their fear that an unhappy teenager can and will do bad things to herself. If anything, excessive permissiveness can make such self-defeating actions more likely. Parents simply have to take command, even at the risk of upsetting or temporarily alienating a kid.

The earlier this power structure is established, the better; it is very hard to institute a whole new set of governing policies when a kid is approaching the age of fifteen. One father informed me that when his kids were young, he told them on several occasions, "Look, this home you're living in is definitely not a democracy. Your mom and I do things our way around here. When you grow up, you can become the rulers of your house." Kids need and want such constraints when imposed fairly and firmly. Limits actually help them feel valued and protected. A child can perceive them as proof of a parent's love and caring.

In preparation for the startup years, children and teenagers need to see that over time they are being given increasing authority and freedom, and ideally this progressive loosening of the reins should be mapped out in advance. For instance, teenagers should know that their curfews will be increasingly lenient in two or three years.

At some point parents have to back off and allow their kid to sink or swim. The more their mothers and fathers hassle and cajole, especially about homework, the more output-resistant the kid may become. That is a signal for parents to retreat. If their child fails to hand in his homework, he'll have to cope with the consequences. Such a strategic retreat can be heartbreaking to a conscientious mother or father, but it is necessary if they don't want him to become his own worst enemy. Some adolescents enjoy a bizarre sense of power and satisfaction from upsetting their parents, detonating nightly scenes at home. That drama is counterproductive and destructive; parents should refuse to participate in the warfare. At the same time, no kid should feel abandoned; parents should make it clear they are accessible—on call, so to speak—to consult on homework assignments and other educational demands.

PARENTAL INTERVENTION AND SELF-HELP

Kids need priming and personal experience to handle the dilemmas and the glitches of life in the startup years and beyond. They have to become resilient in the face of setbacks, and there will be no shortage of minor and major crises. When a child faces a problem, he should learn from his clashes with these barriers. Parents face a tough judgment call in determining whether or not to come to the rescue of a child in crisis. Generally, the answer should be that mothers and fathers should dispense some advice (when asked for it) without actually volunteering for active service. Instead of immediately having a talk with a teacher or a classmate's parent, a mom should help her fourteen-year-old think of what to say to that teacher or how to deal with that kid who is bullying him on the bus. At a certain point the child may need some strong-armed advocacy from a parent, but that should always be a last resort. It would be a shame for the child to grow up lacking his own coping tools and conflict resolution capacities.

FREE PLAY AND PROGRAMMING

In our discussion of brainstorming (page 170), there was mention of the cognitive hazards of overprogramming kids. Parents have to reel in their zeal when it comes to giving their kids nearly every available form of lesson and adult-managed entertainment. They should preserve time for kids to do nothing or else to improvise spontaneously. This is a vital part of the development of creative thinking, independence, and initiative taking. Harpsichord lessons and team sports are worthy pursuits, but they stifle some essential growth processes when they totally eclipse free play. There needs to be the right mix.

Work and play are both essential to a child's mental health and maturity. Kids learn through both channels. But what is of little or no value is what is called "disengaged time," those intervals when someone is neither having fun nor accomplishing anything. In an essay in the collection *Becoming Adult* (Csikszentmihalyi and Schneider 2001), Jennifer Schmidt and Grant Rich write, "Disengagement is characterized by teenagers as being neither productive nor enjoyable, and is commonly accompanied by feelings of low self-esteem. Spending large amounts of time in this unpleasant, unfocused state is unlikely to promote positive development." (p. 93) The authors have found that teenagers who devote large portions of their day to disengaged activities may have the most trouble finding their ways in a vocation. Watching TV, "hanging around" with friends, listening idly to music, and Instant Messaging are some examples of disengagement. Parents should do what they can to prevent disengaged time from displacing more productive leisure and work ventures.

Child's play should include fertile opportunities for exploration. Eva Schmitt-Rodermund and Fred Vondracek (1999) studied what they called exploratory behavior in adolescence and concluded that it was important to help kids acquire broad interests: "We do know that exploration is one of the most important precursors of a good person-environment fit and a choice of an occupation. Considering that most people spend the majority of their life working and that satisfaction with work is very much related to health and a sense of well being, one could hardly value exploration too highly." There is much to be said for having kids shop around activities in music, art, sports, animal life, and the world of politics, in a sense trying on possibilities for interest and continuing engagement.

LEISURE AND WORK

No one would advocate an "all work and no play" approach to child rearing. On the other hand, we may be facing a rampant epidemic of juvenile hedonism. Insatiability is on the rise (page 74), and more and more kids harbor an intense need to be pleasurably stimulated through all hours of their waking days. Might there be a hazardous imbalance between work and fun? That's quite possible.

Earlier in this book, I argued that schools are set up to teach kids how to learn but that parents have the job of teaching them how to work (page 153). Reporting on their research in the collection *Becoming Adult*, Kevin Rathunde, Mary Ellen Carroll, and Molly Pei-lin Huang conclude, "In today's economy parents rarely teach children the work skills they will need as adults. Instead the role of the family in socializing children to an occupational future should consist of arranging for schooling and exposing children to the values, motivations, attitudes, and expectations they will need to find a satisfying productive niche when they reach adulthood." Work routines, practices, and sites have to be nonnegotiable facets of family life: the more consistency on these issues, the better. In table 9.4, I suggested ways parents can turn their kids into workers. Again, the right mix is important. Childhood should be fun. The challenge is to help kids work hard and play hard, but the play segment shouldn't flow into everything a child does. They shouldn't come to feel that washing dishes is unfair because "it's no fun" or that it is an affront to do schoolwork that feels boring. Hedonistic kids will have trouble adjusting to the petty rigors of work in their startup years. After all, the toils of the startup years are not meant to be part of a never-ending arcade game.

CULTURAL ASSIMILATION AND INSULATION

To some extent people become products of their cultural backgrounds, which have two components: one a blend of religious, national, and ethnic identity and the other the evolving norms of the society in which a child grows up. We don't want kids to be so narrow and parochial that they cannot appreciate the value and beauty in other cultures. In any career they will need to relate effectively to people of diverse backgrounds.

Under the influence of mass culture, kids are incessantly pressured and cajoled to go along with the latest fashions and fads. To what extent should parents put lids on their children's blind obedience to such influences? Do kids need protection from commercial exploitation? Should mothers and fathers judge the value or potential harm of their kids' interests? I think so, and that often means setting some limits. If a child is mesmerized by the latest computer games, he may need to be insulated from the cognitive dulling that results from hours spent handling a remote control. Reading, talking, playing imaginative games, building models, and participating in sports will do much more for literacy and socialization than engaging in computer games. Nevertheless, to qualify as a solid citizen of his culture, a kid may need time at his PlayStation. Preset time limits also should be put in place when a kid starts to obsess over Instant Messaging, skateboarding, the latest TV crazes, and other irresistible trends. Many of these offer instant gratification that risks instilling aversions to sustained work and the delay of rewards. Bob Eubanks, a highly successful investment banker, told me recently that the biggest problem he encounters among some young MBA graduates who have come to work for him is that they seem "totally unable to think long-term." If they don't see instant results, they feel crushed. That shortsightedness can be lethal in the investment world and in all spheres of accomplishment.

INDIVIDUAL PURSUITS AND GROUP ACTIVITIES

There's much to be said for rugged individualism. In his book *Leading Minds,* Dr. Howard Gardner points out that numerous remarkable leaders knew how to survive and thrive on the fringes of their society. Many did not feel driven to be popular kids at the center of their peer constellation, unlike some adolescents, who are at risk for a dangerously mediocritizing addiction to their peers. Such teens are desperate to be welcomed into a group and sometimes can think of nothing else. At its worst, this phenomenon causes them to lose sight of their own individuality, the inner direction that can enable them to commit to a fruitful work life.

But addiction to one's peer group is different from sharing values and interests with others, which is a vital part of human development. Parents should stress to their teenager the need to balance his group activities with interests of his own. Together they should list activities that fall into these categories and come up with ways to rectify drastic imbalances.

INTERACTION WITH ADULTS AND WITH PEERS

In his outstanding book *The Childhood Roots of Adult Happiness,* Dr. Ned Hallowell speaks of the importance of connectedness in the life of a growing child—connections to family, to the past, to friends, and to himself among others. He emphasizes the child's need to connect with neighborhood and community. As part of their connecting processes, kids heading toward their startup years need to invade the world of adults, learn to communicate with grown-ups, study them, and relate effectively to them. In an earlier chapter I pointed out that too many kids identify exclusively with their peers. They have little or no experience relating to any adults with the exception of their teachers, whom some may view mainly as evaluators.

There was a time when children learned some of their most important lessons about growing up from their elders. Children should be able to relate to some grown-ups who are not their teachers or close relatives. In doing so, kids need to become students of adulthood. They can form meaningful connections with grown-ups, including relatives beyond the immediate family, neighbors, shop owners, their parents' friends, their friends' parents, and other trusted people in the community. Also, parents should share their insights and stories about grown-up life on a regular basis. If a father is having problems with an employee or a customer or a fellow worker, those issues might make terrific dinner table conversation, allowing a child in fact to serve as a sounding board at the same time she is learning about the realities of careers. Parents can reveal to their kids their own career challenges (past and present). When company is coming, make sure the kids stick around and dine with the adults. Then the next morning there can be some candid talk about the guests or relatives. Each adult can serve as a short textbook chapter for a kid.

Nowadays many children and adolescents are likely to consume an immense serving of their information and values from friends and from television commercials. So make certain that every child vicariously experiences some of the agonies and ecstasies of adult work by "studying" plenty of adults and learning to communicate well with all kinds of grown-up minds.

THE FAMILY LIFE AND LIFE BEYOND THE FAMILY

Kids need to feel that they are loved as indispensable members of a family. As Robert Frost put it in his poem "The Death of the Hired Man," "Home is the place where, when you have to go there, / They have to take you in." When kids are in distress at home, their lives seem to fall apart.

Unhappiness sometimes springs from a child's suspicion that he is not a deserving member of his family. I have seen countless instances of this problem when there is mismatch between a parent and a child. It may be a case of incompatibility of temperament or a chronic personality conflict. Or a child may have a neurodevelopmental profile and a set of interests and assets that are out of step with those of his parents. For example, a father may be a former college athlete and a die-hard sports fan, while his fourteen-year-old son is mainly interested in playing the viola and acting in school plays. They need to be able to laugh at their differences, to tolerate and admire each other for who they are.

A kid should come to perceive his family not just as a clump of loved ones but as a clan of dependable collaborators. In particular, mothers and fathers can strengthen the bonds with their offspring by becoming their partners in exploration. Together parents and their kids should visit and talk about historical places, factories, museums, and zoos. We often associate field trips with school, but they are likely to be even more meaningful when a family undertakes them. During such excursions, families should talk about the people involved in such sites (for example, the zookeepers, curators, artists, and workers). They should speculate on what their work lives must be like.

A number of recent studies have shown that parents can play a powerful role in helping their children develop and pursue exploratory behaviors (Schmitt-Rodermund and Vondracek 1999). In a teenager these behaviors augur well for a goal-directed orientation toward a career. Helping a child collect rocks for his collection, enlisting her help in visiting car dealerships before purchasing a new automobile, going on a nature walk together, or picking out new wallpaper are practical expeditions the family can share in.

Family life can also include sensitive academic support for a child. Parents should show a strong interest in what has occurred in school every day. They should try to learn from their kids, allowing them to talk about new facts or skills they have picked up in school. Parents need to advocate strongly for children who are struggling in school, making sure their profiles are understood and handled well by their teachers. The movement toward home schooling for certain students has saved many a vulnerable child who failed to fit the mold in a school. This action should be viewed as a last resort since being out in the real kid world is an integral part of education.

Parents also can collaborate by sharing interests with their child. Joint projects such as gardening, repairing a power mower, or caring for animals are great ways to help kids see the connection between hard labor and fun.

Kids also need to establish a life beyond the confines of the family. Over time, they will have to seek more and more approval from the outside world and learn how to use it as a resource. That outside world encompasses friends, teachers, bosses, and others with whom they need to interact or collaborate. Children who are too sheltered by their families are at risk for serious work-life unreadiness. So are kids who have somehow grown away from their families or even repudiated them in favor of their peers. There should be a quest for the right mixes between family ties and values, on the one hand, and alliances at work and in school.

GENERAL ABILITIES AND SPECIALIZED AFFINITIES/SKILLS

In their striving to raise a competent child, parents need to watch two brands of performance. They must aim for the right mix between general capabilities, such as reading, math, and motor skills (for example, bicycle riding), and specialized talents and interests, such as raising goats, playing the bassoon, or creating animal sculptures fabricated from objects found at the dump. Schools teach many of the general competencies with the sometime support of parents. Mothers and fathers have to lead the way in helping kids discover their personal affinities, those sometimes partially concealed pockets of talent that can develop into passions and areas of expertise, to say nothing of careers.

General abilities involve the twelve growth processes (chapters 7–10), and parents also assume a fundamental role in cultivating these functions. They can nurture a child's inner direction through regular discussions of his emerging strengths and affinities and those parts of his mind that need attention. Any such talk should be couched in very positive and optimistic terms, recognizing how desperately kids crave the respect of their mothers and fathers. There should be regular speculation about how the child might be using his strengths and interests someday as a startup adult. Parents can help with the second *I,* interpretation, through rich dinner table dialogue and exchanges during car trips (with the radio off). Together they can analyze issues extending from current world events to conflicts the family has with some neighbors, or stresses the student is contending with at school. At home kids can be helped to develop strong instrumentation, enhancing their working capacities, organizational skills, and evaluative thinking. The latter can be honed through sage consumerism—letting a child help decide on the best TV set to buy or jointly critiquing an advertisement or political speech. Finally, parents can be active in helping kids work on interaction, the fourth *I.* They should be reviewing with their child various incidents and social dilemmas involving interactions with peers, siblings, and teachers. A parent can be a child's most effective social tutor.

BODY AND MIND

A kid should be of sound mind and body. We can nurture the physical well-being of a child at the same time we see to it that her mind stays in shape. But blending the two can be challenging. To what extent is a child deriving gratification from the operation, decoration, and fortification of his body, and to what extent is he experiencing the pleasures of intellectual growth? Sometimes there's a serious imbalance in either direction. Some kids are addicted to what I call visual-motor ecstasy. They are infatuated with objects moving rapidly in space. Others become so absorbed in athletic pursuits that the cultivation of a mind seems irrelevant to them, and they may barely put up with formal education. In other instances, kids start to perceive themselves as fashion icons and devote too much of their lives to a prolonged self-beautification campaign that may extend well into adult life, if not throughout a lifetime.

Plenty of studious kids are sedentary and lose out on the social advantages of sports, the character-building elements of physical teamwork, and the emotional benefits that come from feeling adequate (but not ecstatic) about your body. They risk becoming overweight and having to endure the physical and mental burdens of obesity.

Motor and bodily self-satisfaction is a great tonic for bolstering self-esteem in a kid (and in an adult as well). Finally, keeping in shape is important for everyone's physical well-being, a vital contributor to work-life readiness.

THE PRESENT AND THE FUTURE

Some children derive tremendous pleasure from dreaming about the future. In fact, some of their make-believe play enables them to try on different adult roles. During late elementary school, kids often try to act like adolescents, and during adolescence, teens expend considerable energy trying to act like sophisticated and seasoned young adults. This is all part of normal exploration and experimentation.

Many adolescents are myopic and need help connecting the past and the present with the future. Parents should encourage long-term viewing. Ideally, teenagers should visit their parents at work on a regular basis and have discussions at home about different career pathways and what they might offer. A parent may need to point out something like this: "When I look back over the last ten years, it is obvious that you keep coming back to your love of animals. To this day, you seem to be happiest when you're on the back of a horse or fooling around with the dogs. Don't you think this interest will influence what you do when you grow up? You could be a vet, or maybe your love for taking care of animals will change into a love for taking care of people, so you might become a pediatrician or a nurse." In other words, parents can assist kids in the search for their life's recurring themes (page 87) and help them perceive the ways in which parts of their present and past lives connect to the future or maybe even predict it.

Parents should often inject optimism when discussing what might lie ahead for a child, and this should be done without heavy sermonizing. Saying, "If you work hard, you'll be able to . . ." probably won't work. Most kids just ignore such admonitions. In addition, mothers and fathers need to resist the temptation to keep confronting a child with the height of the ladder he has to climb to get somewhere: "If you do well in high school, you'll get into a top college, and if you get into a top college, you'll be accepted at a top law school. And if you graduate from a top law school, you can work for a top law firm, and if you work for a top law firm, you can make more money and can get an even better job somewhere else after that—like you could become an appellate judge or something." Ladder talk like this conveys all the wrong messages and may serve to douse ambition. Overemphasizing the steepness of the climb makes goals seem out of reach, or as one teenager said after hearing his father engage in such ladder preaching, "Sounds pretty grubby to me."

Parents should instead strive to bring up the future without undermining the dividends of the present. Adult success should be depicted as attractive and attainable, something fun to ponder and plan for. Parents should also observe that getting there is not like climbing a hazardous ladder; in truth, it's half the fun! Such parent input can induce the right mix of thought about the present and the future.

Table 11.1 summarizes the various right mixes and offers some advice for parents on how to achieve these optimal blends.

TABLE 11.1
SOME OF THE RIGHT MIXES

Mixes	Recommendations (in the best of all possible worlds)
Praise and criticism	Every six criticisms from parents should be counterbalanced by at least four statements of honest praise!
Discipline and freedom	Certain activities should be declared free from imposed parental oversight and others supervised and monitored closely. For example, at age sixteen, it might be proclaimed (preferably in writing) that homework is not run by parents, nor is the esthetic condition of the bedroom, but nightly curfews, chores around the house, the state of the shared bathroom, as well as spending limits are under tight control.
Parental intervention and self-help	Parents should do more listening than advising and more advising than doing battle for the child.
Free play and programming	All kids should have at least several hours a week during which they are obliged to entertain themselves (possibly with one other child and without TV, musical accompaniment, video games, or structured pursuits, such as organized sports).
Leisure and work	Before finishing high school, all kids should have direct work experience and jobs to do at home. Their lives should include 75 percent work (including school) and 25 percent nonwork entertainment. Of course, ideally, it would be best if they could also derive some of their pleasure allocation from their work!

(continued on next page)

Mixes	Recommendations (in the best of all possible worlds)
Cultural assimilation and insulation	There should be a minimum of several occasions per month when a child is collaborating or playing with kids and/or adults very different in their backgrounds from his own. Also, there should be a maximum total of ninety minutes a day of computer game immersion, TV viewing, and headphone time.
Individual pursuits and group activities	All kids should spend several hours a week engaged in activities few or none of their peers tend to embrace, pursuits that interest them and affirm their uniqueness and perhaps their ultimate competitive advantage.
Interaction with adults and with peers	Parents should ensure that kids are friends of some adult friends of the family and, at least twice a month, have extended conversations with adults who are not their teachers or close relatives, in addition to their interactions with peers in and out of school.
Family life and life beyond the family	Parents should have at least one ongoing project as well as regularly scheduled exploratory expeditions with each of their children. Kids should also have regular community activities that exclude parents.
General abilities and specialized affinities	In addition to general education in school, a child should be spending part of each week working on his or her specialized/unique competencies.
Body and mind	While encouraging interest in body image and motor effectiveness, parents can initiate sophisticated meal talk, cultural activities, and other home-based forms of shared learning.
The present and the future	Mothers and fathers should seek opportunities at least twice a month to discuss a child's future with him one to one in a nonthreatening, nonpreachy, upbeat way.

PARENTING YOUNG ADULTS WITH WORK-LIFE UNREADINESS

Nothing depletes a parent's patience and spirit more than witnessing her precious child adrift in his or her twenties and appearing to be heading nowhere in life. Mothers and fathers all too often are condemned to stand by as their startup adult suffers the aches and anxieties of the unanticipated disillusionment so widespread in this age group. Complicating matters is the fact that the newly formed adult is torn between declaring proud independence from parental influence and seeking early readmission to the womb! Parents need to be sensitive to that ambivalence and proceed with caution as they try to be helpful.

In her book *The Myth of Maturity,* Terri Apter offers a statement that should guide the parents of startup adults who are faltering. "Buying into false expectations, they think their children are ready to fly the nest, when they are simply moving away temporarily and are more in need of support. Parents assume their daughters and sons want to push them away—when they simply need a different kind of closeness."

What is that "different kind of closeness"? In particular, how do parents deal with a son or daughter who is showing signs of work-life unreadiness? Parents cannot waver in their displays of respect for their kid—no matter how they see things going for him. Being a serious disappointment to your mother or father is a wound that's slow to heal. Sometimes a display of respect requires heroic flexibility and tolerance on the part of a parent. Julia Sampson reported to me that her daughter Sandra, a former patient of mine, dropped out of law school because she was bored and despised the competition and adversarial feel of the place. Now she is designing and crafting jewelry in Florence, Italy. Sandra loves what she is doing but hasn't been able to sell a single beaded brooch or bracelet. Her mother doubts she ever will sell much of anything, because she isn't all that talented or original. Meanwhile, Sandra is nearly broke and lives for her friendships and her craft. She insists that she doesn't care if her work sells or not; she is an artist and is creating as a form of expression uncontaminated by commercial influences. Mrs. Sampson, instead of insisting her daughter return to law school, is offering Sandra total moral (but not financial) support. Her daughter knows she is loved; Sandra has to feel as well that she is respected. Love and respect foster closeness. I think Mrs. Sampson is on the right track, although it probably crushes her to think that Sandra's legal career will never materialize. But a sustained positive relationship with her parents is more valuable to Sandra than a law career.

Here's another common real-life melodrama: Dennis was an outstanding student in high school and in college. He worked energetically and always pulled off honor grades. An economics major, at the end of his senior year he decided to forego his acceptance at the Wharton School of Business and instead take a year off to travel. More than four years have passed, and Dennis is still traveling. He "bums" around in Nepal, Burma, and Tibet, managing to land odd jobs. He is bearded, well tattooed, and asymmetrically earringed. Dennis claims to be seeking true spiritual fulfillment and has rejected the values and aspirations of his working-class family, who once glistened with pride at his accomplishments. At first Dennis's dad lectured, moralized, and proselytized his son through letters, emails, and phone calls—to no avail. He recalled all the sacrifices he had made to pay Dennis's "now wasted" tuitions. But without question, the more he preached and vented his wrath, the further he alienated Dennis.

Putting to use sage advice from a counselor, Dennis's parents recently have come to terms with his nomadic lifestyle. It's never too late. They are keeping a scrapbook of photos from their son's travels. They are saving their money so they can meet Dennis in Katmandu, his favorite city, where Dennis will get a chance to show off to his parents his deep knowledge of Nepalese culture and history. They can't wait; neither can he. By his own account, Dennis starting to get restless about his restlessness. He is, he says, starting to think about "putting down some roots and getting going with my life." It would have been a serious mistake for his parents to rush that realization and that readiness. They needed to quell their anger and disappointment and demonstrate tolerance and understanding. Eventually they did, and it worked.

So it is that parents of work-life-unready young adults have no choice but to be heroically and perhaps also stoically patient, respectful, and tolerant. The process can be especially tormenting when a parent has clung to an image of what an offspring will be like, say at age twenty-five, and that budding adult turns out to be heading in an entirely different and less lofty direction. Your former altar boy/future surgeon is now a contented busboy!

Supplementing their generous donations of patience, respect, and tolerance, parents need to be available as career consultants, but only when their startup adult specifically requests such services. Even then, parents should avoid preaching, acting too sure of themselves, or offering glib, oversimplified, and predictable advice. Most of all, they have to serve as attentive and compassionate listeners. In general, confess that you don't know what your daughter ought to do instead of serving up quick fixes that she will find ill-fitting and useless—in which case she may never ask for your input again.

Parents should consider the twelve growth processes when they have a son or daughter who is floundering during the startup years. Are there some critical abilities that are lacking? Does she have adequate insight into herself? Is she sharp enough at understanding job expectations and concepts, or is she misinterpreting important aspects of her work? Does she have the right tools to succeed? If not, what's missing? Finally, is she having trouble establishing working relationships? Once the gaps are identified, parents should share their observations with the startup adult. Sometimes she may need outside counseling from a mental health specialist or a career counselor. Most of all, a startup adult has to be aware of his gaps and decide whether to try to repair them or choose a pathway that bypasses them.

Finally, there is nothing wrong with providing room and board (with or without laundry and dry cleaning services) for a disenfranchised startup adult, a practice that is becoming increasingly common, especially when jobs and money are tight. But when a son or daughter moves back, parents have to be careful to keep their distance and honor the independence and privacy of their adult kid. If feasible, some financial support may be desirable, but it is dangerous to be too generous by bankrolling substantially a young struggler. In the long run, too much financial dependence fosters bitter resentment on both sides.

Table 11.2 summarizes some bad and good things parents do when their offspring have a tough time getting through the startup years. With care, wisdom, and ample love, parents can help their child make it through a work-life crisis. A startup adult may be more needy and more ready than ever to tighten the fragile links between parent and child.

TABLE 11.2
A PARENT'S ROLE WHEN A SON OR DAUGHTER
   REVEALS WORK-LIFE UNREADINESS

Action	Value	Comment
Preaching or lecturing	bad	It doesn't work, and it alienates startup adults.
Being tolerant and patient	good	Some people take more time than others to settle into a career.
Criticizing or accusing	bad	It does no good; it might make the young adult try to punish his parents by failing in life or disgracing them.

(continued on next page)

Action	Value	Comment
Letting a startup adult know you're disappointed in him	lethal	There's no one a person wants to impress more than his parents; it could wreck his self-esteem and motivation.
Bankrolling	good and bad	It can help to subsidize partially (if you can afford it) but total support destroys incentives.
Allowing a startup adult to live at home	neutral	It can be supportive and helpful if parents keep some distance.
Offering advice	good and bad	It can work when requested, but should not be glib, unrealistic, or moralistic.
Protecting	good and bad	Overprotection backfires, but some naïve startup adults need parental protection when they are being misled by others.
Listening and helping to review options	good	It's great for parents to act as sounding boards and low-key consultants.
Demonstrating respect for and interest in a startup's current lifestyle	good	It's crucial, no matter how disappointed parents may feel.
Getting help	good	Outside help is valuable, especially when depression exists; vocational counseling and testing of various brain functions can be valuable for career choosing.
Using medication	good and bad	It may help but should not be depended upon, since it's never the whole cure.

12
EDUCATORS
Offering Life Prep Schools

I found education to be overwhelming. I found to be in school and not be doing something I wanted to do—for this goal that is four years away—made it difficult to be motivated and focused. College was one big goal with no smaller goals to strive for in the process.

I.F., age 22

Schools should never stop examining how they are getting students ready for their work lives. Informed by recent discoveries related to brain function and learning processes, twenty-first-century education can and should introduce revolutionary changes in its missions and methods. I call for new kinds of schools that can combine what is now known about growing minds with our understanding of contemporary career needs to ensure that we turn out a generation of rough-and-ready startup adults.

Numerous public and private high schools proclaim that they are "college prep schools," implying that a sizable portion of their student body blossoms into well-primed undergraduates and that the school is dedicated to getting its students ready for the experience of college life. Often, though, the term "college prep" is not much more than a euphemism for "college admissions prep," because pressure from parents and school traditions may convert a school into a credentials factory, as entry into the right college becomes an end in itself, a trophy for parents as well as the school, to say nothing of the kid. The term "college prep" should be dropped and replaced with "life prep." Secondary schools have to prepare students for what will confront them after college or instead of college. Colleges too should be equipping their students for life after graduation. At present, this need is almost entirely overlooked. We also must recognize and meet the mind-building needs of those students who elect not to enter college. They have an enormous contribution to offer our society, and we never want them to view themselves as second-class citizens.

Influential educators should investigate the contemporary adult world and come up with a clearer vision of what it is we are preparing kids for. What is the modern workplace all about? In what ways have careers and jobs evolved in recent years? How have such changes altered the skills and knowledge required for competence on the job? How have work roles been modified in recent times, and how should these modifications influence our notions of readiness? These are the compelling questions that await informed responses from educational thinkers and planners.

AN EARNEST DISCLAIMER

Ready or Not, Here Life Comes is all about enabling students to face up to the threats and the promises of their work lives during their adult startup years. However, a fruitful school-to-work transition is far from the only aim of education. Schools need to prepare kids to become solid citizens, to appreciate the arts, to be knowledgeable about history, and to germinate an intellectual life. Thus, this chapter represents one rather thick band within a spectrum of educational missions. It is not intended to devalue liberal arts education or to suggest that work-life preparation is a school's entire reason for existing!

TOWARD LIFE PREP EDUCATION

In fostering work-life readiness, secondary schools and colleges should be stressing the growth processes covered in this book (chapters 7–10). Academic institutions can readily determine how, when, and where these indispensable abilities can find their way into the curriculum and pedagogy.

Growth processes can be strengthened in two academic arenas. First, all teachers need to integrate in their classrooms a range of activities, tasks, and projects, including case studies, relevant to what they teach, aimed at what I call targeted mind growth. Second, schools should offer courses, minicourses, or units that teach kids about the growth processes and help them think about the pathways that lead from where they are to where they will need to be over the next decade and then some. Such course work I call mind studies.

Targeted Mind Growth within Regular Subjects

Teachers can fashion some case histories in their subject areas that illustrate life issues that relate directly to what they teach. For example, a history teacher can explore how national leaders have dealt with problems and crises (rightly or wrongly). English classes should dissect growth processes as they are embodied in the struggles of literary characters. Science instructors can point to the ways in which scientists handled or mishandled their brainstorming ventures.

All teachers should introduce some targeted mind growth within their classes. This is the mental equivalent of working out in a gym, and it takes place when specific brain processes are intentionally highlighted and enhanced through educational experiences. There is enormous value in having students learning and acquiring the ability to reflect on their own mind and its workings. Targeted mind growth can help students learn to think about how they think. The process comes into play when a teacher targets a brain function that merits cultivation. She explains the function and teaches her students its name (for example, decision making, expressive language, or prioritization), following which they engage in activities or tasks aimed at strengthening that process. The teacher then ensures that the kids can talk about the relationship between the activity and the strengthening of the targeted function. To use an analogy, it helps if someone working out in a gym to boost the power of his quads can understand the relationship between a certain resistance exercise and the building of strength in his quadriceps.

Here's an example: Let's say a teacher targets the process of brainstorming. First of all, her students should grasp the meaning of that term. Then she might ask them to imagine a solar-powered amphibious car that can run on land and glide over water. Their brainstorming challenge is to think of a brand name for the new mode of transportation. An enlightened student might blurt out, "Oh, I know why we're doing this, Mrs. Vincent! You want us to get better at brainstorming, and by thinking up lots of names and then picking the best one, we're gonna become brainstorming superstars." Yes!

TARGETED MIND GROWTH

1. Specify a growth process that warrants strengthening.
2. Give students the name of the process and explain its applications in school and in future jobs.
3. Design a task, activity, or project that stresses or culminates in the specified process.
4. Ensure that students can recognize and can describe in words the ways in which what they are doing can make that particular process work better.

In the best of all worlds, different teachers in a school would work on specific important functions within each growth process. No one teacher can or should attempt to cover them all.

Mind Studies

Elementary, middle, and high schools should offer mind studies courses that explicitly enlighten students about the growth processes. These may take the form of units within existing courses (such as health or social studies) or else separate courses. Students should study brain functions within the twelve growth processes, such as attention, memory, language, and higher thinking, as they come into play during successful learning and working. Appropriate age and grade levels for this activity will vary depending upon other facets of the curriculum in individual schools. But such teaching should take place at least several times during middle and high school. Other teachers should apply regularly the terminology and concepts introduced in mind studies classes across diverse subject areas, so that the growth processes become well-consolidated learning themes.

Students in mind studies can analyze and discuss case studies of people who have fallen into thorny predicaments as startup adults because of one or more underdeveloped growth processes. Examples might include a person who is having career problems because she is politically naïve or one whose skills are so rigid that she can't bend and grow with the inevitable modifications in technology on the job. Case studies also should introduce the intricacies of different career paths as well as the pivotal challenges most people face whatever their line of work, including getting along with a boss, collaborating with others, and delaying gratification. Cases could strikingly illustrate the setbacks suffered by startup adults who fail to meet the specified challenges as well as the triumphal marches of those who understood what they needed to do and then did it. Some cases should be composed by students themselves. "Okay, class, for tomorrow I'd like you to make up a case study about a really brilliant person with lots of good ideas who has serious trouble collaborating."

BACK TO SOME VERY BASIC BASICS

It's now possible to revisit the four *I*'s—inner direction, interpretation, instrumentation, and interaction—and examine the ways in which targeted mind growth, mind studies course work, and daily learning experiences might promote work-life readiness.

EDUCATING FOR THE FIRST *I*: INNER DIRECTION

Chapter 7 sounded a call for introspection, but most students need prompting and practice to tour their own minds. A major aim of education ought to be to assist students in getting to know who they are and who they are becoming. This is especially vital in the turbulent era in which teenagers struggle fiercely with their own identities, unable or disinclined to piece together the fragmentary evidence that might reveal who they are. Reeling with confusion, they may consider themselves composites made up of their best buddies, a few revered rock stars, a cool older sibling, respected and loved parents, and the odd soccer or volleyball coach. But where and when does authenticity emerge? As part of their adolescent expectations, they need some help discovering their true selves. How is this process assisted in schools?

The Study of Self

Throughout the course of his secondary education, a student's primary case study ought to be the story of his own evolving self. The inside insight inventory illustrated on page 103 can be used as scaffolding for someone's personal story. A template like this one should be modified by each school to teach its values and priorities for the population it serves; items may need to be added or deleted. Ideally, a form of this type would be completed at least once or twice each academic year beginning in the sixth grade. The school should maintain the record digitally (with appropriate privacy protection), and students should be given all of their previous inventories to examine before updating their perceptions. In this way they can watch themselves grow and evolve.

Autobiographies should be works in progress. Students should augment their life histories, and compare their current self-concepts to those from earlier years. This exercise can help them unearth recurring life themes (page 87), leitmotifs that contain powerful implications for the future.

During discussions, possibly in their mind studies classes, adolescents can—if they are willing—exchange notes from their inventories and autobiographies with an eye toward all the "neat" ways people can and should be different from each other. "Nothing's wrong with wide differences among friends" should be the message. Schools can help teenagers overcome their instinctive qualms about being odd or weird or even being seen with someone who appears different, an apprehension that prevents some of them from becoming who they are meant to become.

Through self-analyses and discussions, students also should be able to access their unique competitive advantages and identify their areas of weakness or disinclination. Such pulling together of inside insights also can assist them in grappling with their own feelings about themselves and about the ways their lives seem to be going. All that inner direction is healthy, and it prepares them for permanent self-watching.

In fostering inner direction, schools should require students to journey into their futures. Some parents, understandably, have a hard time doing this. A mother or father cross-examining a daughter about her future may incur strident resentment for applying a subtle form of pressure or coercion. Kids so want to impress their mothers and fathers that they may perceive their natural uncertainty about the future as a weakness they'd prefer not to reveal. A school setting may be a more comfortable site for grappling with uncertainty, especially since your classmates are doing the same.

Fortifying Foresight

Foresight requires rehearsing. As they work on their autobiographies, kids should try making some educated guesses regarding their futures—whether through written essays, oral presentations, or graphic illustrations. There should be a clear understanding that no binding contracts are being signed, but adolescents should be able to answer the questions, "What's your best guess for what you will be doing twelve years from now? What do you think that will be like?" Kids benefit from some long-range previewing; currently too few of them engage in it. It is revealing and fun for them to compile an ongoing archive of their changing views of their futures over the years, for example, "I used to think I wanted to be a nurse, but now I'm leaning toward becoming a social worker."

In addition to looking forward to his own years to come, every kid should learn how to become something of a futurist. Within his mind studies classes he should ponder broad questions such as, "What do you think living in this country will be like twenty years from now? How will things take shape next year in school?" Such inquiries need to be mixed with some vital "what if" questions and speculations: "What will happen if there's an economic depression? What if all our oil reserves dry up? What if someday all of us can travel to outer space and spend part of our lives on another planet?" That "what if" line of thought seeds foresight.

Self-Launching

Schools should prepare kids to be self-launchers. The classroom should be a site where it is safe to take intellectual risks, to propose far-out ideas, and to demonstrate personal initiatives in assignments or projects. There should be plenty of opportunities for independent study and old-fashioned extra credit. Ideally, every student ought to select a topic and stick with it for three to four years of self-study (with supervision). That way each launches himself on a trajectory toward personalized expertise and in-depth scholarship. Such a long-range intellectual quest should be born of a personal affinity or a passion that has long percolated within him.

Teenagers should try on adult roles as if they were getting fitted for a new pair of sneakers. They might write or study cases that feature those roles and ask hypothetically, "What would I do if I decided to run for the senate in this state?" or "How could I own my own jewelry store, even though I started out without enough money?" Their teachers and classmates should join students in exploring the strategies that could assist them in achieving their stated goals. Such thought and talk can stimulate ambition and motivation while opening doors to the future that otherwise would have been slammed shut. Done well, this approach to vocational path finding and clearing can instill students with the energizing notion that "where there's a will there's a way."

EDUCATING FOR THE SECOND *I*: INTERPRETATION

In an age of dazzling technological applications, educators confront a bewildering smorgasbord of innovative options and implications for the art of teaching. In sifting through the options, schools should make the advancement and enhancement of understanding a priority. Throughout much of educational history, schools have allowed rote memory to become the dominant channel for cognitive performance. Classroom tests often have tapped the rote recall of facts or robotlike command performances of mastered procedures. Yet with new technologies for accessing information, the brain's storage silos can become less central to learning than they once were. That shift should free up time and brain resources for deepening understanding. Among other things, it should liberate students to make use of their notes while taking examinations (at least for part of each test). By the way, most career challenges resemble open book tests: the most important thing you need to know is where to find what you need to know!

The examinations a teacher designs and administers reveal his philosophy of education. If it's all memory, that suggests he believes that's what learning mostly entails. What a shame! Can you imagine interviewing a striving twenty-four-year-old for a position in your Internet software company and asking him, "By the way, how's your memory?" That's almost never a job qualification.

The Understanding of Understanding

As part of our effort to help students learn about learning while they are learning, educators need to teach them what understanding consists of. For one thing, they should engage in specified mind building that relates to concept formation. Students have to master the concept of a concept (page 129) and then should maintain a kind of atlas in which they create diagrams depicting important concepts they have come across in a subject. The following chart is an example of such a conceptual map. It illustrates a simple approach to representing a concept graphically. The critical features (principal characteristics) of the concept are listed along with some good examples and some good nonex-

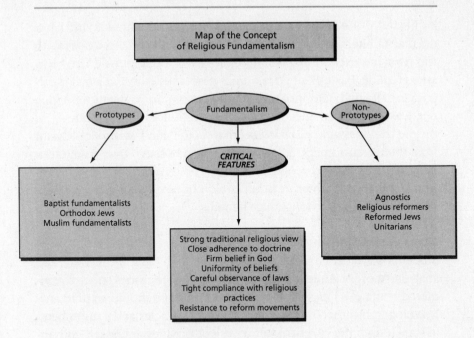

Map of the Concept
of Religious Fundamentalism

Prototypes ← Fundamentalism → Non-Prototypes

CRITICAL FEATURES

Baptist fundamentalists
Orthodox Jews
Muslim fundamentalists

Agnostics
Religious reformers
Reformed Jews
Unitarians

Strong traditional religious view
Close adherence to doctrine
Firm belief in God
Uniformity of beliefs
Careful observance of laws
Tight compliance with religious practices
Resistance to reform movements

amples of it. Students are encouraged to map all-important concepts and save them in a concept atlas.

Students also should learn about linguistics, since many of the raw materials for understanding enter their minds through language. In careers as well as in school, verbally stated ideas infiltrate everywhere and every day. A minicourse on linguistics and how language works should be part of a mind studies class.

Understanding Expectations

Understanding expectations is woefully underdeveloped educational territory. As noted in chapter 8, too many startup adults founder in ignorance because they have only a hazy perception of what is expected of them at work. They misread between the lines of their job descriptions. Once again, the best way to approach this is through the use of case studies; in this instance students should read and discuss accounts of peoples' careers, those that have gone well and those that have not. Did that currently unemployed hardware store salesman realize that you need to make eye contact with your customers or they won't have confidence in what you're telling them? How did the newly appointed assistant principal learn that the superintendent of schools would be impressed if she attended all the meetings of the school board? How did that architect determine what sort of design would be most likely to win over the executives planning that new shopping mall? I recently asked Claudia Barth Bennett, a human resources officer at a major corporation, if she could identify the most common problem hindering her least successful recent hires. She responded confidently, "Oh, they're the ones who just can't seem to understand what people want from them—customers, fellow workers, and bosses." Case studies can help students think through what might be termed "job comprehension." This form of interpretation could outpace reading comprehension when it comes to long-range benefits.

Biographical Education

Students should consume a steady dose of biography reading and analysis. At every grade level, a compilation of life stories should be required reading. As part of this exposure, students should learn to analyze biographical accounts to uncover the intricacies and comprehend in some depth the roller-coaster course of victories, impasses, and setbacks that mark careers. They should be made to share in the decision-making deliberations of biographical subjects (for example, "How would you have handled the predicament Winston Churchill faced?").

Pattern Recognition

Keen pattern recognition is another mode of interpretation that calls for abundant reinforcement, as was emphasized in chapter 8. Teachers across subject areas should raise the question, "What are the salient patterns that keep reappearing in my course?" These patterns may be musical structures, such as sonata form, or may consist of recurring operations in mathematics or grammatical rules in French or certain kinds of events in history. Coaches should tease out the recurring sets of actions embedded in football or basketball plays. Over and over again across subject areas, kids should respond to the inquiry, "What's the pattern here and where have you seen something like this before? And what's a little different about that pattern this time around?" Kids should be engaged in quests for underlying, often partly hidden, patterns.

Evaluative Thinking

The third growth process subsumed under the category of interpretation, namely evaluative thinking, also calls for dedicated time and toil in school. Schools should address explicitly three discrete evaluation targets—ideas, products, and people—and make use of the ten steps in evaluative thinking as delineated in chapter 8 (page 139). The following list provides examples of the kinds of evaluative thinking exercises that could be helpful to secondary school and college students.

SOME EVALUATIVE THINKING ACTIVITIES

Engaging in literary and art criticism
Writing position papers on current issues
Evaluating political leaders
Assessing job opportunities or descriptions
Critiquing proposed legislation
"Monday morning quarterbacking" after a football game
Examining moral, legal, or ethical decisions
Analyzing advertisements/commercials
Writing hypothetical performance evaluations
Comparing several commercial products (for example,
    soaps or cereals)
Questioning the methodology or results reported
    in a scientific article

Whenever possible, evaluative thinking should be documented. The analysis should emerge as a tangible product, in a written report, a graphic presentation, or a version of a completed form, such as the worksheet displayed here.

EVALUATIVE THINKING WORKSHEET

1. Target for evaluation
   TV commercial claiming that pill will give you stronger muscles and let you lose weight permanently.

2. Objective Description of Target
   Commercial says that with two pills a day for three months, results will be seen or your money will be refunded; also says pill has no side effects and is recommended by doctors.

3. Claims and Outward Appearances
Miraculous results are seen in before-and-after pictures of two people.

4. Questionable Aspects

Aspect	Answer	Final Ratings*
1. Does it really work?	Probably not	Very weak
2. Does it work on everyone?	No way	Very weak
3. Does it keep working after you stop using it?	Unlikely	Very weak
4. Is it really safe for everyone?	No way to know	Very weak
5. Who are the doctors who recommend it?	No one we've heard of	Very weak

* Possible Ratings: strong, not so strong, weak, very weak

5. Useful Research Findings or Outside Evidence (If Any)
They don't cite any studies that I can look up—just testimonials.

6. Useful Consultation/Discussion Inputs (If Any)
Called my own doctor; he said it could be dangerous and nothing has been shown to work as well as they claim.
Called my mom's doctor, and he said the same thing; so did my health teacher.

7. Statement of Evaluation Conclusions
These people are just trying to make money selling something that has not been researched well.

8. Action
I'm not going to buy these pills: I'll find other ways to get in shape.

Over time, students ought to practice deriving evaluative conclusions in different subject areas and then justify their stances through cogent arguments. "Here's my take on this year's election for governor. . . . And I'm going to tell you how I came to this conclusion." Not only can such practice help startup adults become far wiser consumers of ideas and opportunities, but it can also help them develop points of view, communication skills, and products of their own that can withstand critical scrutiny.

EDUCATING FOR THE THIRD I: INSTRUMENTATION

Periodically, a school should compile an inventory of the mental tools it is helping students develop. Our society keeps modifying work rules and roles and therefore the tools needed to do jobs; new instruments are forged, some old ones become outdated, and others need recalibrating. For example, technology, skills undergo rapid changes calling for new forms of technical expertise; as global economies expand, previously neglected foreign languages should be taught in school. Education is obliged to keep pace with these changes and provide the equipment needed to succeed in the contemporary work world. As students' special affinities and neurodevelopmental profiles declare themselves, it should be apparent that different kids should be incorporating different mental equipment.

Chapter 9 catalogued some of the tools required to survive and perhaps thrive during the startup years. Below are some academic exercises that equip kids with the instruments they need.

EXAMPLES OF INSTRUMENTATION ACTIVITIES TO EQUIP STUDENTS FOR WORK-LIFE READINESS

Planning, implementing, and monitoring long-range projects
Writing business plans, grant proposals, work plans with
    timelines
Preparing cost estimates and budgets
Implementing new technologies
Designing curricula and instructional plans
Writing screenplays
Producing videos
Making extended oral presentations
Planning, launching, sustaining, and monitoring projects
Editing and revising written material
Designing and preparing visual and graphic displays
Debating current issues
Participating in mock trials

Adaptable Basic and Technical Skills

Traditional academic skills may make us think narrowly of the three Rs. But through formal education, students also can learn the broadest applications and adaptations of these basic skills. For example, they should study ways in which reading differs depending on whether one is appreciating a poem, deciphering the owner's manual of a car, exposing points of view in political essays, or distilling knowledge from a dense passage in a chemistry textbook. As startup adults contend with job demands, what counts isn't how proficient they are in reading, math, writing, and various technical techniques but how agile they are in retooling their skills to meet changing needs and conditions.

Many contemporary employers lament the fact that their young workers have deplorable writing skills. Often they can't even compose a coherent letter or memorandum. I recently asked an eleventh grader how much writing he was doing in English class. He responded, "None." When I asked why, he told me that his English teacher was also the varsity soccer coach and didn't have time after school to read a bunch of papers. I was appalled. Writing is one of the best ways to impose discipline and structure over a student's thinking. It is the skill that integrates the most diverse collection of brain processes, including motor function, language, the generation of ideas, attention, memory (for rules, spelling, and vocabulary), and organization. Therefore, extended writing on a regular basis prepares kids to undertake brain challenges that require the coordination of multiple moving parts, a constant need in adult careers. Students should be expected to write in numerous formats, not just book reports and essays. They should learn to write contracts, persuasive letters, and advertising copy. Writing should become a facilitator of thinking and a communication link for relating to others.

Mathematics and science are especially challenging to curriculum planners, since the extent to which these subjects will play important roles in adult work lives varies dramatically. Students also differ markedly in the ease with which they can acquire skills and knowledge in these areas. Startup adults need to have a framework for understanding, to have some skill, and to not be intimidated by the subject matter. Scientific and mathematical challenges can emerge unexpectedly in almost any career and in daily life.

The curriculum in mathematics warrants very careful scrutiny. For example, all adolescents should be taught statistics and the reasoning processes that surround that discipline. Statistical analytic skills are likely to serve the majority of students as well if not better than inter-mediate algebra. Also, teenagers should acquire a solid grasp of the mathematics of the business world through the study of finance. They should gain experience analyzing stock market transactions, financing alternatives, and the techniques of budgetary allocation. Science courses need to reflect technological advances and place less emphasis on the memorization of facts and more on the comprehension of processes in the physical and life sciences. The study of ecology and the environment also needs emphasis at a time when the world is facing se-rious conservation and resource utilization issues.

The "Soft Skills"

Schools and educational policy formulators also have to respect the rel-evance of the "soft skills," essential capacities that extend beyond the academic core abilities. The growth processes advocated in this book—brainstorming, communication, decision making, evaluative thinking, and collaboration—are among the "soft skills" crying out for academic perfecting. Educators should inspect their curricula to determine the grade levels and subject areas in which such capacities can best be exer-cised.

Efficiency Building

Equipped with an appropriate set of instruments, kids and grown-ups can accomplish what they need to do in an efficient manner. As noted in chapter 9, I meet a fair number of plodding high schoolers I think of as nonmethodologists, people who perpetually do things with-out considering *how* they are doing them and consequently do too many things the hard way, which drains any semblance of satisfaction out of schoolwork. Schools need to help kids become proficient at scheduling, organizing materials, prioritizing, and pulling together endeavors that have a bunch of different "moving parts" (like a science project).

As with other forms of targeted mind growth, these modes of organi-zation should be identified and tied to highly specific tasks, such as the preparation of an exhibit or the design of an organized desk space. Stu-dents should be rewarded as much for how they go about doing things as for what they ultimately produce. They should receive grades on the methods they use, including submitted work plans and timelines, just as they are judged on the quality of a final product.

Productive Thinking

Thinking in a way that can generate a worthy product or decision constitutes an indispensable ability in countless careers. Applying the suggestions contained in chapter 9, teachers can foster productive
thinking among their students. While learning about world literature,
students can learn how decisions get made. They can study the different ways of coping with stress by examining how literary characters re-
covered from or were immobilized by the setbacks and frustrations in
their lives: "How would you describe Ahab's coping patterns?" Or,
"What kinds of decision-making tactics are evident in *Hamlet?*" Classes
in history and in health as well can deal with issues of productive thinking in their particular contexts.

EDUCATING FOR THE FOURTH *I*: INTERACTION

Schools should explicitly address life's social side. Far too many startup
adults get off to a staggering start because they have no idea how to or-
chestrate and monitor their interactions. The three interaction growth
processes (communication, alliance formation and reputation management, and political behavior) should be studied and discussed through
the school years.

Verbal Communication

Terrible verbal communication is rampant in our culture. In the distant
educational past, schools required courses in rhetoric; it's time to re-
vive that practice. Kids need to be taught how to make effective oral
presentations, how to engage in verbal negotiations, how to argue successfully for a point of view, and how to put forth cogent explanations.
They need practice in organized verbal elaboration, and they all can
benefit from direct experience in teaching. Seventh graders should
teach sixth graders, who in turn should have a chance to instruct
younger fledglings.

Verbal communication should be worked on across the curriculum.
In math classes, students should talk through how they obtained their
answers. They should have to write math essays. History students can
perfect their ability to describe human traits and to sequentially narrate
events. Literature classes offer a chance to resynthesize and interpret
fiction both orally and in writing. Links between language and things
that are seen (called visual-verb associations) are vitally important, es-

pecially in the sciences. High school physics students, for instance, ought to be able to lucidly explain spatial and mechanical phenomena. Classes from drama to physical education can offer practice in rhetoric. In every single one of these areas, students may need some prodding and coercing to engage in verbal elaboration; they should be discouraged from talking in instant messages or spitting out verbal fragments.

Language should be a device for comparing and contrasting, and kids should practice deploying well-chosen words and crafted sentences to fuse connections among the scattered ideas or facts they learn. Secondary schools must be committed to alleviating to some degree the contemporary verbal communication famine!

Written communication can be equally important. Students should come to view writing as a way of developing their thoughts. Currently, many kids write reports by cutting and pasting information gathered by surfing the Internet, a form of juvenile plagiarism. They have missed the point that writing is more than reporting; it is a way of transforming and developing ideas. Kids and their teachers need to view writing as a craft rather than an emergency procedure. Long-term writing assignments should be stressed, while timed tests of writing should be de-emphasized. Students should be allowed plenty of time and instead have space limits—for example, "You can take as much time as you need, but you can only write three pages"—a policy that better approximates work-life demands. A great deal of adult writing needs to be relatively brief, but seldom does it have to be produced as rapidly as for a spot-quiz in high school. Additionally, writing is a terrific way to teach kids the art of revising, the sanding and polishing of communication. They should submit multiple drafts of their work. Ernest Hemingway once commented that all writing is rewriting. Student writers should experience the satisfaction of perfecting their creations. Having your writing assessed by a teacher is an excellent way to learn to take and use constructive criticism.

Alliance Formation

Working alliances are a requisite for working productively. The collaborative process should be thought out and implemented to complete projects. From time to time, students should even be permitted to collaborate in taking tests; joint preparation solidifies working alliances. Most of the time teamwork need not involve close buddies working together, even though this arrangement is what most students want for. Kids need to experience joint efforts with classmates whose interests, backgrounds, or abilities differ appreciably from their own: "Hey, you're a good writer, why don't you write the captions and I'll draw the cartoons, since I love drawing and you hate it." Deep respect for variations in abilities is a sign of tolerance and a central feature of productive alliances.

Reputation Management and Political Acumen

Kids should have opportunities to discuss the dynamics of building, living with, and trying to change reputations. All students think about this topic but seldom get a chance to talk about it systematically. A teacher should get kids to describe the reputations they would like to have: "How would you want other students to describe you?" Students should then explore the actions they would have to take on a day-to-day basis to attain their desired reputations and what they would have to do to avoid harming their image. There should also be opportunities to discuss undeserved reputations, how some kids get a bum rap and what their peers can do to help them.

The study of reputations should be combined with consideration of the politics of school and the workplace. A kid needs to talk about the best ways to perform for people with clout, those who impact on his present and future happiness. This group includes student leaders who sway peer group public opinion and help shape reputations, as well as teachers. Participation in the political process of getting your teachers to like and respect you is a way of rehearsing for the role of a well-liked and respected employee.

The Study of Social Cognition

Schools should offer courses in social cognition at two points in particular—early in middle school and late in high school. My book *Jarvis Clutch—Social Spy* has been used as a middle school text to teach students about the specific verbal and behavioral processes they need to relate effectively to both peers and adults. Adolescents can be taught to discover why they or some of their classmates endure trouble with relationships and what can be done to heal these social wounds. They also can be made aware of the less obvious risks of being too popular or overwhelmingly obsessed with peer adulation.

As part of their mind studies course work late in high school, students should read and discuss case studies that illustrate the social and political issues they are likely to face during their startup years. Some of the examples provided in chapter 10 could be included in these discussions. Schools should tailor a collection of case studies compatible with the range of cultural values of their students.

Kids who are sensitive to the social and political nuances and overtones of careers are more likely to shed the painful burden of political naïveté (page 191) that can lead to serious life crises for people during their startup years. As of now, social cognition is pretty much an orphaned subject area. No one claims it; no one assumes responsibility for teaching it. That will have to change; schools will need to incorporate such learning if they want to facilitate work-life readiness among their students.

THE DIFFERENCES THAT DIFFERENCES MAKE

By applying targeted mind growth and case studies, schools can feel more confident that their students are entering the workforce with the tools they need. But they will have to factor in the wide differences that exist among students. One mass-produced toolkit will never work for them all.

The world of jobs and careers accommodates an array of kinds of minds, playing a plethora of indispensable roles. It follows that our educational system has to acknowledge and engage neurodevelopmental diversity, the idea that a classroom is composed of kids whose brains have distinct characteristics, inclinations, needs, and destinies. At no point is this recognition more relevant than during high school. By that time, it becomes increasingly transparent that Tim is the kind of kid whose mind relishes hands-on activities, while Millicent is the consummate verbalist, at her best when thinking in words, and her friend Kysha does her best thinking with visual imagery. Ricardo has an affinity for, practically an obsession with, aviation, and Cindy is all about modern dance. Schools of the future should be receptive to these differences and their implications for individualized educational planning. They need to guard against the prevailing notion that every student's competency can be gauged exclusively through end-of-grade testing. Such tests fail to tap many of the potential strengths and weaknesses that will determine an individual's success during his startup years.

Every high school student should undergo assessment to determine her neurodevelopmental profile and affinities, and she should have a plan to strengthen the strengths and manage any weaknesses obstructing her learning. Classroom teachers wherever possible should manage the deficits in the regular classroom, with special educators and school psychologists serving as consultants. As part of their ongoing training, teachers should be educated in the management of learning differences in their particular subjects. Chemistry instructors ought to have expertise in the breakdowns that can obstruct chemistry learning and how these are best managed in the classroom. Foreign language instructors should be conversant with the brain functions needed to acquire a second language and the specific mind gaps that can get in the way. In a program called Schools Attuned, our institute, All Kinds of Minds, provides such training for classroom teachers.

High-Aspiration Specialty Education

During their adolescence and in some instances even earlier, some students display highly specialized minds. Often they are branded as disabled or perhaps not too bright because they don't satisfy that dubious, childhood-only virtue we call well-roundedness. Some are written off by their schools and by society in general. Some get informed grimly that they suffer from a pathological syndrome (like Asperger's syndrome, if they struggle socially and have offbeat interests). In reality, their differences often represent variation, not deviation!

School can be traumatic and unrewarding for kids with highly specialized kinds of minds. It should not be and it need not be. We should offer specialized education to specialized minds.

I advocate what I call high aspiration specialty education, consisting of programs that enable students to improve in their specialty areas, such as auto mechanics, acting, or welding, while being helped to aim high in life. So in addition to building their technical skills, students of heating and air conditioning could be coached on how to start and operate their own small businesses or how to rise up the corporate ladder at a major manufacturer of air conditioning units or how to brainstorm new ideas for digitally controlled air vents or valves.

While focusing on their affinities, students in high aspiration specialty education still need to be exposed to a core academic curriculum. But many of them would be more receptive to literature, math, and history if they could have their moments in the sun, those learning intervals during which they could do their thing. There are students who could improve their reading comprehension dramatically if they could practice reading automobile repair manuals. School becomes intolerable for many specialized brains because there is never any relief; hour after hour is spent practicing other peoples' specialties. Such relentless mismatching contributes significantly to high school dropout rates.

High aspiration specialty education would include versions of targeted mind-building activities and case study analyses. Students who opt for an early specialty pathway in school will need to acquire work tools that can be used in more than one trade. I was once given a tour of a superb vocational high school in Lexington, Massachusetts. I asked the principal, "What percentage of your auto body students go on and do auto body work for their careers, and what proportion of your electrical students actually become electricians?" I was somewhat surprised by his answer; "Very few of our students have ended up doing what they specialized in while they were here, but in the process of focusing at this school, they picked up skills like decision making, brainstorming, collaboration, and time management. Then they were able to apply these in whatever trade offered them the best opportunities at the time." His was indeed a growth process school. Early specialty education should never close out any options for a student; someone studying plumbing in high school should still be able to go to college if that's what he eventually wants. He might end up becoming an attorney for a labor union representing pipe fitters.

Around the world, there are many models of high school career education. Some European countries provide up to nine or ten years of basic education, following which students can branch out into specialized or academic paths. Often, though, the vocational pathway fails to nurture the important growth processes and instead may focus exclusively on manual or other highly technical skills. Some programs offer formal academic studies interspersed with blocks of time apprenticing in a trade. There are educational systems that seem oblivious to the phenomena of resiliency and late blooming; they track students at too early an age, perhaps eleven or twelve, assigning some to a trade path and others to an academic, university-bound program. They may also labor under the false assumption that a student's academic competency can be captured entirely on a standardized test. I have seen numerous high school students whose academic skills and interests failed to blossom until they were sixteen or seventeen or whose true intellectual strengths were not picked up on the tests. It would have been tragic if they had been branded as nonacademic material when they

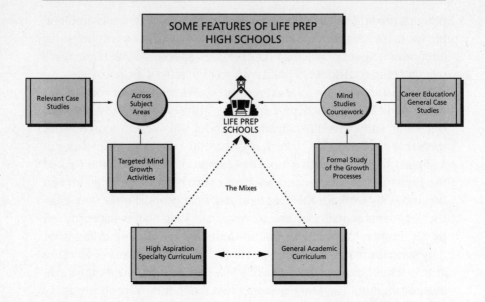

were younger. Their schools might have forced them to take a wrong road at an early age. There must always be ways to switch tracks.

Various mixes of general academic and specialized career education are entirely feasible, and such blends provide relief for kids with specialized minds. They try out some roles, some of which may serve as coming attractions for their future work lives. This model has equal merit for college-bound students, who might spend periods working in a law office or a TV station to acquire their taste of the realities of the work world.

Writing in the *Harvard Education Letter* (2004), Marc Tucker recommends what he calls "fixed gateways, multiple paths." In this model students are expected to demonstrate basic competency in traditional academic skills by the end of tenth grade, after which they are permitted to specialize, attending universities or community colleges. This would certainly meet the needs of many students seeking technical education. As Tucker states, "Very few high schools in the United States can afford the equipment and the faculty needed for technical programs—from welding and auto mechanics to software systems management, hotel and restaurant management, cardiovascular technology, and graphics and design." Early admission to technical schools and community colleges could offer some adolescents these opportunities and spare them the humiliation that comes with school failure or a sense that what you are trying to learn doesn't fit your kind of mind. A current alternative is to have schools within schools, so-called academies that stress particular domains of interest (for example, health care, theater, or computer science). Whatever the format, high aspiration specialized education is a must for many teenagers, but it should never be allowed to create a second-class citizenry composed of adolescents not headed for universities. Again, high aspirations, the goal of affluence, and future leadership roles should be seen as realistic by all individuals regardless of their education paths.

The chart opposite summarizes some key features of a life prep high school, one in which teaching about the growth processes and about work-life readiness takes place in special mind studies classes as well as in classes in traditional subjects. Students are permitted to engage in various mixes of high aspiration specialty education and general academic curriculum.

MEETING NEEDS

It may seem that this book places some heavy burdens on middle and high school teachers and policy makers. It does, but the rewards will be more than worthy of the effort. If teachers get to know their students well and meet their needs more suitably, our society will be relieved of the heavy burdens caused by young adults suffering work-life unreadiness, mental illnesses, underemployment, and reduced productivity. That sounds like a wise long-term investment. The major features of a community's ideal secondary school education plan are listed on the following page.

SECONDARY EDUCATION: WHAT ARE LIFE PREP SCHOOLS?

- Schools oriented toward preparing kids for life
- Schools in which teachers have been well educated in the brain functions needed for learning and whose instructional practices reflect this knowledge
- Schools that help students to know themselves
- Schools that stress the acquisition of excellent communication and interpersonal skills
- Schools that use targeted mind building to ensure that the growth processes needed for adult success are addressed explicitly
- Schools that provide formal teaching in mind studies, including ca-

reer education, key elements of learning and thinking processes, linguistics, oral language (rhetoric), and social cognition

- Schools that apply the case method and considerable biography reading in preparing students for the issues they will face early in their careers
- Schools where all students have individualized educational plans
- Schools that identify and strengthen the strengths and affinities of all kids
- Schools offering high aspiration specialty education as an option
- Schools with credit requirements enabling students to complete their secondary education in less or more than the usual amount of time (three to six years)
- Schools that have multiple ways of assessing the competencies of their students
- Schools that take care not to heap excessive praise and honor on select students and thereby avoid creating future fallen idols
- Schools that require all students to learn about the real world through work-study or community service
- Schools within schools that are subdivided into smaller units with fewer students per class and fewer teachers per student
- Schools that reexamine what it will take to get their students ready for the realities of contemporary work life

All of the above is doable. Pieces of this approach already exist in some settings. There is a critical need to unify the fragments and thereby dramatically curtail the spread of work-life unreadiness.

IMPLICATIONS FOR COLLEGE EDUCATION

Undergraduate and graduate education also have a mission to accomplish for the school-to-work transition. Ideally, professors should be infusing targeted mind building where needed in their curricula. It's never too late to teach such processes as time management, brainstorming, and evaluative thinking. Colleges should provide well-informed career counseling and vocational preference assessment for students who feel they need it. Because there exist so many prototypes of postsecondary education, it is impossible to generalize a uniform set of aims. Community colleges and technical schools have a strong focus on careers; four-year liberal arts colleges, for the most part, are not as directly dedicated to job preparation. Engineering and premedical students concentrate on career-related learning, while many music majors adore music and want to learn as much as they can about Mozart, Lionel Hampton, and the Beatles, although few of them aspire to careers as musicologists. So colleges and universities are expected to satisfy a spectrum of expectations. Nevertheless, all of them should be attending to the growth processes. Just as high school teachers should ask themselves which important functions can best be highlighted in their particular classes, college faculty members can pose and respond to the same question.

Students with fairly firm career plans should have access to lectures or seminars that delve into the social and political intricacies of their anticipated occupations, helping them to think through the life options while anticipating the obstacle course within their intended field. A prospective attorney might learn about the different branches of the law, the day-to-day scenarios of real estate attorneys versus trial lawyers. She should learn about the bumpy career roads in a legal firm or in a government agency. Most of all, students should be exposed to some reality previewing to avoid being ambushed early in their work lives.

LETTING THE FUTURE BEAR ON THE PRESENT

Ready or Not, Here Life Comes asks a lot from education, maybe too much. The recommendations in this chapter may not all be feasible in a single educational institution. Yet I have articulated some shared goals that different schools might realize in their own ways. Educational systems must keep reexamining their goals and practices to determine if they are still as relevant as they once were. What kind of startup adult should we be shaping? Answering that question requires a commitment to the careful analysis of contemporary early adulthood and its implications for growing minds during life's first two decades.

13

ADOLESCENTS

Conducting the Experiments

I am afraid of failure. . . . I think everyone is afraid of failure. I am afraid of failure because I want to make myself proud of myself. I want to know that I have done the right thing for myself.

S.J., age 23

The ages between eleven and twenty teem with tales of trial and error. Teenagers have to shape and reshape the ways they think and act in response to the upheavals in their minds and bodies. They continually inspect and evaluate relationships, including with their parents, their brothers and sisters, their friends, and their teachers. Life is in a state of flux. As if that's not enough of a roller coaster, disappointments in oneself are common—the failed science quiz, the college rejection letter, the three newest acne lesions, the failure to make the field hockey team, or a loss in the city championship football semifinals. Amid such day-to-day turbulence, how can a teenager spare the time and energy to look ahead and prepare for life after adolescence? How can an adolescent get ready for the startup years of adulthood? How can she feel she's moving forward on the right track? It can very be hard, but it has to happen.

Teens can take five forms of action to avoid spinning their wheels on the trip to work-life readiness:

ACTIONS FOR TRACTION

Right reactions
Self-finding

Mastery
Putting everyday life in compartments
Tentative planning

RIGHT REACTIONS

Adolescence is hilly terrain. A fifteen-year-old can have a terrific time with a friend and then be incensed with that person thirty-six hours later. A teacher can make a ninth grader feel like a winner, while another teacher blasts away at the foundations of his ego. Parents can say and do nice things on one occasion only to come across as arbitrary and mean-spirited at other times. The challenge is learning how to react to these heavy crosscurrents.

Contending with Stress

The ability to manage stress ought to be considered a basic skill. Depressing interludes, aggravating setbacks, rejections, and nasty conflicts are leitmotifs that recur throughout life. But teenagers can't let such daily defeats wipe them out or immobilize them; they must learn to withstand and rebound, a capacity called resiliency. Some kids lack coping skills, so they are apt to react to stress by ignoring, denying, or overreacting. A student who is failing geometry tells everyone (including himself) that he's doing okay: he just can't cope with the cold reality of his situation. Such denial almost never works. Other unhealthy copers put down anything they're not good at: "History is stupid, it's completely useless." Still other stressed-out teenagers love to universalize their personal problems: "None of my friends did well on that test," or "No one else likes Mrs. Simpson," or "I don't mind that I wasn't invited; hardly anyone wants to go to Susan's party." Still others explode, fall apart, or develop physical symptoms like lost appetites, headaches, or disillusionment and depression. These are all signs of failed coping.

People are better off when they acknowledge their stress and engage their problems. Then the sufferers can react more directly and work to heal the wounds. Adolescence is when both good and bad coping patterns become established. In the future, making derogatory comments about a supervisor behind her back won't make that manager vanish from one's life. Making believe you're doing well at a job you're really messing up is likely to have catastrophic consequences. When a kid has a problem, he can start by admitting it. Then he can discuss his stress with someone, a really good friend or an adult who can use some crafty techniques to help him cope with the challenge.

I frequently encounter a teenager whose patterns of reacting to problems are more problematic than the problems he's reacting to. Such maladroit coping skill can return to haunt him during his startup years. Here are some typical examples:

• Ralph has trouble writing. He hates to write, so he keeps telling his parents he has no homework. Distorting the truth is Ralph's mode of dealing with some of his problems. But his ill-conceived strategy backfires when he fails English and has to go to summer school. In adulthood, his truth-bending tactics may become a habit. Lying may serve his purposes some of the time, but sooner or later that practice will get him fired.

• Susan is intensely jealous of her little sister's popularity, so she starts spreading ugly rumors about her in school. Pretty soon everyone finds out that Susan's stories are fabrications. She ends up looking contemptible. If, as a startup adult, she went about spreading false rumors about someone at work, she would soon be despised and distrusted by her colleagues and might even be fired. She needs a better way to cope with jealousy—maybe by finding her own way to excel or impress others.

• Grant spends lots of time and energy fuming at his dad, who criticizes him constantly. Grant feels there's no way he can be as smart or as successful as his father and believes his parents consider him a failure because he doesn't do much work in school and his grades aren't what they should be. Grant reacts by completely giving up on schoolwork. He abuses drugs, smokes a pack of cigarettes a day, gets a metal ring inserted in his umbilicus, and dyes his hair lime green. He hangs around with other kids who do nothing but hang around with other kids. Maybe without realizing it, Grant is trying to punish and embarrass his parents because he feels there's no way he can please them and earn their respect. He has overreacted (and misre-acted). Who will he humiliate during his startup years? His parents won't be in the picture as much. His self-defeating strategy won't work on his boss, who has no genetic loyalty to Grant! He is inflicting more cruel and unusual punishment on himself than on anyone else. The kid is self-destructing. If he can't find a healthier way to react to his oppressive father, he may never learn to rebound from negative feedback. And there will be no shortage of criticism to react to during his rapidly approaching startup years.

Positive reacting, first of all, demands slowing down and thinking things through. Some of the worst reactors are people who do or say the first thing that enters their mind, kids who explosively tell off a teacher, and adults who do the same with a boss or collaborator.

To avoid establishing bad patterns, adolescents have to groom their inner reactions. When something goes haywire, how sad does it make you feel? If it makes you feel blue, how long do the doldrums last? Can you bounce back and sink that rebound shot? There's nothing abnormal about feeling low, but are you so depressed over something that you become emotionally paralyzed? That incapacitating pattern can be habit-forming, so adolescents have to work on overcoming their anxieties, recovering from bad moods, anger, and serious disappointments or losses.

Sometimes kids have to tune in to an internal voice or cheering section that can give them reassurance when they feel they are sinking into a black hole of despair. That voice might say, "Okay, Jared, this too will pass. You've had these kinds of defeats before, and they always work out. You have to keep going. You can't let things like this wipe you out." This is called self-coaching or verbal mediation, and it's one great way to cope. Kids should rehearse this kind of script and be encouraged to talk to themselves—honestly.

From time to time, I have lunch at a cooperative market not far from the campus of the University of North Carolina. Many of the employees there are startup adults, and quite a few of them appear to be struggling in life to establish an identity and a pathway. Recently I overheard a manager say he had just interviewed a job candidate who obviously had a lot of personal problems. I could not resist chiming in, "I thought that was a requirement for working here." He laughed and said, "I don't mind them having problems as long as their issues don't interfere with their work." A startup adult can't let problems interfere with the way she performs. When she comes to work, she should leave her troubles behind her. That takes some practice, but adolescence is a great time to practice separating preoccupations from performance.

Finally, a person must know how to react in a healthy way to positive events and victories. Overdoses of adolescent success are sometimes far more damaging than chronic failure. I've known some kids who were superstars in sports or extremely popular or securely atop their classes academically, and they let their success inebriate them. They became some of the fallen idols described in chapter 3.

SELF-FINDING

Becoming acquainted with oneself is often a highly confusing teenage mission. It can be almost impossible for some adolescents to distinguish between who they actually are and who they want others to believe they are. In their quest for identity, teenagers constantly test out different ways of coming across to others and to themselves. They are in search of an image that feels right for them. In chapter 7 I described the building of inside insight. This quest for self-identity plays a huge role in adolescent development.

A ninth grader once groused to me that he gets evaluated from the moment he wakes up in the morning until he falls asleep at night. "Before I even start eating her burnt raisin toast, my mom is checking out how clean my ears are and what I'm wearing to school. I think she even smells me to make sure I brushed my damn teeth. At the bus stop and on the bus, other kids are checking me out to see if I'm cool or some kind of dork or geek or something. My teachers all day long are testing me and calling on me, trying to find out if I studied enough. They would like me to be a perfect nerd. In the afternoon, the coach never stops criticizing the way I play. Then it's back home, where my mom and dad look over my homework and hassle me about my 'careless spelling' and my lousy handwriting. My big sister evaluates the way I comb my hair; she tells me I'm weird (another test flunked). It never stops. It won't go away—even on weekends. I wish I could have a whole day, one entire twenty-four hours, when everyone just accepts me just like I am without trying to find out if I'm any good or not!"

Throughout high school and college, students seldom get any respite from performing and being judged—academically, socially, and often in other arenas as well. Their teachers, their parents, and their classmates are constantly checking out how they're doing. The relentless pressure to impress can make it hard for a person to get to know himself. So much energy may be channeled into performing that there's not much left in the way of resources for exploring the inner caverns of one's true self. The growth processes described under inner direction (chapter 7) have to be built up like muscles to endure a successful landing in the startup years.

Recurring Themes and Differences

How can adolescents get to know themselves? In chapter 7 I dealt with the search for themes that reappear in different guises as a child grows up. Kids need to look back to find themes that repeat themselves. A high school college student may discover that she has always savored activities connected to the arts or that she has always felt most fulfilled when helping someone in need. It's those recurrences that provide important clues about who someone is and where he ought to be headed.

In perceiving their own uniqueness, adolescents can start to differentiate themselves from the pack. Most of all, they need to find what Po Bronson in his book *What Should I Do with My Life?* calls their "sweet spot." The discovery of this often-hidden inclination fosters long-term career gratification. As Bronson put it, "Educating people is important but not enough—far too many of our most educated people are operating at quarter-speed, unsure of their place in the world, contributing too little to the productive engine of modern civilization, still feeling like observers, like they haven't come close to living up to their potential. Our guidance needs to be better. We need to encourage people to find their sweet spot. Productivity explodes when people love what they do." Adults are more likely to love what they do when they learn what they love as kids.

Having Values and Causes

An awareness of what really matters to a person is closely tied to the act of self-finding. Adolescents must become active believers in their beliefs, feeling profoundly what is important to them. Not all teenagers have causes that inflame their thinking or points of view that burn like hot coals within them. But those who do should blend their values and beliefs with their career plans. A student may become a veterinarian or a park ranger because she is adamant about wildlife conservation. Another may go into law or politics out of an intense conviction about the civil rights of minorities. Someone may become a policeman because thieves and murderers really stir up his outrage. A desire to ease the burden on other people or a belief in religion may influence the way a person approaches any career. When teenagers find out what they believe in, they can determine the ways in which their values can influence their chosen careers.

MASTERY

The chapter on instrumentation described the skills that enable a person to get off to a good start in a career. Adolescents should be aware of abilities they are lacking so they can decide whether to work on their deficiencies or start to think about roads to take that work around their shortcomings. Equally important, kids need to know what kinds of things they are mastering well and how they want to keep building on those assets.

I believe strongly that success is like a vitamin; no one can grow up well without it. Every teenager must find what she's good at and do it well, enjoying the satisfaction and the recognition that it brings.

Athletes and artists attain motor mastery. There are kids who savor mastery in one or more academic subjects they really enjoy (as opposed to just getting good grades to break into a college). Some very popular students achieve a kind of social mastery, although popularity alone tends to wear thin when your friends disperse and go their ways in life. If you have no other kind of mastery to feel good about, that can be a terrible let down during the startup years.

There are different kinds of creative mastery, such as designing dresses, making ceramics, or writing songs. There is also the mastery of a subject or topic. For example, a kid may know a lot about trucks or computers or audiovisual equipment or archeology. Expertise is like a dietary supplement; it helps a mind grow and thrive. A person feels validated and important when she knows more about something than anyone else around her.

Every kid should be on a diligent mastery quest. Each individual must find the realm of accomplishment that feels right and fits right. And it's best to have more than one kind of mastery, without having so many that none of them ever fully ripens. Eventually areas of mastery can guide a person toward a career that's just right for her kind of mind.

A kid and his parents should realize that no one should have to master everything he comes up against. Sometimes an adolescent is expected to be elegantly well rounded, impressive at each and everything he tries to do. Being too unflawed might even pose lethal dangers; if you're good at everything, how do you find the right good thing to do with your life? That's why some very well rounded kids may come to a crash landing during their startup years; it's as if they can't figure out what they do best.

Not being able to master certain things teaches you how to deal with failure and a sense of inadequacy. That's something everyone has to experience sooner or later—the sooner the better. Dealing with weaknesses can make someone a stronger and tougher person. Maybe that's why so many people who barely remained afloat in school come into their own as notably masterful and powerful adults.

PUTTING EVERYDAY LIFE IN COMPARTMENTS

Although raspberry sorbet and marinara sauce are both delicious, it is not a good idea to mix them together. Compartmentalization involves keeping the different parts of a life separate enough so they don't compete or interfere with each other. But figuring out how to compartmentalize is hard. Many teenagers and grown-ups have never met this challenge.

First of all, the adolescent asks herself, "What should I put in my compartments?" The answer is the different activities or parts of life that are important to her. The diagram below portrays one teenager's compartments:

BEN'S COMPARTMENTS

family life	social life	schoolwork
my dog Reggie	religion	computer games/TV
football	things I worry about	job at the pet store

Using this diagram, Ben can think about how and when he will tend to each compartment and, most of all, how he can make sure that he deals with or thinks about them mainly one at a time, although he may see important connections between them.

Some students have trouble hitting the books because their social compartment overflows into the others all the time. One high school senior admitted, "In the middle of my work I start thinking about girls, and then it's all over." Unfortunately, for too many kids, family life and schoolwork deteriorate because there's so much social excitement in their lives. Grades go down, family arguments flare up, the dog doesn't get fed, and that socially obsessed teenager quits his job at the pet store.

There's a trite old saying that admonishes everyone to "work hard and play hard." The truth is that there's enough time to do both well if activities are not allowed to interfere with each other. That's why adolescents need to concentrate on getting their interests and responsibilities tightly compartmentalized.

TENTATIVE PLANNING

I can't believe how often I ask a teenager what he wants to do when he grows up, and he says, "I have no idea" or "I never think about it." This is usually followed by the unreassuring comment, "And none of my friends do either." That's an unacceptable answer. A kid needs to have *some* idea or else the future is just an ugly blur.

In past generations it was common for kids to do what their parents did; observing their parents provided teens with a preview of what their adult life would be like. In many parts of the world, most students attend vocational high schools, where by age sixteen they have acquired a clear notion of how they are to earn a living someday. This practice is based on the flimsy assumption that by age fourteen or fifteen a kid can be certain what he'll want to be doing as an adult. That's just plain wrong. Nevertheless, it does help a kid think through his future so that he is less likely to be ambushed by reality at age twenty-two.

I tell kids that they must have an idea of what they are likely to be doing when they grow up, but that they can change their mind hundreds of times between now and then. Many people do. But to have no view of the future can lead to anxiety and hard times in the early twenties. Every time a teenager comes up with a fresh new idea of what she wants to do, she is actually trying that ambition on for size. She lives with it for a while and then either keeps it up on her screen, modifies it somewhat, or deletes it and uploads another possibility.

Teenagers, including college students, should shop for future work. In recent years, internships or apprenticing opportunities have become increasingly available. These experiences enable a student to test the waters, to spend some time assisting (and hopefully observing carefully) people in their daily work in a specific career. Summer internships can give students opportunities to preview some options. I have known resourceful teenagers who have designed their own internships, volunteering for a local newspaper or a political campaign, helping out in a welding shop, or doing clerical work for an Internet company. While on the job, an adolescent should engage in active spying, keenly observing the permanent workers, thinking about what it might be like to have their activities and their lives. They also can decide if the daily subject matter interests them while getting a taste of some of the drudgery.

While kids need to have some fun during vacations, at least a part of every teenage summer ought to be spent amid a cadre of working adults. Such experiences should be seen not solely as a way of harvesting credentials to get into a prestigious college, but also as an indispensable means of shaping the way teens think about work. It can help them become keen interpreters of their future world (chapter 8).

For many years I served on a Rhodes Scholarship selection committee, picking young men and women to attend Oxford University for two or three years. We interviewed some of America's most extraordinary college students, many of whom were destined to become leaders in their fields. Almost all of them had pursued fascinating, often original and unselfish, activities during their summers. Those months are like a blank canvas, and I think that kids who spend these weeks just perfecting their tennis, horseback riding, swimming, and other self-indulgent recreational talents do not do themselves justice. A chunk of every adolescent's July and August ought to be spent in serious pursuit of a future.

In planning ahead, kids can think about the numerous roles that come up within a career. Someone who studies business may end up selling real estate, running a restaurant, operating a car wash, or becoming head of a major corporation. A person interested in religion could become a clergyman, a teacher of religion, a writer about religion, or a missionary in Tanzania. The good news is that a teenager doesn't have to decide on the exact job, just which areas look like strong possibilities. Most students entering medical school have no idea what specialty they'll end up in, but they're really excited about becoming physicians.

How should teenagers ponder what they want to do with their lives? They need a combination of approaches. First, they should follow their instincts and passions. Second, they should think back over experiences that have most interested them. Third, they should consider adults they know or have learned about and ask themselves if they'd like to be like any of them. Finally, they should try to find out as much as possible about work that attracts them. Someone interested in health care should visit or volunteer at a local hospital. A person who wants to do something in aviation should talk to some pilots and visit an aircraft maintenance facility.

Some kids become too negative too soon. A student might declare, "I'd really like to be a doctor, but I don't think I could get into medical school," or "I'd give anything to be a policeman, but I'd never be able to pass the examination," or "I want to study to be a curator at a zoo, but those jobs are too hard to get." Those kinds of statements slam the doors for promising people, doors that would stay open if they had the courage to dream. Adolescents should focus intently on what they want over what they think they can get. There's a good chance they'll end up getting much more than they ever thought they could—and enjoying it more too.

14
STARTUP ADULTS
Looking Ahead from Behind

I wanted to work in an environment where people were truly passionate about what they were doing. They weren't working just for a paycheck, but they had a mission, a cause I could believe in. I reason that at this point of my life I am young and can invest the time and can afford to take the risk to work with some of these people. If things don't work out, I can start over, where I may not be able to in a couple of years.

C.T., age 24

T he startup years can be a period of disquieting ambivalence and self-stocktaking: "Where am I?" "Do I like what I'm doing?" "Is this leading anywhere?" "Who am I, and what really matters to me?" "Is this where I should be right now?" "Do my plans still seem to make sense?" "Am I happy?" Such questions can create discomfort, sometimes agony.

Relative stability during the startup years depends upon maintaining the delicate and precarious balances depicted in the chart below. This chapter will explore these balances.

SHORT-TERM VIEWS AND LONG-TERM OUTLOOKS

The fragile balance between short-term gains and goals, on one hand, and long-term visions and ambitions on the other stymies many a startup adult. Can she feel ambitious and nourish a desire to rise to near the top of her field or company while dealing with a swirl of day-to-day routine? Does she come to feel that the hour-to-hour demands of the job feel too much like a treadmill out of control? How can you think big while doing small things? The answer is you have to. A startup

THE STARTUP BALANCES

Short-Term Views	←→	Long-Term Outlooks
Idealism	←→	Decline of Naïveté
Looking Back	←→	Looking Forward
Self-Defining	←→	Self-Redefining

adult may be shackled with menial work, but she can't allow herself to resent it so fervently that she performs her job unsatisfactorily.

Bruising and Healing

In the book *Quarterlife Crises,* Alexandra Robbins and Abby Wilner warn, "Young adults and recent graduates are learning now that the twenty-something years aren't supposed to be a consistent high but rather a journey full of both successes and setbacks." Further, a startup adult is likely to feel exploited, underpaid, and horribly unappreciated by the powers that be. She may not even be able to fall back on her parents to win the effusive praise she hungers for at work; her dad's unlikely to say, "Gloria, you did a nice job preparing those spreadsheets for the Collins deal." And if Gloria is well accustomed to raving accolades from her teachers, family members, and the minister at church, she definitely now feels the pain of a fallen idol. How does she handle this letdown? Everyone envied her when she landed the job. Now the sheen has worn off. She's beginning to realize she may never become

a top executive at her company. But there are other high-tech companies out there—lots of potential advancements in the industry. Gloria
should never forsake that perspective. She needs to cope with the
mundane burdens that beset her while keeping one eye on her long-
range targets. She can't let herself become downtrodden; she needs to
think of her present work as part of a life cycle.

Here are a few typical early career bruises:

- Scott, who has been with the company for eight months, was taken
  out of his roomy corner office to make room for a new administrative assistant and relocated in a tiny cubicle without windows. He arrived at work one Monday morning to find his materials had been
  moved. He was never told this would happen, nor was he asked how
  he felt about it. He couldn't figure out why it was he who had to be
  exiled to an inferior space. The experience was humiliating.

- Mary Beth can't comprehend why Millie, her project manager, never
  invites her to lunch. Most of the others in the office seem to dine
  with Millie on a fairly regular basis. Mary Beth feels slighted and
  deeply hurt by the oversight. Who you go to lunch with is important
  in her organization.

- Raj, a software engineer, is bored in his present position. He applied
  to head the information technology section of a young company. He
  knew he was eminently qualified for the position, but he lost out to
  a person less experienced and skilled. Raj felt sure that his Indian
  background and accent were the reasons he was passed over. This
  was the third time he had endured such disappointment.

- At a meeting of the entire staff (over 150 employees), there is praise
  for the new software Wayne has installed and taught everyone to use.
  But Wayne's name is never mentioned. He receives no credit, even
  though he stayed until after midnight many nights to get the program set up and debugged on everyone's desktop.

- Rita, who is pregnant with her second child, has an eleven-month-
  old who gets frequent ear infections with high fevers. Because she
  doesn't feel comfortable leaving the baby with anyone else when
  he's ill, she has missed a lot of days over the last six months at the

fast-food restaurant where she has worked behind the counter for four years. Recently they fired the manager, and Rita, who had gone through management training, assumed she was in line for the high-paying position. But the chain brought in someone from the outside, an older woman with grown kids. Rita felt angry, helpless, and discriminated against for the stage of life she was in.

There's always light at the end of the tunnel. Unfortunately, some startup adults get discouraged and may compromise on their long-range plans because they have trouble healing the inevitable ego bruises along the way. These wounds have to be seen as nothing more than temporary setbacks; they can't be allowed to discourage ambition.

Pacing the Climb

Timing is everything, and timing takes planning. Most efforts to get rich, powerful, or famous overnight during the startup years end up in humiliating busts; of course we hear mainly about the very few who somehow defied gravity and soared precociously to the top. For each such example, there are vast numbers of startup adults who tried to move too fast and paid a price.

Startup adults would do well to go for minor victories, chalking up a winning streak of modest results. That sometimes requires some radical downsizing of short-range expectations: "Did I have to go to engineering school to do this stuff?" Such downsizing must be done skillfully. Our center in North Carolina has had to hire temporary secretaries from time to time. I've always been astounded by the wide differences in the jobs they do. Some of them work extra hours without even asking for additional pay, display initiative, and deliver top-notch work with remarkable gusto. Others barely get by; some have to be replaced. I believe a commitment to consistent excellence—no matter what work you take on and how you feel about your job—instills powerful career momentum that is bound to carry a person to the highest levels of gratification and mastery at work.

At the same time that an individual is meeting and preferably exceeding current demands, he should be looking ahead, studying other people above him in the pecking order, and setting his sights on the main act (page 93), that moment in his biography when he will occupy the limelight, have a chance to lead, to make a lot more money, to be creative, to do good, and to feel fulfilled. Day-to-day routines and aggravations should never be permitted to cloud that vision. Modest salary increases and glimmers of recognition have to be sought and valued during the gradual ascent.

Part of the pacing process consists of a march toward stability in life. Marriage and having a child can offer some anchorage to a startup adult who has been meandering. In other instances, these events may come late or not at all during the startup years. For his book *Emerging Adulthood,* Jeffrey Jensen Arnett studied many individuals in their twenties and discovered that instability is very much a part of their time of life. Most of them change their places of residence with great frequency, and it is not unusual for them to sample a chain of jobs as well. Quite a few are undecided about their future work, but this may not trouble them. As Arnett notes, "Although they may not have found what they want, few doors seem closed for good to them. . . . Even in their late twenties people are still looking and still hopeful of finding a job that fits better than the one they have now. But the options often start to narrow once people reach their late twenties, as they leave emerging adulthood and take on adult roles." So by the end of their third decade people may find themselves under some pressure to accelerate the pace at which they settle into a fairly stable career commitment.

IDEALISM AND THE DECLINE OF NAÏVETÉ

Many folks are totally naïve when it comes to the unforgiving realities of the workplace. Unexpectedly, they suffer seemingly catastrophic setbacks that differ in impact from the painful bruises described above. Following are several examples of painful ego wounds that result from the naïveté of startup adults:

Naïve Expectations

- Janine enjoys her work in the biochemistry lab. She has her PhD and is involved in promising and important research. She thinks her boss is "a jerk." He's brilliant and widely respected in his field; he publishes prolifically and wins generous grants from the National Institutes of Health (NIH). But he treats Janine like his personal servant. He almost never says anything nice to her, acts like the ultimate male chauvinist, and keeps taking credit for things she does. But she's petrified of him; he could make or break her in the field of enzyme biochemistry. She believed that any boss she might work under would serve as her benevolent mentor. Somewhere along the line, Janine should have been warned that deep disillusionment with a boss or supervisor is an all-too-frequent scenario during the startup years. And some bosses feel so insecure themselves that they can't protect anyone beneath them on the career ladder. Janine never suspected that something like this could happen and now feels like a hostage.

- Bob is crushed. He just got passed over for a promotion at the oil refinery. He thought he was doing everything right and knew he was getting stellar performance reviews. He was affable and helped out whenever he could—the very model of a team player. Bob often showed up early and stayed late. He dressed right, talked right, and acted right as far he could tell. Yet one of his colleagues got promoted over Bob. The guy who made the grade was younger and less experienced than he, never worked even half as hard, and clearly wasn't as skilled. But Rodney went out of his way to play up to the top executives, and he had graduated from the same college as the CEO. Bob felt as if he'd been maimed by a land mine; his pride was amputated by this defeat. The day after the public announcement, he didn't know how he could face anybody at work. He felt a churning mix of rage and humiliation in the pit of his stomach. Bob naïvely had clung to the belief that the race always went to the swiftest.

- Curt got all kinds of kudos during his first four years at the Dodge truck dealership. He was salesman of the month on several occasions and cultivated a nice following among well-heeled frequent pickup purchasers. Curt really liked the company he worked for, and he got regular encouraging feedback from the owner himself. He harbored the fantasy of becoming sales manager some day. But then, during a moderate sales slump, Curt was summarily laid off with two weeks' notice and one month of severance pay. He was dumbfounded. "How could they do this to me?" They could and they did. Curt made a naïve miscalculation when he counted on institutional loyalty. He kept thinking, "I gave them my best all the time." But in the real world, organizations look out for themselves; they have limited gratitude. Curt had no idea how to react because he had never thought of such a contingency. He was not in the habit of asking those healthy and potentially protective "what if" questions, such as, "What if I get laid off someday?" He should have.

Naïve Misplays

Melinda left her job because she found it "totally tedious, a real drag" and she didn't much like her boss. Besides, she found a position that paid a lot better. Just before she left, she badmouthed her boss to everyone who would listen and told him a few things in a crass, arrogant tone. She felt great after this denunciatory catharsis. There was no way he could hurt her now that she wasn't going to be working under him. Wrong! Two years later she applied for a new job at a new company. It seemed like a perfect fit for her. Although she didn't list her first boss as a reference, the CEO at the new company called him. Her old boss found it hard to say anything favorable about Melinda. She was crushed when she didn't get hired, but she should have known that you never burn your bridges. In fact, how you leave a job is even more important than how you start it.

I've had people leave my employ and give much too little notice. I remember one person, aged twenty-seven, who told us on Thursday he was leaving the following Monday. He never asked anyone if this would be a problem, nor did he seem at all concerned about how we would get coverage for him. He claimed we owed him some sick leave time anyway. A few years later a prospective employer called to ask about him, and one of our administrators objectively described this man's departure. He was turned down for the job. I have had trainees who after two years with us never came around to say good-bye or thank you to me, their boss. It's not that they were mean-spirited or angry; they were naïve. Startup adults who keep burning their bridges behind them may never stop leaving behind ill will and tarnished reputations.

A startup adult may make the fatal mistake of playing up to the boss on every possible occasion, ignoring the cultivation of good relationships with people on his own level and below. His conspicuous apple polishing alienates fellow workers, who eventually come up with ways of undermining him, perhaps even badmouthing the guy to the boss. Focusing exclusively on impressing a superior is another naïve misplay.

No Surprises

During their startup years, people should anticipate the kinds of lurking hazards described above. To deal with them, they need contingency plans. They can't bail out of their life mission whenever they feel sunk in the undertow. A startup adult needs to keep aiming high, even when he senses he is being dragged down. While recuperating from the effects of naïveté, he may suffer a morbid combination of pessimism and fatalism and become a conservative non–risk taker, surrendering all ambition and playing life safe—nothing ventured and nothing gained. If so, he has forsaken his idealism. He should actively combat those negative sentiments and convince himself that he can lose some ballgames and still win the World Series. It happens all the time.

LOOKING BACK AND LOOKING FORWARD

Coming to terms with the startup years depends partly upon maintaining a clear mental windshield and a properly adjusted rearview mirror. Startup adults should look ahead to decide where and how they want their lives to go in the future, and review the past, since where they are coming from will have some bearing on where they are heading.

A Diagnostic Process

When startup adults lose their bearings, where should they look for guidance? Many career counselors would urge them to discover and follow their passions. In *What Should I Do with My Life?* Po Bronson asserts, "We all have passions if we choose to see them. But we have to look backward even more than forward, and we have to chase away our preconceptions of what we think our passion is supposed to be, or not supposed to be." A startup adult who feels stranded should take stock of the past. Too many people plunge into their futures while blindly disregarding the covert clues embedded in earlier years. They should excavate any buried passions, treasures that may inspire future directions.

Ready or Not, Here Life Comes advocates a diagnostic process that should be used by any struggling startup adult. To begin with, he needs to determine which descriptions in chapters 2–5 pertain to him. For example, could he have some sort of mind debt? There might be a lingering gap in reading or math. A festering neurodevelopmental dysfunction, such as a chronic problem with language communication or memory or attention, could be sabotaging key aspects of work. Interpersonal problems are a common source of debt. As I pointed out earlier in the book, difficulty relating to people, a dysfunction of social cognition (chapter 10), is a mind debt that frequently causes early careers to implode. Trouble interacting optimally with others at work is a flaw people have the hardest time seeing in themselves and acknowledging to themselves (and others). Denial often prevails and obscures a person's true picture of his circumstances. In chapter 5, I illustrated some ways in which neglected strengths evolve into mind debts. A disillusioned startup adult should identify strengths and affinities that have gone untapped recently.

Someone with work-life unreadiness may discover that he is having trouble giving up adolescence, that he is feeling the letdown of a fallen idol, and/or has taken one or more wrong roads. Pinpointing the destructive pattern can be a big step in overcoming its destructive effects.

When significant job impasses occur, startup adults should give some thought to the growth processes (chapters 7–10). Have they missed out on some of these in significant ways? Do they lack inside insight? Have they had recurring problems understanding some on-the-job concepts and procedures? Do they lack key mental instruments needed for mastering the career they are pursuing? Are they having problems with on-the-job communication? Are they sufficiently aware of the political forces at work?

Building on the Past

Whenever a startup adult feels the need to take a new road, she should first go back and seek out autobiographical patterns, such as reappearing affinities. She might excavate from her past history: "Wow, you know what, since I was little, I've always been happiest when I was taking care of animals," or helping people, or doing things outdoors. She might conclude, "I do my best work late at night and when I listen to music." Seeking work that builds on a life's recurring themes is often the most promising way to look forward. It can help get someone back on track after she has temporarily lost her way.

Recurring themes also include traits that pop up in various contexts: "I think I've always been the kind of person who overreacts," or relates best to people through humor and friendly teasing, or doesn't like to talk very much. These clues need to be taken seriously, especially in framing job values (page 88). In reviewing the trends and traits of the past, it is important to get as much as possible down on paper. There's too much information to hold in one's head. By jotting down notes on circumstances, growth processes, and recurring themes, one can reexamine, update, and augment one's self-studies.

Once a vivid self-image comes into focus, the move from the past to the future remains a balancing act, calling for careful strategic planning along with some realistic opportunism. The plan should contain a range of desirable options, with some backup plans in case the first choice goes awry. Then it's time to look around for opportunities. What are the specific choices available? Often that's where patience, a willingness to compromise, and risk taking come into play. For example, a startup adult may need to take a job at a lower salary or rank than he was planning on in order to get where he wants to be ten years from now. Or it may be best to snag a short-term job that would be an excellent credential or a source of useful experience, although it is not something he would like to do for very long. A startup adult can't have everything he wants, nor can he have what he wants whenever he wants it. That can be a hard lesson to swallow in an age where intense pleasure and rapid gratification are the rule.

Two final ingredients facilitate a successful move forward—luck and opportunity. They are harder to plan for, but a competent startup adult knows a lucky break when he sees one coming down the road, and he knows how and when to be opportunistic.

SELF-DEFINING AND SELF-REDEFINING

Everyone is an actor at work. How a person plays his role helps him define himself. It's not the whole definition, because people are also defined by who they are in a family, in a community, and within the intimate privacy of their own minds. This section focuses on the all-important work part of self-definition.

Who do you think you are?

"I'm the one everybody goes to when they're having a problem."

"I'm the one who handles all the little details."

"I'm the one who gets to work the earliest every morning."

"I'm the one who works the hardest around here."

"I guess I'm the idea person in this place."

Changing jobs multiple times during the working years is the norm, whether the transitions are forced or voluntary. In either instance, the process of deciding what to do next is dependent, at least in part, on how an individual thinks of himself at that time. When all goes well and someone knows himself, job changes have a fascinating continuity to them. Take Mark Grayson, who is the CEO of All Kinds of Minds, our nonprofit institute. Mark has done a brilliant job of expanding our work nationally and internationally and has enabled us to enhance our programs and market them effectively. He has also done a magnificent job of raising money and keeping the institute on an even keel over its first decade. Mark started out as a Hollywood agent and then was an executive in children's television programming. How in the world does that qualify someone to become the CEO of a large nonprofit institute? He was a brilliant networker, which is crucial when a program like ours needed to go national. He understood production. His years in Hollywood taught him how to deal with prima donnas (such as Dr. Mel Levine) and how to market good ideas. His experience in children's television gave him a grasp of the potential of technology as well as some insight into the needs of kids. So Mark never had to reject or deny his past in order to move into his future. He used previous definitions of himself as he redefined himself. Each chapter contributed meaningfully to the one that followed it. That's definitely the way to go.

Careers are most apt to move onward and upward when there's stability but not total stagnation in how a person defines herself. Some startup adults change their self-image almost as often as they change their socks. Here's an example from Simon, whom I met while he was in college. He first told me, "I'm the kind of guy who likes working with people. I want to help others, cooperate with other people, get to know everyone real well that I work with. I think that's the kind of person I am and will always be." When I met him a few months later, Simon pointed out, "I don't care what I do and who I do it with; all I care about is having a chance to be creative, to do my own thing, on my own." While Simon's second analysis doesn't necessarily contradict his first one, he has undergone a wide swing in emphasis. There are many adults with work-life unreadiness who, like Simon, seem to be trying on all sorts of new identities as they progress through their twenties. They keep changing jobs to fit their latest version of themselves because they can't stabilize any sense of who they are. Some degree of exploration and experimentation of the kind that permeates adolescence is actually desirable during the startup years, but not to the point where a person is unable to commit to any kind of self-image or work for any length of time.

Career momentum may decelerate dramatically when a startup adult suffers from ambivalence. Many unready startup adults are infected with this virus and so work with mixed feelings about everything they're doing. To some extent, ambivalence is a natural state of mind, one that may reappear throughout a career. Harboring a trace of skepticism about your work life is healthy. But it causes paralysis when it erodes the commitment needed to perform at a peak level. Back in the seventeenth century, the French philosopher Blaise Pascal advised his readers to bet on the existence of God even if they didn't believe in a deity. He argued that this was a sound wager, since they had nothing to lose and everything to gain. The same applies to the embryonic stages of a job; a startup adult should bet on it, convince himself that, at least for the time being, this is definitely what he ought to be doing. Some individuals fail to apply any form of Pascal's wager. They may not realize that ambivalence can be a very tough habit to break. Their lack of fervent commitment is likely to be transparent to those who work alongside or above them. The result may be chronic vocational discontent, mediocre performance ratings, and a conspicuous dearth of accomplishment.

The Medicalization of Self-Redefinition

More and more adults suffering from work-life unreadiness are finding out or deciding they have a disease of some sort. By acquiring the diagnostic labels, they somehow feel redeemed. Here are some examples:

- Andrew finds out he is "adult ADD." He wished he'd known that earlier in his life. The diagnosis explains everything, including why he's never been able to settle down, why he had such a hard time in school, and maybe why he has a drinking problem. Medication is making a huge difference.

- After reading an eye-opening magazine advertisement, Jan has been telling everyone she has a chemical imbalance and that's why she has such a hard time finishing her work on the job. She believes her new daily dose of "heavy metals" is helping her a whole lot. She now has her children consume the same minerals.

- Hank's psychologist has informed him that he is chronically depressed. He kind of knew that already, but he didn't think of it as a mental illness. Also, he wasn't aware that his profound unhappiness at work stemmed from his depression until the therapist opened Hank's eyes. The psychologist failed to raise the possibility that his depression stemmed from his unhappiness at work. Hank is being referred to a physician for "appropriate medication."

- All her life Vera has shown signs of performance inconsistency. Some days she seems up for work, and others she feels a great deal of fatigue and lacks ambition. Several months ago her gynecologist told her that it sounds as if she has bipolar illness. She was delighted to have an explanation for her erratic performance. Vera has felt better on medication, but she seems to be as inconsistent as ever at work.

Many young adults feel genuinely relieved to get a diagnosis, but it can be frustrating and hard to determine if such diagnoses are accurate. In some cases, they conveniently provide a simple explanation for some chaotically complex life scenario. They also serve to get startup adults off the hook; you don't have to assume responsibility for your shortcomings or failures if your "ADD" has caused all your woes. Clinicians may be only too ready to label a patient. After all, it's a lot less complicated to write a prescription than it is to try to sort out a tangled career!

Attention deficits (without the label "ADD"), bipolar illness, and depression do indeed exist and are worthy of expert medical attention. (I'm not as sure about all those "chemical imbalances.") However, sometimes disorders may be overdiagnosed or decided upon without a close look at a person's life circumstances. Unquestionably, problems with attention or mood can be caused or triggered by a painful experiences.

When unready startup adults are put on medication (and so many of them are), the results can add confusion to their already baffling existence. Typically, the drug results in some improvement, but it is almost never the whole answer to the problem. Medication is a bit like applying a bandage to an infected wound. Things *look* a lot better, but the underlying condition of work-life unreadiness is not addressed at all. What often occurs with startup adults is that a drug works for a while but then, over time, its effectiveness tends to wane. That may prompt a clinician to raise the dosage or try new drugs. Each drug alteration results in some improvement—but only for a while, unless that therapy is accompanied by a new sense of direction in the patient's work life.

Undeniably, some floundering startup adults benefit from antidepressants, mood stabilizers, and stimulants, but these treatments are only a part of their solution. Drugs should never be seen as magic bullets or panaceas. With or without medication, a person is likely to need help defining and then redefining himself. The best clinicians use a multifaceted approach to turning a life around when it seems as if it's not going anywhere.

To the Rescue

Frequently I receive a call or an email from a desperate parent who wants me to see her son or daughter who seems have some learning and adjustment problems. The "kid" turns out to be twenty-eight years old, unemployed, sometimes abusing and even distributing drugs, and profoundly depressed. I wish this were an unusual scenario, but it's all too common. I explain that I am a pediatrician and therefore do not evaluate patients over the age of seventeen. Next comes the inevitable heartrending question, "Well then, who can see him?" I may recommend neuropsychological testing to help identify his strengths and weakness, but while it can be extremely revealing, the findings may not translate into a plan of action. There are specialized psychologists and counselors who can administer tests of vocational preference or style that can reveal some helpful patterns, but quite often a startup adult has trouble acting on the results. I might try to locate an adult psychiatrist or clinical psychologist, but what if he or she leans on their *Diagnostic and Statistical Manual* simply to pin a label on the patient? The prescribed answer is apt be medication, which, as we have seen, is at best only a part of the answer.

A team approach works best. A faltering startup adult needs career guidance based upon accurate assessment of his neurodevelopmental profile to uncover any lingering mind debts, plus an evaluation of any emotional damage and possible therapeutic needs. Career advice is likely to fail when it is not based on a thorough knowledge of the person receiving it.

Following a careful evaluation, unready startup adults should consult a good career counseling coach. Sometimes young adults who struggle have trouble using advice on their own. They need to be chaperoned through the first two career stages (page 90) and require close follow-up plus long-term guidance. Specially trained counselors, possibly psychologists or social workers, can do the job but may be hard to find. Some colleges and universities offer good career and placement services, but they don't generally provide the continuity and ongoing monitoring many unready startup adults will require. In *Quarterlife Crises,* Robbins and Wilner are very skeptical about the effectiveness of college career counseling offices. They note, "Essentially the career centers help students prepare their resumes but they don't suggest what to do with them. . . . If career centers would just tell it like it is—that recent graduates might have to 'put in their time' by doing administrative work, that they could be in for some emotional turmoil when they have to lower their standards, that their ideal jobs may have nothing to do with their majors—then twenty-somethings might be better prepared."

Helpful services are available, but they are sparse. We don't yet have the delivery system to provide such sorely needed diagnosis and counseling on a wide scale. Nor is it clear how these services ought to be paid for. In the long run, public investment in constructive school-to-work assistance will save money that might otherwise have to be diverted to the justice system, drug rehabilitation programs, and unemployment benefits. Unready startup adults are entirely salvageable if we can help them redefine themselves and use their insight to locate the niches that fit.

The Other Sides of Life

To fend off an endless volley of outrage and accusation, this author hastens to reemphasize the point that self-definition and personal gratification are not exclusively determined by jobs and careers. Every individual must decide what proportion of his satisfaction and pleasure in life he wishes to extract from work. It is a very personal decision. Most people never overtly make it, but they reveal it every day. There are numerous non-work-related sources of self-definition and gratification, including raising a family, spirituality, recreational activities, outside interests, sex, and varieties of pleasantly mindless amusement. Some people argue that what counts in life is not what you do but who you are. I think the two are very closely bound.

While writing this book, I had a conversation with a leading investment banker in New York. I asked him what advice he dispenses to his junior employees in their twenties. He responded, "I assure them that their work will not be much fun at this point in their careers. So they need to make sure they have very enjoyable interests and activities outside of work." Outside activities provide layers of insulation from the vexation that rumbles through the startup years. Paradoxically, it turns out that some of the most helpful diversions are the ones that involve effort. Immense value can be found in leisure activities that require some hard work, as opposed to passive, disengaging pastimes. Practicing the flute, weeding the rose garden, taking golf lessons, obeying the seemingly sadistic commands of a personal trainer, and stripping the old paint off an antique oak credenza are examples of hard work outside of work. I find the long hours I spend engaged in arduous chores on my farm therapeutic and stress-reducing, although they often feel like forced labor. People whose extracurricular life involves little more than watching TV, going to movies, shopping, and other entirely effortless forms of recreation are less apt to experience a constructive escape from the rigors and perhaps the monotony of the job.

Each of us decides how much time we spend on non-work-related activities, as well as how much satisfaction we derive from these pursuits. The decision often is made by default. Repeatedly, I have discussed with my own trainees and employees the puzzling equation that determines how much of their satisfaction they hope to derive from their careers and what proportion from outside the workplace. The grid below reveals a partitioning of a startup adult's waking day.

The grid below partitions an individual's work and nonwork pursuits. A person must determine the proportion of her time and gratification derived from each of these areas. The grid above will differ in the relative size of the boxes from person to person.

WORK AT WORK	
work at play	work-free play
friends and social life	spiritual, cultural, and altruistic life
raising a family	autonomy and time alone

SOME ADDITIONAL MATTERS STARTUP ADULTS NEED TO CONSIDER

- They are accumulating experience at work—no matter what kind of work they're doing. That means it's better to work than to be unemployed and have to contend with the costly stigma of being "inexperienced," a common reason for being turned down for a good job. I remember one young woman who told me she wanted to work in an art gallery, but every gallery she applied to rejected her as inexperienced. She wondered how she could become experienced if no one would ever hire her. The answer is she could gain experience (in customer service, aesthetic appreciation, and business in general) by working in the makeup department of a department store or at a shop that sells dinnerware. Many of the skills are transferable.

- Parents are often good sounding boards, if they can be asked not to preach or dispense too much glib, oversimplified advice (chapter 11).

- Startup adults should avoid pure money chases (if possible) or get-rich-quick gimmicks that in the long run have a tendency to not pan out and to leave their victims at a loss. Financial rewards are more apt to follow when someone goes after a career that resonates with his kind of mind.

- People should never feel they can't backtrack. Poor decisions are always reversible. Life is full of trials and errors; no one should let an error put the brakes on their forward motion. A startup adult can learn from taking a wrong road, and he can always make a legal U-turn.

- Careers can be regulated in intensity over the years. For example, a woman who wants to devote considerable time to raising her baby should find ways to work from home or in some other manner keep a hand in her career, realizing she can rev it up at a later stage of life. It is probably not advisable to close off a career path, as it might be hard to come back to.

- Startup adults should never give up on their passions. They should keep finding ways to get where they want to be, namely, getting paid to do things that they love.

- Startup adults have to realize that there is no work entitlement. Their boss doesn't owe them anything, and he is not losing sleep worrying about their self-esteem. But they are being watched, and they need to perform as if they are being scored on their performances. Being impressive actually can be fun.

- Early in a career, it is a good idea to explore diverse roles within a field. That means that a person who wants to become a screenwriter and is having trouble selling her scripts should consider a job as an associate producer or assistant casting director—a job that might eventually lead right back to screenplay writing or branch out into something else worthwhile within the movie world. Early insistence upon a particular role can be counterproductive.

- It is important for startup adults to keep sniffing out the connections between what they are doing and what ultimately they hope to be doing. A person might say, "Eventually I'd like to manage a restaurant; working in this coffeehouse is teaching me a lot about customer service, and I'm observing closely how my supervisor operates; she's terrific." By the way, such connections are very effectively mentioned during a job interview.

- Everyone should have some well-thought-out alternative plans and then be ready to change course when an excellent opportunity presents itself that fits with someone's overall career aspirations. It is hazardous to wait around for such golden chances and foolhardy to get so stuck on a plan that potential windfalls are missed.

In Search of the Genuine Self

The French philosopher Jean-Paul Sartre once wrote, *"Il faut choisir, vivre ou raconter"*—in English, "One must choose whether to live one's life or tell it." That advice suggests another formidable challenge faced by startup adults—and the rest of us as well. People have to live a life that's right for them, not an existence that *sounds* right. The world is replete with posers, folks of all ages, who are telling their lives rather than living them. A startup adult needs to be especially careful to avoid making important choices solely because a choice would embellish a "cool" story. Although it can be tempting to try to emerge as a charismatic character in one's own biography, there has to be more to life than that. The best success stories are about people who have refused to be anyone but themselves.

EPILOGUE

Carol Carter's Soliloquy

*I*t's been pretty hellish, but I think I'm finally on track with my life. I feel like I've done it all over the last ten years—waited on tables, made sauces for spinach linguini, sold lingerie, worked as a telemarketer, resuscitated crashed computers. I went back to school, moved in with my parents and then out again, got depressed, took medication for that, slogged through a bunch of sickening romances, drank and smoked too much, finally got married, and produced a baby boy. And you know what? It got real bad at times, but I think I learned a whole lot, about life and about who I am.

Now I have this job at an advertising agency, and it fits me; it fits just right. You see, I've always been into art, things you can see, images (including my own). Ever since I was a little girl, I liked drawing and writing poetry. I also loved trying to talk my friends and my sisters into things, like to sell them whatever I believed or wanted them to believe. So there you have it. I was born to deal with things arty and to become a person who sells! I'm managing some nice accounts at Image Star, Inc., and I'm starting to bring in new business. This is all a fantastic challenge, and best of all, I feel as if I'm succeeding. That makes me a better person and a better mother and wife. I only wish I had put it all together when I was younger, but sometimes I think that all the grief I went through maybe toughened me up. Looking back over the last ten years since I was twenty, I can say it was a helluva trip, but as long as it turned out okay, I can't complain.

I know lots of people who didn't luck out the way I did. They're my *age, and some are still sliding backwards downhill; their lives are just one disaster after another. And I have some friends who just plod and plod without going anywhere. They have to be very unhappy and totally bored and trapped in what they're doing or not doing, but they may not even realize how low they feel. I wish I could help them. I wish all of us could have been more ready for all of this.*

REFERENCES
AND SUGGESTED READING

Apter, T. 2001. *The Myth of Maturity: What Teenagers Need from Parents to Become Adults.* New York: W. W. Norton.

Arnett, J. J. 2004. *Emerging Adulthood: The Winding Road from the Late Teens Through the Twenties.* New York: Oxford University Press.

Beckman, M. (2004). *Crime,* culpability and the adolescent brain. *Science* 305:596–599.

Bregman, G., and M. Killen. 1999. Adolescents' and young adults' reasoning about career choice and the role of parental influence. *Journal of Research on Adolescence* 9:253–75.

Bronson, P. 2003. *What Should I Do with My Life? The True Story of People Who Answered the Ultimate Question.* New York: Random House.

Brooks, R., and S. Goldstein. 2003. *The Power of Resilience.* New York: Contemporary Books.

Brown, M. T., M. J. White, and L. H. Gerstein. 1989. Self-monitoring and Holland Vocational Preferences among college students. *Journal of Counseling Psychology* 36:183–88.

Clifford, P. I., K. A. Katsavdakis, J. L. Lyle, J. Fultz, J. G. Allen, and P. Graham. 2002. How are you? Further development of a generic quality of life outcome measure. *Journal of Mental Health* 11:389–404.

Cohen, C. R., J. M. Chartrand, and D. P. Jowdy. 1995. Relationships between career indecision subtypes and ego identity development. *Journal of Counseling Psychology* 42:440–47.

Csikszentmihalyi, M., and B. Schneider. 2001. *Becoming Adult: How Teenagers Prepare for the World of Work.* New York: Basic Books.

Darden, C. A., and E. J. Ginter. 1996. Life-skills development scale—adolescent form: the theoretical and therapeutic relevance of life-skills. *Journal of Mental Health Counseling* 18:142–64.

De Botton, A. 2004a. *Status Anxiety.* New York: Pantheon Books.

———. 2004b. Workers of the world, relax. Essay in the *International Herald Tribune.* September 7, 2004.

Erikson, E. H. 1966. Eight stages of man. *International Journal of Psychiatry* 2:281–300.

———. 1997. *The Life Cycle Completed: A Review.* New York: W.W. Norton.

Gardner, H. 1995. *Leading Minds: An Anatomy of Leadership.* New York: Basic Books.

Hallowell, E. M. 2002. *The Childhood Roots of Adult Happiness.* New York: Ballantine Books.

Johnson, M. K. 2001a. Change in job values during the transition to adulthood. *Work and Occupations* 28:315–45.

———. 2001b. Job values in young adult transition: change and stability with age. *Social Psychology Quarterly* 64:297–317.

Leung, J. J., B. W. Wright, and S. F. Foster. 1987. Perceived parental influence and adolescent post-secondary career plans. *High School Journal* April/May:73–179.

Levine, M. D. 2000. *Jarvis Clutch—Social Spy.* Cambridge, Mass.: Educators Publishing Company.

———. *A Mind at a Time.* 2002. New York: Simon and Schuster.

———. *The Myth of Laziness.* 2003. New York: Simon and Schuster.

Levy, F., and R. J. Murnane. 2004. Education and the Changing Job Market. *Educational Leadership* 62 (2), 80–83.

Mau, W. C., R. Hitchcock, and C. Calvert. 1998. High school students' career plans: the influence of others' expectations. *Professional School Counseling* 2:161–67.

Otto, L. B. 2000. Youth perspective on parental career influence. *Journal of Career Development* 27:111–18.

Phillips, S. D., D. L. Blustein, K. Jobin-Davis, and S. F. White. 2001. Preparation for the school-to-work transition: the views of high school students. *Journal of Vocational Behavior* 61:202–16.

Robbins, A., and A. Wilner. 2001. *Quarterlife Crisis: The Unique Challenges of Life in Your Twenties.* New York: Tarcher/Putnam.

Schmitt-Rodermund, E., and F. W. Vondracek. 1999. Breadth of interests, exploration, and identity development in adolescence. *Journal of Vocational Behavior* 55:298–317.

Seibert, S. E., and M. L. Kraimer. 2001. The five-factor model of personality and career success. *Journal of Vocational Behavior* 58:1–21.

Seligman, L., and L. Weinstock. 1991. The career development of 10-year-olds. *Elementary School Guidance and Counseling* 25:172–82.

Watters, E. 2003. *Urban Tribes: A Generation Redefines Friendship, Family, and Commitment.* New York: Bloomsbury.

INDEX

Page numbers in *italics* refer to illustrations.